Unstill Life

Art, politics and living
with Clifton Pugh

Unstill Life

Art, politics and living with Clifton Pugh

JUDITH PUGH

ALLEN&UNWIN

First published in 2008

Allen & Unwin
83 Alexander Street
Crows Nest NSW 2065
Australia
Phone: (61 2) 8425 0100
Fax: (61 2) 9906 2218
Email: info@allenandunwin.com
Web: www.allenandunwin.com

National Library of Australia
Cataloguing-in-Publication entry:
Pugh, Judith, 1944- .
Unstill life : art, politics and living, with Clifton Pugh
1st ed.
Includes index.
Bibliography.
ISBN 9781741754773 (pbk.).
1. Pugh, Judith – Biography. 2. Pugh, Clifton, 1924–1990.
3. Feminism – Australia. 4. Australia – Politics and government – 1972–1975.
5. Australia – Politics and government – 20th century.
994.060092

Index by Fay Donlevy
Cover and text design by Ruth Grüner
Typeset by Ruth Grüner
Printed in Australia by Griffin Press

1 3 5 7 9 10 8 6 4 2

This project was supported by the Peter Blazey Fellowship 2007

The Australian Centre
making links

THE UNIVERSITY OF
MELBOURNE

FSC
Mixed Sources
Product group from well-managed
forests and other controlled sources

Cert no. SCS-COC-001185
www.fsc.org
© 1996 Forest Stewardship Council

This book is printed on FSC-certified paper.
The printer holds FSC chain of custody
SCS-COC-001185. The FSC promotes
environmentally responsible, socially beneficial
and economically viable management of the
world's forests.

Think where man's glory most begins and ends

CONTENTS

PLACE

Charred sheep, bread, rough red

Sometimes on a hot, clear summer day, when the sky is high, there is at Dunmoochin that astonishment of sudden revealed beauty. Then the grass, the fine pale clay, the stones, the eucalypt leaves melt into a shimmer of light, so that the detail of each element is lost in a haze of palest pink and yellow and silver grey. Clif painted this one year when we were very happy, when everything seemed possible, healing even, and love itself. The show sold out, and I've never seen any of the pictures again in auction catalogues or galleries. Perhaps their joy remains with the families who keep them.

But mostly, the word for Dunmoochin is delicious. Its charm is of domestic scale; tiny flowers and birds, the trees a comfortable height, the spaces between them laced with delicate grasses. There is always the sweetness of the air and the song of magpies, easy walks on the gentle hills.

It was such an ordinary day, delicious, when I drove up the pale clay road from St Andrews and for the first time onto the road through Dunmoochin. The painter Margot Knox had told me about a place for rent belonging to Myra Skipper. Myra and Margot knew I wanted to return to the bush; we'd met when I lived in Research, Margot agisting a pony with me, Myra, one day on her way back from a painting trip, stopping to use the loo.

The cottage snuggled into the ground, cosy and welcoming. But as my housemate and I walked around and talked about it, I knew I would live on top of the hill. I explained this to Jan. She asked if there was a place there to let. I didn't know. The extent of this certainty was limited. I just knew that I would live on the top of the hill. Up we drove, to find a rambling mud-brick house with an external gateway consisting of a nineteenth-century entrance door. It had a stained-glass surround and a bit of tin on the top to keep out the weather. It was meant to be built in to a house. Door-as-gate worried me; it always would. I understood that I'd live there, but further enquiries as to what this meant were impossible: no one answered our calls.

I'd been teaching for some years, untrained, doing arts after leaving a law degree at Melbourne. But in 1970, after a bout of glandular fever, I was a full-time student again, sharing a house in Greensborough with two fellow La Trobe University students. I had been senior resident in college, at twenty-five a few years older than Jan and Penny. They'd come in wet and upset after a demonstration against the Vietnam War and we'd made friends over cocoa and dry towels in my room. They thought of me as conservative, and I suppose they were right, although my reluctance to demonstrate was to do with doubt about its effectiveness, coupled with distaste for crowds. I prefer broader strategies, and directly to influence the political moment. But their commitment made me want to act. I wanted to see Australia out of the war, but my main concern was with schools. I had been teaching in the poverty-stricken state-school system in Victoria, and wanted it to change.

I like to think about order, the constitution. It's not only early legal training, it's about living in and with history: ideas and systems transmuted from Greece and Rome and the Bible through the British, then stretched across Australia. I decided to join the Australian Labor Party, the ALP. Early that September in 1970, off I went to my first meeting, at the Eltham branch.

It was the most extraordinary night. I'd thought it would be boring and bureaucratic, people discussing fundraising. But I'd arrived to join on the day that the executive of the Victorian branch had been dismissed by the federal ALP. The meeting might have been out of the Russian Revolution; people argued passionately about principle versus pragmatics, about politics and religion.

That day, Clyde Cameron had supported the intervention by the federal ALP in the affairs of the Victorian branch of the party. Clyde, who would be the most sophisticated and efficient member of the Whitlam Cabinet, had decided that the principle of a decent education for all children was more important than the principle that no state funds should go to religious schools. The executive of the Victorian ALP was being replaced. Clyde's decision meant that it had become possible for the ALP to win Victoria and, after more than twenty years, for a federal Labor government to be elected. He sacrificed years of friendship and had to tolerate contempt and anger from many bitter men on the left, but his gesture absolutely altered Australia's social fabric.

Within the white Australian population at that time there was a deep religious divide, affecting every facet of daily life. Cameron's choice delivered the death blow to that division. In the early twenty-first century, the issues of our living together in Australia are about what multiculturalism means, about fundamentalism of all kinds, about political correctness, about dealing with racism and religious intolerance. One forgets the cheerfully racist, sexist and religious attitudes that shaped generations of Australians. The significance and intensity of the dividing lines sustained into the mid twentieth century between western Christian sects – Protestant, Anglican, 'Roman' Catholic – are almost impossible to conceive. Then, religious identity meant everything to most white Australians. It managed class, affected marriage, job opportunities, sport at every level, union membership, political affiliation, business. Being Catholic or Jewish was not an absolute barrier to success, but it was a barrier to overcome. When Clyde Cameron made the decision to support intervention, the end of that time began.

At my first riveting ALP meeting we were reminded that on the coming Friday, after the moratorium march against Australia's involvement in the Vietnam War, there would be a barbecue.

Jan and I had left Dunmoochin that lovely spring day and driven back to Greensborough. I don't remember now if I rang Margot, if we discussed the house. Perhaps Jan told Penny and they decided politely not to mention my odd notion about living on top of the hill.

The moratorium day came. I telephoned my mother, who said my brother was marching; she didn't know how she'd managed to have such radical children. Jan, Penny and I drove in to the march in my Mini Minor, picking up a couple of people on the way. It was a happy atmosphere, festive, hardly radical; as soon as we got to the city it was clear that there would be no trouble. Melbourne was then truly provincial, and it seemed as if everyone you knew was on the streets. We were nowhere near the front of the crowd or able to hear the speeches, just part of an unusually large, good-humoured gathering, self-consciously well behaved and aware that, because of these elements – the good manners, the number of people, but most of all that so many were so suburban – this was more than the usual radical protest. It was a demonstration in the real sense of that term. Middle Melbourne wanted Australia out of the war.

After the moratorium, the barbecue. There was a fashion at that time to dig a pit, light a fire, lay on the fire the carcass of a whole sheep, cover the carcass with dirt, light another fire on top, shovel on some more dirt, and begin to drink. The idea was to provide an easy cheap meal, but rarely was it appetising. After some hours, half-raw, half-burned chunks of meat might be distributed; with any luck on paper plates, as any bread had been eaten much earlier. I've never drunk much, so for me these evenings were particularly difficult: the enticing smell of the cooking meat, the increasingly drunk men increasingly boring. And in those days many women, even on the left, even in bohemian Eltham, hardly expressed an opinion in public.

That night was cold, nearly frosty. We were clustered around the pit, talking about the war and the march, the firelight intense, so it wasn't possible to make out the features on the faces opposite. One silhouetted figure began to hold forth on the principles of pacifism. Apparently he had recently returned from France, where he'd talked to people involved in the riots of 1968. He had fought in World War II, and had during that war made a decision that all war was wrong. The principles he articulated were somewhat original, though; he was saying that if he had been in Paris during those heady days, and if any trouble had then blown up, he would, as all good men should, have joined in on the side being attacked. On reflection, it's a wonderfully Australian pacifism: a sort of larrikin scheme of fair's fair, innocent of notions of provocation or provocateur. It was cold, I was hungry, and I was young enough not to worry about the response of the group. I took him on. I can't remember what I said; I just began to point out the logical flaws in his position.

It's as though I'm there. The bright heat of the fire, the figures merging into a group, the cold at our back, his curly hair a wayward halo against the night.

'You're intelligent,' he said. 'Do you want to have dinner on Monday night?'

I'd thought he was old, his halo in the firelight had appeared white, but as he moved forward I saw it was a dark blond. Before I could answer Myra Skipper said, 'Oh yes, that's a good idea, Judith and Clif.'

There were other murmurs of support. I asked who he was.

'Clif Pugh,' said Myra. 'Clif's a painter.'

I asked where he wanted to go.

'Two Faces, it's the best restaurant in town.'

Indeed, Two Faces had wonderful food, but I can cook. When I go out I want atmosphere, as much as food.

'I'd prefer the Florentino.'

'Okay, the Florentino.' There was a pause, as this talk of food had reminded us all of the sheep at our feet. Then he said, still across the pit, 'Look, if we go out on Monday we'll go to bed. Why don't you come home with me tonight?'

Penny was standing beside me. 'That's a good idea, Jan and I can borrow the car.'

An entirely public transaction, negotiated without sentiment, without a scintilla of flirtation. Clif had learned etching in Paris, but not romance. My previous affairs had been with people I'd met and got to know at the university, or through work. This was a leap in the dark, across the pit, as it were; but the mood of the day was radical and public, and I trusted Myra's instinct as much as my own.

So some time later, after a small amount of raw charred sheep, we drove off in Clif's ute. I have a very intermittent sense of direction; the night was starry, but there was hardly any moon. We arrived, at a place in darkness. He led me along a path through an entrance-way and heavy glass doors, and turned on the light. On the mud-brick wall opposite hung a large romantic somewhat abstracted landscape. Underneath it was a tartan-covered couch. They looked terrible together.

One can find various ways to overcome the awkwardness of casual encounters; redecorating wasn't my usual form, but I had the same feeling of confidence as when I had understood I would live on the top of the hill. I did wonder if I was impolite to ask, it was after all his furniture, his painting, his house. But I knew the couch had to move.

I went up to it. 'Can you give me a hand?'

So we moved his couch, and he went to get coffee. The house was very cold and my feet began to go numb. Without thinking that I didn't know where the bedroom was, I went, through an unlit passage, into the unlit bedroom, and got into bed.

When I walked into the garden in the morning, it was without astonishment that I saw we had come through the entrance gate with the stained glass and tin.

The next afternoon, back at Greensborough, I began to pack. I knew he'd come for me that night. I explained to Jan and Penny that this was what would happen, and they became a bit alarmed when I made it clear that no, he hadn't said he'd come (he had already been taking someone to dinner that evening, he was still taking me to the Florentino on Monday), it was just that I knew he would come that night to take me back, in the same way I had known about the house I'd woken in that morning. At about nine, after some discreet murmuring, they both showed unusual signs of sleepiness, and suggested we all go early to bed. I thought it best to go along with this so I put my voluminous flannelette nightgown over my clothes and we all had what was obviously meant to be a soothing cocoa.

The phone rang. No mobiles then, and when the line went dead I pointed out that it would be Clif trying to ring en route from a public phone. They seemed worried, and went on with the cocoa and chat. The phone rang again; he'd stopped at the next phone box. He asked if he could pick me up and I said yes. He showed only marginal surprise when Jan and Penny, still concerned and wanting to keep an eye on me, put their rapidly packed bags in my car, and my things in the back of the ute with my borzoi, and we told him they were coming too.

And he took me to Dunmoochin, to live on top of the hill.

2

FAMILY, BEFORE FAME

Tea, porridge, leg of lamb with herbs

Beside the road to the house there was a depression that was almost always filled with water. It was just on a bend, you had to slow down, and every time, in every season, a blue wren would dart from the bushes, fiercely defending his territory. Domestic detail makes our lives and is our structure; routine and meals together, books on shelves, clutter from travel and gifts, fireglow, washing on the line. My memory of events at Dunmoochin, of people, of art, of all our other places, is filtered through minutiae: magpies outside the kitchen each morning, the blue of the kitchen tiles Marlene made for me, the light on the main room table, lavender scenting the linen in the cedar chest of drawers.

Fame overwrites all these for the observer, and the subject, the observed, is invested with fantasies. We were to become famous, hardly a week without a story in the newspapers, television crews part of our lives. But the wren, the lavender, the substance of the life we built in our early days protected us from the unreality.

Narratives and styles which at the time had their ironies now control the facts, the substance of our history. Our story, how we lived, is told to me again by his latest biographer, who emails me that 'Cliff bargained with life', and that she sees me, too, bargaining with life as I changed my surname when other women were reclaiming their birth names. She suggests that my family name would have given me less access to people and places, that I had saved valuable time as the name Pugh opened doors and gave me direct access to publicity.

Cart before the horse. This biographer is about my age, but seems to think that the new feminist movement had had effect by 1970. Women began to use their birth names in that decade, but at the time I knew no one yet who had. Nor was the gesture political, or even for political reasons. My family had all the access to power it wanted. When my parents left school there was only one university in the village that was Melbourne before the war; there they met each other, and all of Melbourne's people of influence that they hadn't already met at school. My paternal grandfather had trained in medicine like my father, my paternal grandmother studied music, and my mother's mother economics. My family, with professions and private means, were part of a comfortable connection that comes with sharing values and experience in a provincial place.

It wasn't my idea to change my name, but on the day after I moved to Dunmoochin Clif remarked, 'I suppose you'll want to get married.'

My instinct was not to think about this, but he was serious.

'Well, you'll want to have a child, women of your age do, and it would be better for you both if we were married.'

Remarkable now to remember the stigma attached to unmarried mothers and even unmarried partners, but he was very conscious of the implications for me.

He didn't want to have another unpleasant divorce on adversarial grounds, but mutually to divorce from Marlene, his second wife, on grounds of separation, which meant a wait of some years. He rang a lawyer friend who drew up a deed poll document, and I declared myself to be Judith Pugh. I rang my mother.

'This is Judith Pugh speaking.'

'Oh, you sound just like my daughter Judith.'

'I am your daughter Judith. I'm ringing to ask everyone to lunch on Sunday.'

'Oh . . . Where?'

I dropped in to tell Margot Knox I was living with Clif. She had been a friend since I'd moved to Research in 1968: I'd taken a house on several acres while I was teaching at a nearby school, and come to know her and her husband Alastair Knox, who designed and built in mud brick and timber. She was a sort of older sister to me, always a point of reference for uninstitutionalised good sense. Every year she had a show of paintings, no matter what else took place in her life – babies or illness or any other event – and she brought up a most creative set of children. The atmosphere in the house was always calm, Margot always interesting and interested. She and Clif had had an affair when they both had small children. I knew it had been serious, because he'd painted her twice. Although people in that pre-pill Eltham bohemia sometimes separated, in the main they kept the family unit as a place for their children to shelter, and their affairs apart. I suspect too, that both Clif and Margot wanted connection with a non-painter, so that the imagination feeding their work was not clouded with another's visual images.

'Be polite,' said Margot. 'Treat openings and dinner parties as if you were a diplomat; don't allow yourself to be upset.'

Good advice. Clif had just come back from six months in London and Paris, and everyone wanted to catch up. He was a successful painter in that little Australian society. There, in the art world, businessmen relaxed with journalists, actors, academics. Constituting himself by dress and manner a blunt bohemian, he had made a comfortable niche, with patrons who thought his directness arose from his war service and lack of university or public school education, and excused the unironed jeans, the army shirt, the beard, as evidence of artistic commitment.

Clif was twenty years older than me, but despite our age difference we had a great deal in common. We were both born in Melbourne. His parents, like mine, were educated professional people in a society articulated by class, in which family connection and occupation were as essential for influence as talent or money. He had all the discipline and focus of a tough ex-serviceman and successful athlete, and was extremely intelligent. I had grown up with uncles and a father just like this, decisive men who got on with their lives and expected their wives to do the same. Born during the war, I was just old enough to be part of a generation where a *wife* was an acceptable model. Although some of my mother's friends worked – as scientists, physiotherapists, in art galleries or their own businesses – many did not. There was much entertaining in those Melbourne circles. Where power is based on family and class, the *taken for granted* is connection through social activity. So it was natural for me to concentrate on the house and Clif, and see what could be done to change the federal government.

Artists often bluntly articulate things over which society takes time, and Myra Skipper had acknowledged the likelihood of our companionship. We were blessed by Myra's encouragement, but we were both confident. From the first night we shared the assumption that we would be together. This must have been confusing for people who were used to his cynicism about relationships. But he was sure.

If the abruptness of our commitment was confusing, it added to the myths that developed later when reputation morphed into fame, as our life, or, rather, an image of our life, was displayed in newspapers and on television. But this was before fame, when the detail of our days meant meeting family and friends, when pots and pans were packed up and settled into new cupboards, as we met each other's lives.

On my first Monday in the house I was woken by a young voice.

'Excuse me, how do you have your tea?'

It was Dailan, his younger son. I grabbed Clif's dressing gown and cooked porridge for the two of us, hearing about the junior classes at Hurstbridge High School. Clif joined us, and they told me about shopping for food and cooking in Paris.

We decided to have open house on Sundays at lunchtime. At other times, unless there was an arrangement in place, I would give visitors a cup of tea and say he was busy. This controlled people dropping in unannounced to catch up with Clif and protected his routine, because at first I could not filter the friends from acquaintances and strangers.

The covered entrance opened into the large room where the couch had fought with the painting, a Fred Williams. It had been Clif's first studio, and its big glass wall gave onto an indoor garden, connecting to his present studio. With a long table he'd made from railway sleepers, the room had the architectural effect of a formal hall, so that unexpected arrivals stayed there looking at paintings and the pre-Columbian artefacts Clif and Marlene had brought back from Mexico. Early in that first week I found a slim and obviously nervous woman waiting there.

'Can I help you?'

'Is Clif around?'

When he came, he was wary. 'What is it?'

'I've come to get some things.'

'What things? Everything here is mine.'

This seemed odd, who was this person? I asked to be introduced.

'This is Marlene, my wife.'

Oh. What things did she want, had she left something behind? And it transpired that they'd agreed before he left for Europe that their separation would be permanent, but as she'd been travelling and then he had, they'd not gone through the house to sort domestic objects.

Begin as you mean to go on.

'Marlene, this house is yours and it represents your life. I know that you helped build the walls and decorated them. You will always be welcome here. Clif and I are going up to the pub now, and when you've finished here you could come and have a drink with us. We will be able to buy whatever we need, so please take what you like. Clif, if you don't agree with this then I will leave now.'

Marlene looked at me. 'I will never forget this.'

I realised, much later, that she was astonished. And later still I envied her . . . no one would speak up for me. But it was thus we became friends.

Tim Ealey rang from Monash University Zoology Department: a baby kangaroo needed care. Marlene and Clif had been an informal outstation since the department was formed by Jock Marshall, Clif's commanding officer in wartime New Guinea. In that same first week another kangaroo, and a wombat about a year old, injured by a car. The house was filling up.

My family arrived for lunch on Sunday, my sister Sue with a little baby. The weather had warmed up again, so the doors were open. About twelve of us at table; my brother Christopher beside me, carving a leg of lamb. Serving dishes circulated, everyone had food and drink. A pause before I began to eat, just to think it through. The borzoi where it couldn't get to the kangaroos. The baby in its pram, safe from the burly wombat. The big brown snake curled up in the warm patch inside the open door. I turned to my plate, then thought aloud. 'We don't own a snake.'

Christopher picked up the carving knife. 'Where is it?'

'There, beside you on the floor.'

He reached down and cut off its head.

I'd asked Clif to have his mother up but, confined to a chair, she was content to meet me in her hostel in Melbourne. One had the impression of willpower and intelligence. In a refrain to be repeated on every visit we made, he complained that she'd tied him to the clothes line when he was three. She replied that he wouldn't stay in the garden. I would watch the two pairs of eyes in those Welsh features, and listen to them talking about not his painting, but hers, discussing her latest clouds. More than a duty, not a pleasure. But they seemed to enjoy the old battle.

Friends and family, the house and the bush focussed and held us. The certainty about being in place gave me confidence as we stepped into politics and life in the public eye. But most of all, we were heard when we spoke out because the issues that engaged us, about which we sought to influence politicians and public opinion, always came from our lives and our experience. Clif's friends from Monash would teach me the science of the environment; his commitment was from observation. After the death of his tamed wild cat he had seen native birds return to the bush around the house. In the Second World War, a soldier, he had refused to go back to the front. My determination to see the ALP made respectable and elected federally came from teaching in facility-bare and teacher-deprived schools.

Mischa the borzoi, too exotic for Dunmoochin, had to go. I would have no dogs or cats, but I learnt the unsurpassed pleasure of a cuddling wombat. That lovely spring drew on, wattle bloomed and pale pink blossoms formed, tiny spiders floated on the morning breezes. In the evenings when we were alone he'd bring the day's painting in from the studio, and prop it beside the television. As images from the Vietnam jungle flickered on the television screen, as he was asked to speak out from his experience and known pacifism, memories came back, stories from the war.

3

BACKGROUND

Ice cream, chicken with honey, soy and ginger, billy tea

Surprising at first to find Clif and his artist friends watched television. After all, they moved among intellectuals, writers, academics, and in those circles, in those days, there was considerable disdain for popular culture and for sport. But the issue is visual language, and television is visual language that moves. He put the painting he was working on beside the television set to keep an eye on it, so he was conscious of it. If he'd left it in the studio and dropped in to visit after sunset he might have been tempted to work in the wrong light. Artificial light alters colour and the relationship between colours.

When we were alone for the evening we would have dinner watching the ABC news and current affairs. Then, as scenes from the Vietnam War played on the screen, as young draft resisters argued their cases and were pursued by the police, his angry mood began. In our first weeks together it seemed to be vehemence at the idea of war again, at the idiocy of Australia following the United States into a hopeless conflict.

He had been on attachment to the Americans for a time in New Guinea, and had no respect for American soldiers.

The tough experienced soldier, glowering on the couch.

'They walked about in the jungle with their radios on. They called out to each other. There were desperate snipers tied to trees, starving fanatics ready to use their last bullets to get as many of us as they could. You had to move quietly, to watch out. You never drew attention to yourself.'

Such careless behaviour was astonishing, but so had been the luxury in which the American troops lived.

The incredulous teenager who had joined up.

'And they had ice-cream. The refrigerators came up with the second wave.'

The manner in which it was served, just when he'd seen his first ice-cream for years.

'They queued for a meal and it was put in the dixie on top of the rest of their food.'

Not people to fight alongside.

But we weren't much alone. Dunmoochin was the name adopted for the co-operative Clif founded when he wanted to settle in the area, and which had broken up after some years as marriages and partnerships of individual members dissolved.

The word Dunmoochin (itself a take on D.H. Lawrence's reference in *Kangaroo* to 'Wyewurk') referred both to the area and to the house in which we lived. The sense of co-operative and community was still strong in those who'd been there since the beginning; neighbours would often join us, inspecting me and catching up with Clif. Dailan lived with us, and Clif let out studios he owned on the blocks of land he'd retained after the co-operative ended. The painter John Olsen and his wife Valerie were living in one of the studios, and John worked in another.

He arrived to look me over and they came to dinner. I made honey soy and ginger chicken, so commonplace now, so exotic then. John decided I was an exciting cook.

'This could be interesting, very interesting, Clif, you have something here.'

John talked about food and wine and Europe, wrote poetry and quoted it. He seemed a delightful friend and neighbour. I was wary, though; he tended to arrive with a bottle of wine for lunch. And the bonhomie perhaps had an edge. Clif had a clear routine, he didn't drink when he was working, which meant not until dark. John was just a bit disparaging of this, as if we were somehow less sophisticated than he. He would ask Clif, who was slightly colour blind, to name colours, and be amused by his answers. Clif appeared not to notice.

In look and manner John was a contrast to Clif. I wondered about the differences. Both were artists, unconventional. Perhaps that John seemed to operate only in the art and literary worlds, his focus the paint and the brush, poetry part of his output; Clif always thought about issues beyond paint. Our individual personalities react with the culture of our family and the society around us as we develop. Was the difference that John came from Sydney? Perhaps that John was those crucial four years younger than Clif, so that he was at school during the war when Clif was a soldier.

Clif and I had no courtship or even a period of friendship to get to know each other's families or histories. There was a lot to discover, but we didn't set about conveying information systematically; memories and opinions were triggered by events, by places we passed as we travelled, in response to news items, in the usual ways. One of the things we had in common was that as children we were each close to a man of science, and also to an engineer. These men taught us about the history of science in the social and political structures in which we lived.

'If you can imagine it, it will happen,' Clif would say, and I could hear his grandfather speak.

Clif left school in his early teens. But the basis on which he would develop his ideas and values was already laid. His sense of personal and social responsibility, ideas of structure, systems of enquiry, his family culture, were of that Anglican and protestant liberal tradition that gave Australia its values. As important as the particular Anglican ideas of connection to society that he learned through his maternal grandfather, and the protestant discipline and independence his father taught, there was another tradition which formed his character and his views. This was to be a source of friendship and of passion throughout his life. Clif's father was an engineer, and he taught Clif to make things, how design related to production. Clif's maternal grandfather, Ernest Cooke, was a renowned astronomer.

The industrial revolution has a bad name these days, because it gave us carbon emissions on a grand scale and mass production. But that revolution sprang from and nourished the philosophies of the enlightenment. Science, innovations in technology, rail, and telegraph, meant the democratisation of communication, in a way as profound as that produced by computers and the internet. Clif was conscious that Ernest Cooke had been at the fore of the nineteenth- and early twentieth-century international telecommunications revolution, and he thought about the continuity of ideas in history. Technology – innovation – was a family matter.

When he was a child in Melbourne his grandfather was living in Adelaide, so Clif did not know him well. In 1935 Clif's father, Thomas Pugh, took a position in Brisbane, and, the house and Clif's pony sold, Clif and his mother joined him there a year later. But after his father's sudden death in September 1938, when Clif was not quite fourteen, Violet sold her piano to pay for a term's fees for Clif at Ivanhoe Grammar, and returned to Adelaide to live with her family. Money ran out, and Clif had to leave school after this one term, so he too joined the family in Adelaide. There he had the comfort of connection and class to balance the loss of his father and the financial strain it brought. Here, at a crucial time in his early teens, the boy learned from Ernest Cooke to observe, and to consider the implications of his observations. Family, and time with a grandfather whose intelligence he had inherited, were sources of Clif's later confidence.

Shortly before we met, his mother had given Clif the letters he'd written to her during the war. He'd joined up in Adelaide, twice in fact, the first time putting up his age, at which point Violet intervened and had him discharged. He'd rejoined as soon as he turned eighteen. He read a letter each day in the studio, and in that early summer of 1970, as he went through the first letters, he recalled the time before he'd joined up, the things he'd left behind, the time in South Australia.

Ernest Cooke was born in South Australia. His London-born father Ebenezer had arrived in Adelaide in 1862, just twenty-seven years after South Australia's foundation as the first Australian colony of free settlers, to take up a position as accountant for a large smelting company. He soon became manager of that company and won a seat in parliament, later retiring in order to be appointed the Commissioner of Audit. Exercising authority through his personality more than by precise legislative precept, he established fundamental principles of civil service accountability for the colony. Ebenezer was an impressive man. He was an art collector, a cultivated, confident man of the Adelaide establishment, influential and well liked. But his son Ernest, Clif's grandfather, became much more.

Such a small society in those days. A child of the Australian establishment was part of British society. The most talented academically went to Cambridge or Oxford, often remaining in Britain for at least the early part of their careers. Ernest Cooke was a brilliant scholar at St Peter's College and at the University of Adelaide, where he was awarded the South Australian Scholarship. But instead of taking up the scholarship and choosing the British option, Cooke chose to work with the great Sir Charles Todd, South Australia's astronomer and meteorologist, one of the most important and influential men on the continent. Cooke joined Todd in the major undertaking of the surveys of the borders of South Australia with the three eastern colonies. This had been the first step on the way to Cooke's international reputation.

Cooke's artist grandson was to have the same quiet confidence in his abilities and commitment to this country, and indeed to draw his inspiration from the vast spaces his grandfather knew. Clif saw Australia as the essential place for a creative Australian. It is unremarkable to make this claim now, in a thriving competitive art world, but it was astonishing in the 1940s and 50s, when every young artist clamoured to get away. However, Clif's vocation had been encouraged by an internationally connected family of cultivation and taste. He wasn't fleeing a stultifying suburban family that feared artists. Nor did he suppose he could not live as an artist in Australia. The walls of the houses in which he'd grown up and those of his family's circle were evidence that there was a market, and he knew how to operate in those circles.

In that liminal time while he waited in Adelaide to join the army, his grandfather was – as grandfathers tend to be – more apparently indulgent and gentle than Clif's tough austere father. The survey with Todd had meant months on foot with packhorses, camping out under starry skies; his grandfather encouraged the young Clif to take a horse into the hills for the weekend, camping out and observing the country, learning to be independent, to be alone in the bush. He found the boy work, drafting maps, just as he had made maps all those years ago. From that time Clif would always gravitate to the company of scientists, and would measure men by the standard set by Cooke.

Such a vast world in those days. It is almost impossible to imagine. All the calculations by which we order our daily lives – the maps, processes, the physical structures, their systems – were planned and made by such men as Todd and Cooke. Exploration and wilderness are concepts made common by colour television, but once they carried a different meaning. Road signs and maps, however minimal, mark the landscape for us, and speedometers measure our travels.

When we travelled in the desert, Clif would think about his grandfather and the survey. 'Relative time came to the desert with the border survey.'

Relative time is a recent concept, a product of the industrial revolution, of rail technology and the telegraph. Before it was necessary to synchronise the train timetable and possible to send telegrams, time was local.

'They still have their own time in some of these places.'

He meant that they didn't need relative time, and he meant the settlers; it was not a remark about indigenous culture.

At the border, as I drove the borrowed ute across the gibber plain, where three states meet in abstract geometric imaginative concepts that we carry in our minds, he spoke as the young mapmaker.

'Latitude, that is, distance from the equator, is not a problem. The sun and stars' courses are understood, so that, provided their position is visible or known, you can fix the north–south location on a map, or on the map you are making.'

Clif's imagination was supported by precise observation; his paintings incorporated representations of distance informed by a mapmaker's skill and a knowledge of terrain. His training as an artist was added to his understanding of scientific method, and how the scientist approached the world. He felt his way into the landscape, wanting to be at one with it, trying to give up the control of geometry and physics.

At night the space and height of the desert closes in, the air cools. Fire is for cooking and warmth; its crackling and its glow make an intimate place where sleep will come with contentment. Time becomes irrelevant, so he talked about time as we looked at the stars.

'Calculating the east–west bearing, longitude, is dependent on the concept of relative time, of knowing the time at a fixed point and the time at the point where longitude is being measured.'

The image is through waves of heat, of quaintly dressed men pacing the miles, dust stirred by the packhorses' hooves, the creak of leather, a trail of smoke as they pause to boil the billy, make notes and confer. But the word is *physicist*, and for these scientists the laboratory was the desert. Until the survey, for a nineteenth-century European in Australia, journeys were made across land as trackless as the sea; surveying the continent was crucial to its development for settlers.

Todd came to Australia convinced that the speed of transmission by telegraph was a vital tool for establishing longitude, the east–west position, and mapping the colonies. Because we've had radio and telephone and facsimile for so long, because the internet stores information as well as sends it, we think of the telegraph as a communication system. In the desert Clif taught me to see that the telegraph, its almost instantaneous delivery of signals, was also about geography, about place. Calculating position by longitude is time over space, telecommunications. By the telegraph, Todd made longitude available, and changed the way Europeans could navigate the continent. Telecommunication was of consequence then as now: the telegraph to the nineteenth century, as the global positioning system to the twenty-first.

One must think of these men as a cross between astronauts and those who built Microsoft. Colonial society valued them because it understood the connection between research and result, the importance of recruiting the most intelligent and taking their advice. The rewards of public service were enough for them; they didn't want riches. Clif always made the distinction between 'academics' bound up in systems, and practical imaginative scientists and scholars.

'If you can imagine it, it will happen.'

Ernest Cooke was to develop the use of photography, and make meteorology a tool for farmers and shipping. In 1896, Todd suggested his protégé as government astronomer for Western Australia, the first such post in Australia. Cooke's time with Todd and his observation of the career of his own father, Ebenezer, prepared him for the discipline and politics of public service, and he developed a remarkable reputation as an astronomer. His entry in the *Australian Dictionary of Biography* notes that 'His work was acclaimed internationally, quoting the Astronomer Royal's advice to "follow implicitly the lead of the Perth Observatory and copy their methods"'. Cooke had his new observatory equipped for the photographic mapping of the stars, and in 1909 an international conference in Paris adopted his proposals for this global project. He had believed, and he had demonstrated, that one could stay in Australia and develop an international reputation from the continent.

No wonder his grandson was without his contemporaries' colonial cringe.

Clif's father Thomas Pugh, like Ebenezer and Ernest Cooke, had used his training in the public service for the public interest. Knowing his father and grandfather, Clif had particular contempt for power-hungry or inefficient public servants, and respect for intelligent men who might have made a great deal of money in business, but joined the public service to provide objective information and advice. He was lucky when he left the army to find such a man running the National Gallery School. Bill Dargie (later, in recognition of his service as Chairman of the Commonwealth Art Advisory Board, Sir William) had principles and exercised judgement about people. Clif was to benefit from this.

The school, established in the National Gallery of Victoria when it was built in the nineteenth century was still, when Clif was there, *the* place in Australia to be trained as an artist. Louis Buvelot was its founder; Eugene von Guerard taught in those studios.

Clif had not been accepted when he first applied. 'I just scraped in. I talked myself in, my work wasn't good enough. Dargie rejected the work. But I was determined to be trained. So I just kept talking, until he said, "All right, if you're so determined, come in, then."'

Dargie was an extraordinary figure. At the time he had a number of ex-soldiers as pupils, and imposed strict discipline. The first stage of training involved drawing plaster casts of classical figures every day for months, until the drawings were photograph-perfect. Only then could you start to paint. Dargie's ex-pupils did not think him a great painter, but all of them respected him as a teacher and as an official, both within the school and as a member and Chairman of the Commonwealth Art Advisory Board. Clif had affection and admiration for him, and gratitude.

Dargie had effectively been Clif's patron as well as his teacher. When he was still a 'junior' student, Clif had persuaded Dargie to walk up from the Gallery School to see a show of Sidney Nolan's Kelly paintings at Tye's gallery. He never analysed Nolan's pictures when he told this story, just saying that he'd seen 'something different'. Years later we focussed on Dargie's response, on the moment when things changed.

He wanted Dargie's approval; of the work and of his own excitement.

'Dargie looked at them, he looked at me, and said, "I think it's all rather decadent."'

Dargie had brought with him his 'top student', who echoed the disapproval.

Clif was disappointed but determined. He kept going, but when the teacher can't see what the pupil can, there is a point when it seems improper to sit at the foot of a master from whom you can no longer learn.

This was a crisis for Clif, but not just of conscience. He was paid to train as an artist by the Commonwealth Reconstruction Training Scheme (CRTS). A wage, it was enough for food, lodging and materials. He would be taking a great risk to leave the school. No choice, though. He felt he had learned all Dargie could teach him. He decided to give up the CRTS income, to say from this moment on that he was an artist. When he arrived to tell Dargie he wanted to leave the school he found not disapproval, but a welcome.

'He said, "Come in, Clif," and when I explained that I disagreed about the Nolan paintings, I thought they had something in them, a way of seeing the landscape, that I felt I needed to understand that, he said, "Yes, I thought you'd want to leave." He had this piece of paper, this blank piece of paper. "Now, come on, write your signature here." On a blank piece of paper. "Why?" He knew the rules, he worked in the system. He said, "I'll have to sign you in and out each day, or you won't get the CRTS money." He practised my signature, until he got it right.'

By this gesture Dargie gave Clif months of freedom, and also gave him acceptance.

'He went way beyond his line of duty for me because when I left, before my time was up, I still got paid. He did keep an eye on things, on me, for me and for the government. He was honest. He used to come up to see if I was working up here. He was very good; he could have got himself into trouble. It doesn't matter now, but it was possible, he might have lost his job. He put himself on the line for me, he knew he'd taken me as far as he could but he trusted my determination, at least I think he did. I painted the paintings for the travelling scholarship here, not in the school. You were supposed to paint them there, under supervision. He used to come up and see me. He was a great man.'

It was not about rank or class. All Clif's army talk dismissed officers unless they were effective, and although class negotiations in Australia were more flexible than in Europe, class was a very obvious part of life. Clif had the luck of the upper class, to be able to dismiss it. The Cooke family was ironic about its own status, or at least Clif's mother Violet was; when I last visited her, some time after we separated, she asked if I thought Clif's latest affair was 'one of us'.

Violet's manner was contained, and ironic. Her hostel room was full of her conventional landscapes, but the atmosphere was of constrained intelligence, not embroidery or lace – one did not think 'ladylike'. Her grandfather Ebenezer Cooke had been known for his cultural pursuits; her father Ernest was not only a research scientist but also an inventor, winning a gold medal at the 1924 Wembley exhibition for a sun-dial which could be used to determine local time and true north.

Perhaps his inventions, rather than the small social circle in Perth,

Violet. Marie. Colin Pugh. Barbara

led to Violet Cooke meeting Thomas Owen Pugh, Clif's father. Clif used to talk about his father's as well as his grandfather's inventions; Thomas Pugh devised the first egg-washing machine. An engineering draughtsman who came to Perth from the United Kingdom with a diesel rail locomotive he had designed, Thomas was also an amateur painter, a cultivated man.

Violet and Ernest had moved to Melbourne after their marriage. Clif was the youngest of three boys, and until his early adolescence the family lived in comfort. Whenever we went to Kew we'd drive past the house they'd owned when he was a toddler, and he'd mention the clothes line, and whenever we visited Violet, they would talk about him absconding, and the clothes line. Her dignity and authority were entirely to be expected in a woman who had grown up in that well-connected group from which her father's international reputation had developed.

It was no wonder, then, that John Olsen's little teases had no effect on her favourite son. John wore a beret, a kerchief, and a colourful waistcoat; Clif jeans and an army shirt. They were durable, comfortable and cheap, from army disposal stores. He had spent time in army prison for various forms of casual insubordination, especially his attitude to clothing, but his objection was to a particular style. One can imagine the frustration of his sergeant. 'Some shirts had no buttons.' And always the gesture, as he ripped open the imaginary shirt front.

He never wore a tie, regarding them as silly. Which they become, when logic is applied. Most men wore a uniform of suit in those days, so most artists were immediately recognisable, as they tended to casual. Except lovely tubby Fred Williams, always wanting to look respectable, wore a suit to go out.

We adapt to our circumstances as best we can. Clif's beard and relatively long hair were a hangover from days of straitened circumstance, and for convenience (haircuts and razors cost money and take time), not from a desire to outrage. In the early days of struggle he'd had to deal with people who thought the decision was a deliberate style choice. They commented without questioning his motives, and this re-enforced his determination to dress as he wanted. When I encouraged him to buy clothes, personal taste for vivid colours and comfort moulded his choice. Quite early on I found a sheepskin vest. It features in so many of the photographs; temperature, not occasion, the deciding factor.

The paint-stained clothes weren't bad business. He had the measure of the men who ran that small Melbourne society. *Effete* was hard for them to accept, but they could enjoy eccentric, especially jeans, which were the working man's clothes, manly, framing Clif's appearance as artist. And the shirts were a reminder that he'd been a soldier, a patriotic man of action. Every exhibition catalogue mentioned his war service; and there he is in photographs at those openings, dressed just as if we were at home watching television, with the painting beside the set.

4

PORTRAITS,
IN A MARRIAGE

Sausage sizzle, crème brûlée

Clif articulated the way we'd live together. He wanted, he said, to have a house where he could entertain. His dealer Rudy Komon was responsible for exhibitions and all deals were accounted through him, set off against the running account that included Clif's retainer. But the house was a gallery, people interested in the work would want to come up. Clif wanted portrait clients who came to the studio to be comfortable. It was interesting, but it was not comfortable. He had originally camped on the site, then built a wattle and daub shack, to which he added in mud brick when the kids needed a room, and when he wanted a separate studio. In the mornings and at night we needed fires, even on a warm spring day.

The weather was warming up, and as Alistair Knox pointed out when he and Margot came up for lunch, the ambience of wattle and daub, of rustic posts beside mud brick was one thing, but mosquitoes and wind would find their way through the gaps. He and Clif decided that Alistair should design an extension to sit above the kitchen and laundry. I look back and see Alistair, who had employed Clif in the early days, and was fond of us both, using my arrival in Clif's life to persuade Clif to accept the rewards of his success.

I plan, I organise; but I have no memory even of discussing the elements of the way we began to live, simply of what Clif told me. How to explain, even to myself these days, when women have such different relationships with men? Probably because Clif spoke aloud my taken-for-granted, both its general and the particular. For instance, I'd known what the house would look like, and when it didn't, I would wait for it to change. I knew there would be the three rooms Alastair Knox would build on, they were in my mind's eye before I went to live at Dunmoochin. I was not at all surprised when Clif and Alastair made the decision to build them, or other changes came about: when Phyllida Hodgkinson suggested a brilliant alteration, when Marlene decided I should have a room of my own. I lived much in the moment, and this worked well for me. When Clif gave me a carpenter for two weeks as a birthday present, I designed and built myself a new kitchen.

The house was in many ways a symbol of the way we lived, adapting to changes, unconstrained and individual. Sometimes it changed unexpectedly from one day to the next. I would go to a meeting or to the market and return to a huge hole in a wall, mud everywhere. This was interesting, never an issue between us. What made me anxious initially, perhaps a residual effect of the law school at Melbourne University, or perhaps of my engineer uncle, was that the local council was never involved. No planning or building permits, rarely any plans. Clif was uninterested in official views about the shape and structure of his house.

'If an inspector arrives I'll explain that there are no plans because it's a very old house.'

Indeed, the mud bricks made on site, the second-hand doors and windows, lent verisimilitude to this argument, at least until we added the white Colorbond roof. The joy was that every change was a visual improvement, and also meant I could patch the holes around the doors and windows. Eventually the house became the lovely light-filled series of rooms I'd seen in my mind's eye.

The mornings remained cold in November, and as we had breakfast one day I realised that Dai and Clif were both shivering. I looked for winter clothes. Hardly any; after two consecutive summers Dai had outgrown all his warm things, the spring that year had been warm, and this was a very cold morning. Alastair had known that the years of struggle had meant not considering comfort, but it wasn't apparent to me. Clif had money in the bank, so we went shopping to the local store. The unaccustomed choice of several pairs of cords, jeans, and sweaters arriving in Clif's life at the same time as he not only agreed to allow Alastair to design an extension with an indoor bathroom, but to pay for someone else to build it, installed me in Clif's mind as a symbol of luxury and abandonment.

He wanted to buy two houses in Melbourne. We would use the first as a townhouse, he would let the other. These would mean security; he would always be able to rely on rental income to support us, in case the work stopped selling. He had just achieved this goal when he and Marlene separated; she was to have the houses he owned in Fitzroy and Shoreham as her divorce settlement. Clif had given her a few paintings, but it was clear that this had been reluctantly. I thought the financial ruthlessness was a symptom of a sort of panic. One quite practical reason for his reluctance to give Marlene pictures was that he managed his market well, being very careful about prices, ensuring that supply did not quite meet demand. He was afraid that giving pictures as part of the settlement would mean that he would effectively be competing against himself in the marketplace, and not have control of price.

He wanted me to find a housekeeper, someone who would do the dishes and clean, and take care of the animals and house when we were away. He gave me one hundred dollars a week to cover all the household expenses, including the wages for the housekeeper. This was a not unreasonable amount at the time. Rudy sent wine, that was no issue, and I managed to employ someone who lived in one of the cottages, and light, heat, feed and clothe the three of us. One stand I did take: I refused to pay for his cigarettes.

Clif was pleased that I assumed I'd care for Dai. As Marlene was next door, Dai could see her on the way home from school and, when we were out, have a meal with her. Shane, the fifteen-year-old, returned to use us as a base soon after I arrived at Dunmoochin, with those difficulties frequently seen between powerful tough fathers and their sons. The focussed energetic Clif had not taught his boys the discipline that gave him the power to articulate an objective and adopt strategies to achieve that objective. Shane, like Clif, had left school at fourteen; when I met Clif Shane was rather unfocussed.

The problems between them were fairly conventional. Clif was irritated with himself for not being a better parent, conscious that his commitment to his work during their childhood meant the boys had not had great advantages. Shane also had the teenage boy's problematic relationship to cars: never enough money to buy a good one, and it always breaks down. Eventually Clif settled on each boy a block of land from the parcel of titles he owned at Dunmoochin. Shane found expression of his talent by training in art and stayed nearby; Dai went north and became an environmental activist.

Clif liked to get up and work around the house, fencing, repairing and digging for a couple of hours, then to go to the studio. I took morning coffee to him, he came in for lunch, and I often joined him for tea in the afternoon in the studio. The strength of his habits made it easy to fit in, explore the house, find places to put flowers and books and get to know the paintings, his and his friends', as I would get to know the men who painted them.

Like most people who had lived through the Depression, even those who'd kept jobs and income, Clif was careful with money. He was concerned when we met that the art world and Rudy's clients might not like the work that was to come after Paris. He was struggling with the celebration of beauty, the very insouciance of the way the School of Paris made light and water – the elements of nature – its own. But Clif was not known for beautiful paintings, and that was his worry.

In that post-Depression, post-war Australia, people could live well if they painted society portraits and landscapes in the tradition of the Australian impressionists, the 'gum-tree' school. But the more sophisticated art world – centred on the National Gallery of Victoria and galleries thought of as 'contemporary' – had embraced modernity. Clif had made his own way within this market, confronting darker images than most of his post-war contemporaries. In general market terms, in an area of absolute discretionary spending, he had successfully introduced a challenging, unconventional product to a market segment in which beautiful and enjoyable items ordinarily triumphed. Clif's concern was that, even if his work became beautiful, it might lose support.

I was to learn that the money fears could be ignored when a curious or beautiful object came into view. He was okay for money at the moment; the London show had done well. He intended to do a couple of portraits that had been lined up, and expected these would keep us in the immediate future. There was no need for me to earn money. He needed me to be there for visitors and clients, and I would be able to take an active part in the local ALP campaign. There were friends, official guests, and there were fundraisers, mainly for the environment or the ALP. Clif was a member of the local Hurstbridge branch so I joined it soon after we met, almost immediately becoming the branch representative on the Casey federal electorate campaign committee.

The branch was left-wing; Race Mathews, the ALP-endorsed candidate, was right-wing, so they said. Factional boundaries were not quasi-official in those days, and divisions perhaps more deeply felt. These divisions are and were along fascinating ideological strata of history, religion, family and culture. Interesting that a man with Marx's sense of irony articulated ideas that led a hundred years later to bearded men in a weatherboard cottage at the other end of the world debating Item 4 on the agenda: *whether to support a right-wing Left-Party candidate or allow the people to continue suffering so that they would rise up to overthrow the whole constitutional system;* followed by Item 5: *what to charge for the sausage sizzle.*

I travelled across the electorate and into suburbia to the first meeting of the committee, to discover more sausage sizzles on the agenda. Casey electorate sprawled across the outer eastern suburbs of Melbourne, where families had followed the dream of fresh air and their own homes to find it materialised beyond public transport, with no infrastructure such as libraries and swimming pools, no childcare, with under-resourced and overcrowded state schools, without sewerage, without pre-school education. Areas of natural bush were being developed without regard for habitat or species conservation; even residents uninformed about science could see the bush degrading. Boys of eighteen, their brothers and sons, were being conscripted to fight a foreign war. Women, their wives and sisters, were paid less than men doing the same work; once married they lost job security, and if an unmarried woman had a child she was ineligible for income support soon after the baby was born.

Thus local concerns were in the air, beside the larger ones. The task for the Labor Party was apparent: to articulate and consolidate the agenda with clarity. The election in two years time could be won. The challenge was to harness anxiety about the Vietnam War to less dramatic concerns – to highlight the injustice of the paternalistic constraints under which Aboriginal people lived, the effects of degrading the natural environment, the ephemeral yet personal issues such as women's unarticulated longings for a fuller participation at every level in the community, education at every level – and to ground these ideas with material local concerns, such as sewerage and transport.

Although the ALP had some candidates who seemed electable, for a long time its controlling ideologues held that the press was the enemy. Media ineptitude, even of capable candidates and MPs, meant the party's image was disastrous. But first things first. One might imagine snappy posters and well-designed leaflets, a lively engaging series of ads in the local papers, but before one could mention such luxuries money would need to be raised. A lot of sausages, or I could talk to Clif.

After that first meeting of the campaign committee, as I drove back across the electorate to the wombat and the artist, wondering who had arrived while I was out and what I would cook them for dinner, it seemed that anything was possible. One might influence a future federal government, and the price of a sizzled sausage.

Clif and I shared physical intimacy, political views, and the culture that formed us. We both wanted a comfortable and beautiful space in which to live, to nourish us, our friends, and our ideas. Twenty years apart in age, we were at either end of that last generation in western culture to take for granted that the man earned money and the woman kept house. Within all this, there was the intuition that had brought me to Dunmoochin; his intuition, and the wartime pain he began to share with me. All this might have happened for either of us with someone else. The structure that kept our relationship going for so long – through changes in power and dependence, through illness, disaster, career, travel, lovers, mistresses – was what we did together with the portraits. He had anticipated I'd run the house and entertain; this was the model in the culture. But the portraits were a different level of involvement.

Dame Mabel Brookes was the first of 'our' portraits. Clif did not use photographs or begin with sketches. He spent as much time as possible with his subjects who, ideally, came up to Dunmoochin as often as he needed, for the day or to stay with us. If we went to them, for instance when we were interstate or overseas, he would spend time observing them at work, when relaxing. He might do a sketch or two to 'note' something. But such sketches were more to keep the internal conversation going when he wasn't near the easel; they weren't planning the look of the work. The painting as *painting* developed on the board.

Of course each painting was a product of years of training, of practice, of experience. Clif loved to tell the story of Whistler's response in court to the question 'How long did it take you to paint this picture?' 'All my life.'

All my life, my whole body. The neuro-physiologist Dick Denton remarked to me when he was writing *The Hunger for Salt* that he thought the very act of hand-eye coordination allows the brain to access levels of information and helps sort it. For an artist, one can add that imagination is accessed too, and for the portraitist, intuition. Clif had been an athlete, wrestling in the army (you got steak if you agreed to wrestle or box). Every morning he worked physically on the house or around the property, or, if we were away from home, walked or swam. After the war he'd worked as a ballroom-dancing coach. We used to dance when we were alone, fishtailing across the new slate floor in the main room. But the most pleasurable physical activities were painting and drawing. He stood at the easel and his whole body was engaged in the act, moving from board to table where his paints sat. As I write I remember him, balanced and concentrated.

He had always painted portraits, all his contemporaries did, indeed many artists still do. It is just another way of articulating the world. He began, as most artists do, with self-portraits. The model being always available, co-operative, and free. Then he painted friends: the philosopher David Armstrong, poet Noel Macainsh, the actors Peter O'Shaughnessy and Barry Humphries, musicians, potters, lovers such as Margot and Marlene, and the boys. Visitors saw the portraits, he exhibited them as part of his practice, the word got around, and he began to be asked to paint people he didn't know. He'd had establishment support from his early days and that had helped. Daryl Lindsay, director of the National Gallery of Victoria, and Bill Dargie were both on the Commonwealth Art Advisory Board, and they'd arranged for him to do the official portrait of Viscount De L'Isle when De L'Isle was Governor-General.

There were two problems with painting portraits of strangers on request, for money. One was that the normal arrangement delivered the finished product and its copyright into the hands of the person or body commissioning a picture. The Commonwealth Arts Advisory Board (CAAB) had insisted on taking the De L'Isle, a painting with which Clif was unhappy. He resolved this at the time by painting De L'Isle again, and subsequently by never accepting a commission. He would 'have a go', and the sitter or the institution that wanted the portrait could have first option if the picture was for sale, that is, if Clif were satisfied with it. He thus retained freedom and copyright if he did sell the work. This left the second problem, getting to know the sitter.

Clif didn't want *pose*. The brilliance of his drawing made 'getting a likeness' easy. He wanted to paint the substance of the person, what they were like, not what they looked like. But the problem with portraits, not only portraits of strangers, was that once he was concentrating, he would lose track of the conversation, and the sitter tended to freeze up. Visual language, painting language, is managed by a different part of the brain from talk. Marlene had been a help if she liked the person and was not in awe of them. But by the end of the marriage she had lost interest in distracting clients, especially if she disapproved of them. And if, in the absence of Marlene, the subject brought a friend or a partner, that person's presence might intrude. Clif didn't guard his studio as closely as some painters, but he did want psychological control of the space.

For me, engaging his sitters was part of being there, of making Clif a comfortable home, taking pressure off where I could. If the issue was getting to know his subjects so he could do good portraits, then the trick was to encourage them to be themselves. My opinions were irrelevant; theirs were what counted for the exercise of portrait. If I found their ideas or personality unattractive I could enjoy encouraging their wildest expression, just to make sure that Clif got the picture.

At the time we met, a young businessman, Terry Whelan, had arranged for Clif to paint Dame Mabel Brookes, as a wedding present for her nephew. Clif asked if I would mind talking to her while he painted. Not at all. At seventy-nine she was a powerful force in the studio, undeterred by the mud brick and the wombats. She had never been a beauty, so 'What do I look like?' was not a question; indeed she was interestingly incurious about the exercise. As I describe her I match her in memory with Clif's mother: the same conviction and confidence, from a comfortable childhood at the highest level of a small society.

There was a recurring phenomenon in my communication with Clif's portrait clients who, after a while, realised that what looked like a child could actually make conversation. It happened when I was talking to Sir John McEwen and to the Duke of Edinburgh. They would suddenly, out of the blue, give me advice. It was always apt and practical and unrelated to our conversations. The first time was while I chatted to Mabel Brookes, who said suddenly, 'I want you to write this down' and gave me a recipe for crème brûlée. 'You will be doing a great deal of entertaining. This will be easy to prepare in advance. Only use this recipe, they use it at Trinity College Cambridge and they call it Burnt Cream. It's richer and better than any made with milk.'

As indeed it is, and she was quite right, very good for entertaining. Prescient, because the real entertaining was yet to come, these were our early days. Mabel Brookes was known as a society hostess and for her charity work, but these alone did not define her. She had written several books and travelled the world. Framed by the time into which she was born, she was a woman who would these days have an independent career.

On St Helena, the island to which Napoleon Bonaparte was exiled and where he died, the defeated Emperor was at first housed in a pavilion on the estate of Dame Mabel's ancestor, Alexander Balcombe. Dame Mabel had grown up with gifts given to her family by Napoleon. These tangible reminders of the association, as a consequence, had encouraged an interest in the Emperor. Curious, that Clif's first portrait after his return from Paris should have been of someone so connected to France;

but we didn't know about the association. In her silk dress and jacket she looked luxurious, as if she should be in an opulent interior, not our rustic setting. Clif finished the portrait for Whelan in mid-October. We went to Sydney for the Travelodge Art Prize in late October, but when we returned to Melbourne, Dame Mabel's image, and his own of her, came to his mind in the empty studio.

It was be a homecoming for both of us, back to Alastair's addition, my furniture and books and cooking utensils added to Clif's. For years he'd suffered the winter cold in the gap-walled house, worrying about money to buy paint, to keep the family, and in the last few years he and Marlene had lived through their unhappiness. He'd left the Australian autumn for a gilded European summer, where his intellect and imagination were stimulated. He'd lived in comfort and with affection. This trip had provided no dramatic incident to stimulate a set of images. On his earlier trip to Mexico it had been the penitents and the role of the church; in the outback the condition of the Aboriginal people had produced the St Francis series. His European experience was about art, about centuries of technique and representation, about the pleasure of paint.

Occasionally Clif's intuition was almost material. In his mind's eye was the work he'd seen in Paris early that year. Ideas about light, space, the moment, about life's pleasures: Bonnard, Degas, Vuillard, and also . . . Mabel Brookes, powerful, brooding, and somehow . . . *French*. You have to begin from where you are. Clif began to paint her again, using the device of repeating the pattern of her jacket on the settee behind her that Vuillard and Matisse employ to such effect, the device which somehow implies that claustrophobic atmosphere of French nineteenth-century interiors, their sumptuous over-decoration, yet conveys movement, immediacy, and the personality of the subject.

He sent the picture to the Archibald Prize, the richest art prize in the country.

5

OUR ART WORLD

Steak, wine, glasses of milk

Dunmoochin was only an hour from the city. We drove into Melbourne a couple of times each week for exhibition openings, staying afterwards for dinner and talk, sometimes films. The scene was active and there were plenty of parties. The art world is the business of an artist, keeping in touch. Violet 'Peta' Dulieu had her gallery in South Yarra, Anne Purves ran Australian Galleries in Collingwood, Joe Brown was in Collins Street, the Moras were in St Kilda at Tolarno's, the new NGV had regular exhibitions.

Early in October, soon after we met, there was a John Brack opening at Georges department store. Rudy Komon, who was also Clif's dealer, hired the gallery on the top floor to show his artists in Melbourne. This was the first time we were at an opening as a couple, and John Olsen had publicised me. John was a Sydney painter, and assumed I knew nothing about the art world. In fact I knew South Yarra Gallery well, I'd handed out drinks there while I was at school, and I knew the National Gallery of Victoria; but this part of the art world was very much Rudy's, managed by him and his artists.

Astonishing now to think. We saw John Brack's brilliant *Ballroom Dancer* series on temporary stands, the sort used at Rotary exhibitions, in a department store gallery. Sydney was Rudy's base, his gallery was in Paddington. Most of his major artists were based in Melbourne, so he had to show them in their own city, but he would not deal through the Melbourne galleries.

Other dealers were puzzled at the loyalty he commanded, but Rudy understood the practical nature of the people whose work he handled. An artist, like anyone running their own business, needs capital – for materials, for studio space, enough to eat and to wear – and time, to make work. Capital comes through sale of work, for which the manufacturing artist needs a retailer, or must become a retailer, which may affect the work itself and will certainly affect the amount of time to make the work.

Rudy paid his artists a retainer, a monthly income that covered all their expenses so they did not need to think about money. He paid retainers regardless of whether he sold their work. In addition, they wanted freedom: never to be told what or how to produce. With considerable courage at first, and with commitment and élan, Rudy never interfered. He took what they sent him and either sold it, or bought it for stock.

At the Brack opening Clif began to introduce me; people were rude and abrupt. Remembering Margot's advice, I was polite in return. To no avail, and soon I was looking at the pictures alone. New members of a group can expect to be scrutinised, but the level of emotion, of antagonism to me, seemed a bit exaggerated, and I complained to Clif.

He gave me my first lesson in the effect of art, of the lurid figures with their garish clothes and staring smiles: 'It's not you, it's the pictures, they are very good, very aggressive, and they're making people angry.'

By this time I was not happy. 'If they are so good why doesn't someone buy them?'

'They will. You can come in to Georges tomorrow and see red stickers; but the atmosphere is bad because the paintings are upsetting people – that's a good sign. Listen tonight and see which ones sell.'

He meant listen *over dinner*. Rudy took his artists out as a group after each opening. This time to his favourite, Vlado's, all red meat and red wine. The opening crowd might have been aggressive, but around the table was a group of men who were articulating the culture in paint. I expected an evening of ideas, art and poetry: after all, Olsen was like this. But although he is a poet as well as a painter, in this group John was one of the boys.

Len French, Clif, John Brack, Olsen, Fred Williams. They talked about tax. Tax, accountants, business, gossip. Except that every now and again someone would turn to John Brack and remark on a painting or a bit of one.

'I liked that yellow one.'

John, Clif and Fred

'I liked the dress on the red one.'

Abrupt comments, concrete language. It was like hearing children speak. I was contemplating this when Fred Williams' wife Lyn told me that I had to get Clif involved in politics.

'Really?'

Yes, Fred had asked him and he'd refused, but it was very, very important.

So I said I'd talk to him about it. I'd been worried about the way he was affected by the political news on television, and even though we'd met because we'd both been at a moratorium march, and I did want to see the ALP elected to run the Commonwealth Government, I'd been thinking I should perhaps encourage him to concentrate on his work. If he continued chairing the ALP Arts Policy Committee it would be a distraction. But she was an older woman and I would take her advice.

The next day I went into Georges. Several of the paintings had red dots, the indication they were sold. At home that night I told Clif he'd been right.

'Which ones, did you notice?' He pointed out that the pictures that had sold were the ones the artists had talked about. 'Rudy has bought those pictures for stock. He knows nothing about art, but he listens.'

'Nothing?'

'Nothing.'

I was sceptical about this. But when Clif and I went up to the first Travelodge Art Prize in Sydney I saw this in action. Each painter had been asked to submit two paintings, which were hung in pairs. I watched John Olsen, Len French, Fred Williams, Clif, and Don Laycock talking about one, but not the other, of the two Olsen pictures. I was beside Rudy at the time and I saw he was watching, too. I found the paintings almost impossible to read: covered in little marks, swirls, narration and abstract gestures at once. I thought, well, he's the dealer, he must be able to explain, I'll ask. I turned to him and noticed for the first time that he was wearing dark glasses. At 10.30 in the evening. Under artificial light.

Inside. Perhaps Clif was right.

I asked Rudy why the artists were talking only about one of the paintings and not the other.

After a long pause: 'You see,' (this was a frequent preamble) 'this one has a moon, the other one does not have a moon.'

Clif was right.

I'd been to Sydney briefly before, but this was the first time I was able to drift and get used to the city; we were staying on while Clif painted Alan Greenaway, the Travelodge chairman. Paddington, where Rudy had the gallery, was more like Melbourne in those days. It was still a bit raffish; some academics lived there, but not people interested in status; it was not over-invested; there were pubs which were quite old-fashioned. Sydney is subtropical, her buildings of golden stone. The jacarandas and flame trees glow, the sparkling harbour beckons, the place demands a life of pleasure. Melbourne's grey stone and cold winters force us inside, to think. The harbour was not the advertising symbol it has become. The city seemed to have a soul, perhaps because we mixed with men like the writer and critic Laurie Thomas and the ABC's Charles Moses, educated, ironic; men who loved conversation and with whom one felt on safe ethical ground.

I know now that the convicts who laboured in the early days of New South Wales were slaves who had to buy their freedom with obedience and work, that the three-tiered society of slaves, corrupt officials and decent but powerless administrators made the state a place where principle, power and money are still continually in flux; that by contrast with Melbourne and Adelaide, Sydney has always been a flashy tart. In 1970, I was an innocent newcomer to the city.

We dropped in every day to the gallery, having lunch with Rudy, Len French and winemaker Len Evans, whoever was around. It was clear at first that Rudy didn't really enjoy having me along. Newcomers are always an issue in a group, he'd been very fond of Marlene; change is more difficult as you get older. And Rudy in particular had dealt with a great deal of change.

Every year, as winter closes in, I think of Rudy. He was born in Czechoslovakia on 22 June 1908. Clif wrote on his affectionate oil sketch *For Rudy on His Birthday The Shortest Day 1965*. I think of the timing of his birthday as a profound symbol of his life, because during his childhood in Europe his birthday had been celebrated at midsummer, that magical time of long delicious scented twilights. In subtropical Sydney the night comes suddenly, and in June it is becoming cold, although the city is never softened by snow as Prague must have been. Rudy's father had been an antique dealer, and Rudy's a gracious and civilised childhood in that wondrous city.

So much loss for so many refugees, and yet from this loss, such gain. Rudy's contribution to Australian culture has not been widely celebrated, yet he initiated a truly professional art world, was instrumental in setting up the wine industry, and in educating a generation about the relationship between enjoying wine and food and the arts. He encouraged a sense of the collective, of artists working together to articulate the culture, that went out of Australian art when he died in 1982. For Rudy represented most of the prominent artists of his day and, with them, profoundly affected the management of the art world.

The story Clif told was that Rudy was a Reuters correspondent when the communists took power. He was anti-fascist in sentiment, but committed to reporting what he saw. Then, after the communist coup d'état in 1948, a telephone call at night warning he was on the Communist Party death list.

'Go. Now.'

Coat on, wallet I suppose in pocket, with whatever cash was in the apartment, perhaps a little food, perhaps not; and a life abandoned. He took the dog on a leash as if for an evening walk, left it tethered to a fence some way on, and walked to Switzerland. Whenever we walked down the street Clif kept an eye on the ground, often collecting bits of change. Rudy had taught him that when they first travelled together.

Rudy didn't talk about his past. But that mysterious abandoned life must have been interesting and comfortable, in a beautiful cultured city. He arrived in Sydney with a friend he made in the refugee camp, knowing no one. He found work as a chauffeur, and began to deal first in oriental rugs, then in Australian paintings, from the boot of his employer's Rolls Royce. Until one day the employer opened the boot. And, so the story went, put up the money for the space in Paddington.

Portraits of him show his bright, searching eyes, shrewd and intelligent. I hear his all-purpose complaint, 'Barbarians . . .' It was a useful insult, describing the not-us on any day, and often enough he used it as crowd control, the crowd being the unpredictable alcoholics in his stable, not the least of whom was Clif. I used to wonder just how much 'Barbarians' reflected for him what he had lost, and whether he had replaced the pleasures of Prague, the company of European intellectuals, with the Australian wine industry, Australian companions.

He was perfectly polite to me, and so was his assistant, Gwen Frolich, but they didn't chat. Clif had taken Julia to London and it hadn't worked out, so I might well have been temporary. Wait, be polite. Besides, I could see the point. I was conscious that people would see me not only as young, an appendage, not even a wife, in those conservative times; but as a possibly short-term liaison. In Australia in 1970 women were unseen even when present in the professions, academia and business world, and although in the arts some women were influential because they owned or ran galleries, or worked as performers, they were ignored where possible.

We read often of change in the 1960s, but in regard to feminism, to women coming to consciousness of the many ways in which the culture limited their lives, this memory of change in Australia is an appropriation of American history. Change indeed began in the United States, in the 1960s, where in 1963 Betty Friedan's *The Feminine Mystique* was published. But it wasn't until after Alewyn Birch of Granada published Germaine Greer's *The Female Eunuch* that the consequences of such analyses began to be felt in this country. Australia's small, culturally coherent society has the capacity readily to disseminate ideas, and when these ideas are accompanied by enabling technology, Australians adapt rapidly. The mid-twentieth-century feminist movement was supported by technology of the contraceptive pill. Choice about reproduction gave women freedom not only to time childbearing but, like men, to have sex without fear of pregnancy. Arguments for sexual equality had been articulated throughout history, but this was the first time the ideas were practical. Once re-introduced, feminist theory, or rather mid-twentieth-century feminism, began rapidly to change the culture, because, at last, it could be changed.

I had never felt constrained to avoid thinking or doing anything I wanted, nor, like Clif, intended any action simply as a defiant gesture. I was the child of privilege, with very funny and intelligent parents who brought up a large family to care about ideas and principle, and to resist conformity. I grew up making decisions about my life and acting on them, all the time with the constant of intuition. The intuition had brought me to Dunmoochin. But although on one level I was content, I did have a problem, which interrupted that lovely drifting Sydney spring. It irritated Rudy and affected my relationship with Clif, but in the end it meant Rudy took me seriously and it gave Clif an idea of my resilience.

I'd had a persistent pain in my side since the Travelodge opening. I didn't drink much; alcohol has always made me sleepy. Because of the pain I kept asking for milk, which persuaded Rudy that I was a sort of female barbarian. Not only an influential art dealer, Rudy was one of the most important figures in developing Australia's wine industry. He was president and a chief judge of the Wine and Food Society, and of the wine competition at the Royal Easter Show, then the most prestigious industry trophy. He'd had to battle with beer drinkers for many years, but my milk requests were anathema to him. Then one day Charles Moses came with us to lunch. As usual it was wine, red meat, not much else. We'd had a couple of reds, then Rudy asked the waiter to bring a white wine, which he described in detail while we waited for it. It was his process of educating palates; everyone, even the sophisticated Charles, was learning to distinguish and discuss each wine.

The white wine came, and everyone had to say what they thought. A table of tough powerful older men who had had quite a bit to drink, and I could see that Rudy almost didn't ask me for my views. But he did. I did not know about wine, but I had been cooking since I was seven years old – cooking was my deep pleasure – and I knew about taste. I was in just enough pain not to pass. I said I didn't agree with his description of the wine, and described what I was drinking. Perhaps the restaurant owner hadn't brought the right wine? Rudy was spectacularly sarcastic. Fred Williams was desperate to settle things down, when suddenly Moses intervened.

'I agree with Judith.'

Chaos. Dramatic demands for the bottle we'd had. Oh. The restaurateur had brought the wrong bottle. Rudy had described the wine to which he'd awarded a prize, and which he'd ordered, but not the wine he'd drunk at that table, and everyone else had gone along with the idea, not the reality.

Except Charles: 'Well done, Judith,' and he pointed out that Rudy should take me seriously. Rudy began to respect and talk to me then, even remarking to Clif that he was lucky. But still a way to go to be accepted.

The pain became constant and was getting worse. Bending, dressing, making love became painful, and my right shoulder began to hurt. We had no doctor in Sydney, so Clif rang Hal Hattam, his gynaecologist friend in Melbourne who was also a painter. Hattam told me I should exercise, there was no problem. Some time later Clif told me that

Hattam had said to ignore my complaints, that as I was a Catholic I was probably anxious about living with him. I'd not been in a church for years. My father had spent half his education at an Anglican school in Sydney and my mother was entirely Presbyterian, having barely agreed to be received into the Catholic Church so they could marry. I could not have been less like the Catholics I knew. Clif didn't tell me then about the conversation, but he made me walk everywhere, when each step was agonising. I was confused, Clif irritated that I kept complaining. The ease, the happiness was going. Then one night at an opening Rudy spoke to one of his friends, a client who happened to be a surgeon. Peter Eliot came up to me as I stood chatting in the gallery. I could see Clif and Rudy behind him, watching me.

Peter was rather deaf, with an accompanying loud voice: 'Hello, I'm Peter Eliot. Clif says you have pain during intercourse.'

The opening suddenly silent, as everyone turned to look. Oh well.

'Yes.'

'Pain in your right shoulder?'

Clif looked astonished and then worried; he obviously hadn't told Peter this.

'Yes.'

Peter pressed his hand on my stomach and abruptly took it away. Excruciating pain. I tried not to yell.

'Okay. Gwen, take over the opening. Rudy, put her in the car, I'll meet you at the King George V.'

Everyone stared, no one moved.

'Rudy, Clif, she has peritonitis, and you've told me this has been going on for more than a week. She's dying.'

Such activity. They threw me into the car, not just Clif and Rudy but a carful of artists hurtling along, full of concern. With visions of admittance procedures and privacy I made them stop and get me a nightgown, but when we arrived outside the entrance there was Peter, gowned beside a stretcher with a couple of orderlies. He told Clif to get my clothes off, immediately. Much enthusiastic assistance. I was picked up naked and put on the stretcher. They threw a sheet over me, another gowned figure stepped forward, explained he was my anaesthetist, and found a vein. Some time later I woke up with an anxious Clif and Rudy beside my bed, Peter announcing to the world that he'd left me some of my right ovary.

I left the hospital to recuperate in comfort at the Rushcutters Bay Travelodge. We'd made friends with Alan Greenaway, the Travelodge chairman, as Clif painted him and I 'kept him occupied'. Flowers, visits and concern from Rudy. Peter Eliot had been quite cross with both him and Clif. Like all men of his generation Rudy respected a stiff upper lip. He was delighted when, a couple of days after I left hospital, Alan and Clif brought the entire Travelodge Board to see the painting, and Alan asked that I talk about it to them. So I told them why I thought it represented Alan, and they decided to buy it. Apparently there had been some hesitation.

Rudy told the white wine story to my other visitors; he was solicitous, and Gwen became warm. As Rudy drove us to the airport it was clear that he would be telling the art world that the new woman in Clif's life would not be a problem, and might even be a good thing.

December 1970 was filled with end-of-year parties and moody hangovers. Not that a hangover ever stopped Clif getting out of bed and physically working, then going to the studio by eleven; not even heart attacks intervened in that routine. Even if he didn't have a painting on the go, he always, always went to the studio each day: tidying up, looking at art books, keeping the lists of pictures up to date, checking accounts, preparing boards. But although he had routine, Clif's painting had not yet settled.

Pinned up on the walls of the main room were 'look and put' gouaches from the Tibooburra trip, the rich oranges of the earth, the vivid blue skies; he passed them on the way to the studio. Each day he walked through the Dunmoochin bush: pale clay, pale yellow, soft greys, rose.

These two places had been the source of his work for so long. But there were new experiences and images to integrate into the paintings that he made in the studio. These paintings, oil on board or canvas, could be worked over and changed and, once finished, had permanence. They were considered and reworked until they satisfied him. Infused with his emotions and experience, they talked about society, about ideas, about art.

6

RETROSPECTIVE

Lentils with smoked ham hocks,
fresh bread

We had met at a very particular moment in Clif's career and his personal life. After a retrospective of his work in London in May 1970 he'd stayed for some months in the United Kingdom and Paris, and he was unsure of the direction his painting would take after his exposure to so much historic and early twentieth-century work. By every measure he was a successful artist. The retrospective, organised by the British Council when he was only forty-four years old, consolidated his position in the art world.

Clif's reputation had developed steadily throughout the late 1950s and the 60s. During that time he'd been noticed by critics and academics such as Laurie Thomas and Alan McCulloch, and included in the important official travelling exhibitions. An illustrated monograph on his work was the first of a series published in 1962 by Georgian House for Melbourne University under the general editorship of Bernard Smith. His work was studied as part of the school art curriculum, was in important private collections and the public galleries. After early years of financial risk, his work was selling regularly.

In 1968 Andrew Grimwade had published *Involvement*, a scholarly limited-edition volume about Clif's portraits, remarkably sumptuous for the time, reproducing ninety of the portraits he was able to find, forty-five paintings in large colour plates, each opposite a black and white photograph of the sitter by Mark Strizic, commissioned for the book. With supplementary smaller black and white images of the other forty-five, the book was a superb catalogue raisonné of the portraits. With an essay by Geoffrey Dutton, then perhaps the most influential man of letters in Australia, and another by Andrew, it included interviews by Andrew with Clif and with Mark about each sitter. For Clif, this meant reflecting on each painting and, therefore, on his whole career. The launch of *Involvement* at the National Gallery of Victoria was accompanied by an exhibition of his portraits, so Clif saw many of them again, in reality as well as in reproduction. And the development of *Involvement* overlapped with the selection of paintings for the retrospective.

Amongst all the publicity and critical evaluation and curatorial comment attendant upon a retrospective, one can forget that it gives the artist, as well as everyone else, a chance to look back and think about work collected together from different shows and different periods. Because *Involvement* was produced during the same period, Clif's life had processed before him in a formal and celebratory manner, over the previous three years. The accolade of the British Council choosing to stage a London retrospective of his work before that of any of his contemporaries confirmed his status as one of the most important painters of the post-war generation. This was a crucial time to think about his work. And in late 1969 he and Marlene had agreed at last to separate.

Marlene had talent and intelligence, great instinct for goodness, and decency. But she didn't want business to be part of social connection.

She'd loved the stimulation of the early days, when friends like Barry and Ros Humphries came up most weekends, when the dinner table was full of committed idealists discussing politics, making fun of the pompous and pretentious. She resented the way that success for its members broke up the happy and chaotic group of young creative people at Dunmoochin. She wanted to go on living simply, and for Clif to concentrate on producing work, not mixing with his buyers. She generally regarded conventional businessmen and their wives as pretentious, and never saw that their grasping at convention might mirror her own anxieties.

It had been a tumultuous fourteen-year partnership. At first both delighted in their attraction to one another, in the challenges of living on a very small income while making art. Marlene was an art student when they met. When she moved up to Dunmoochin, occasionally when time permitted during the marriage, and after it ended, she worked beautifully in clay. But she had fallen pregnant very early in the relationship, and was distressed at the thought of an abortion. Clif had already lost a woman he loved because he didn't want children. His acceptance of Marlene's need to continue the pregnancy in fact represented the depth of his attachment to her, but in the way of Australian men, and with the fierceness of worry at the responsibility he faced, he did not show this, perhaps even to himself. Soon Marlene became pregnant for a second time, and there were two boys to keep.

Children demand energy and attention. Even women with money, household help, dishwashers and washing machines find it hard to develop their own creative work. Marlene had no help, intermittent money, and a house that was technologically in the early twentieth century, if not the nineteenth. She had to manage with a small amount of tank water, initially no pump, walls with gaps, leaking second-hand iron on the roof, gas bottles, and to boil water in old kerosene tins in order to sterilise nappies. She had struggled through this only to find that the pleasure in the relationship was gone. They had both begun to drink too much, to seek other intimacies, and to resent each other. They made the final break as the London shows drew near.

Getting out of Australia for an extended time helped Clif to settle in to life without Marlene. He took gentle Julia to London with Dailan, his younger son, but she left him and returned to Australia.

In London he'd been embraced by the art world. There were contemporary shows as well as the traditional riches of the public galleries. Every day in Paris he'd visited galleries, finding the experience surprising and overwhelming, the more I think because it happened when he was already a formed and mature artist.

When he was young he had seen a few good examples of some masters, even modern masters in the public galleries in Melbourne, Adelaide, Sydney and Brisbane. There were travelling shows. But colour reproductions in large glowing art books weren't abundant, nor, until after he died, was there access to every major gallery through the internet.

Often in interview or in response to a client he'd say that he was influenced by Kandinsky. I wondered: how? Which Kandinskys could you see in Australia in the 1950s? Perhaps he meant what Kandinsky said about painting, about the work of the artist. To ask in front of an interviewer or even immediately after an interview might have seemed like a challenge, as if I actually thought the paintings didn't reflect the influence, so I waited for the moment. One must be polite. It was some years before the moment presented; we were in the studio, and he was talking about the Bonnards in the Musée d'Art Moderne, so I wondered somehow where he saw the Kandinsky that so inspired him. One thing is certain: artists are influenced by what they see. Clif produced the influential image. About five centimetres square, one black and white reproduction, in a little textbook about the history of art. There were the black outlines he used and which were inimical to the tonal tradition in which Dargie had trained him.

When he left the Gallery School he'd not really been interested in going to Europe. During his scholarship interview, Gallery Director, Daryl Lindsay, remarked, 'And you'll go to study at the Slade School.'

Clif on the instant making the decision to lose the scholarship, 'No, I want to go to Mexico.'

'You'll go to the Slade School.'

'No, I won't.'

And the scholarship awarded to 'a woman who got married on the boat'.

Every now and again when he was in a mood to tease women, he'd make this remark, but it was clear he wasn't really bothered. He would have found a way to Europe if he'd wanted to go then. It was the money that mattered. He wanted the scholarship for financial support while practising what he'd been taught, it was not about getting out of the country. He'd lost time in the army; he just wanted to get on with it. Like his grandfather, he didn't consider the relative lack of sophistication of Australian society as a problem, nor the issue of who would buy his work, which he fully expected to challenge the 'gum-tree' school. The priority was to paint.

His first overseas venture as a painter was to Mexico, to see the development of modernism with a political edge. With Rudy's help, Clif and Marlene had lived there with the boys for some months in the mid-1960s, and he'd seen the work of Tamayo and Rivera. He'd had shows in Mexico City and Los Angeles, and with Rudy had gone on to Chicago, where there is a big impressionist collection. But this European journey in 1970 had been different.

To arrive a stranger in a metropolis can be interesting, can be exhilarating, can be alienating. Confident or apprehensive, one is always conscious of the need to deal with both the geography and the culture of a city, to find one's way, literally and metaphorically. The way around London physically is on the buses or the Tube. Used to breathing fresh clean air and to travelling by car on spacious roads in relatively empty Australian cities, Clif had not been looking forward to public transport or going underground. But the Tube was easy and efficient. It was also remarkably personalised. The British Council had promoted the retrospective, and the official advertising included huge posters on every Tube Station. Clifton Pugh was welcomed by *CLIFTON PUGH* and an image of his own, whenever he took a train.

The London art scene, familiar with his work, was delighted to meet him. The connections between Australia and the United Kingdom through commerce were then very strong and on a personal level. British culture is shaped by class, and that was readily transacted. His paintings had made the social connections long before he came in person. Nine years earlier, when Clif was thirty-six, his work in the Whitechapel show had been praised by the critics, one bought by the students' common room of Magdalen College, Oxford, another by Dick Mitchison, Lord Mitchison, for his wife Naomi, in whose collection in Argyll it was seen by many of the British intellectuals of the time. People could not have been more welcoming. Lord De L'Isle, now retired, had him to Penshurst, and there were dinners and parties in his honour.

He painted a double portrait, a couple named Dawnay. Kit was chairman of Dalgety's and also of the Worshipful Company of Fishmongers; his wife, Patsy, a JP on the local bench, was a descendant of Hereward the Wake. Clif had canvas, paint, the physical, imaginative and intellectual engagement he needed. He stayed with the Dawnays at Longparish House. Its builder had decided to model the house on a chateau he'd seen in France en route to the crusades: the family lost it at one time but Kit had bought the estate again. Each room looked across a lawn to the cool mill stream. There was no reminder of the tension between the bush and the imported animals and vegetation. Here the landscape was lush, productive, made by humans to nurture and delight them.

In Melbourne, in that small social group, where *artist* might mean *challenge to comfort*, Clif was the taciturn painter, blunt, tough, and masculine, to carve out his position in the art world. London is an old society, and has welcomed and sheltered many artists. There, sophisticated people, especially in the art world, are used to visitors from many cultures. The manners and habits of his childhood simply fell into place. He did not have to worry about Marlene's response to the social demands, and, as they were alone for the first time, found delight in Dailan, now thirteen.

And Rudy was there, the happy avuncular European, given context by London urbanity. Rudy had taken a comfortable furnished apartment, which they made their base. Clif and he had travelled together before, but it was in London that they relaxed like father and son. Rudy had left his family in Europe after the war, he and his Ruth were childless, and he guided, supported and cared for his artists as if they were his children. Clif's father was a childhood memory, but here again in his life was a provider who gave advice and material comfort. There was no leaking roof, no worry about water in the tanks. There were shops, theatres, and restaurants within walking distance. Clif had a taste of the depth of culture Rudy had left in Prague. He could accept Rudy's paternal affection.

The public galleries were full of old acquaintances: pictures and sculptures, works he'd read about or seen in reproduction, and there he found many new images and ideas. These gave context to his two shows: his official retrospective at the Commonwealth Institute and the commercial exhibition at the Kalman Gallery in Brompton Road. Both were praised by the London critics. The show at André Kalman's sold out, Kalman too proving a sophisticated and wise dealer. So Clif had an opportunity to reflect on the historic body of his work, in the context of his current work. This combination of material and emotional factors allowed him to relax and be open to the art with which he was surrounded. It was spring in the northern hemisphere, and he experienced for the first time that unsubtle burgeoning of life that renders nature in Europe so unsophisticated. André encouraged him to see Paris with Dailan before they went home.

André was close to the printmaker William Hayter, and suggested

Clif visit him in Paris. Hayter, from seven generations of artists, was one of the most influential British artists of the twentieth century. He had trained and worked as an industrial chemist before deciding to become a professional artist, moving to Paris in 1926 when he was twenty-five. His scientific and technical training were the basis for a confident exploration of traditional, and development of new, printing techniques. In 1927 he set up an atelier where equipment and materials were available for professional artists to make prints. Hayter had a reputation as an artist as well as an innovative technician; he was close to Miro, Arp and Tanguy, and worked with writers such as Samuel Beckett. Picasso collected his work. He'd left Paris for London when war broke out, ending up in New York, where he again set up, printing with exiled European artists and young Americans such as de Kooning, Motherwell, Pollock and Rothko. He had returned to Paris, re-establishing the atelier in the 1950s.

Clif delighted in Hayter. Here was an artist and man of science, of the tradition of enquiry and co-operation that had formed Clif's own father and grandfather, at sixty-nine as energetic and confident as the forty-five year old Clif. But Hayter was limiting the number of people in the atelier.

Nevertheless. Just as he'd talked his way around Dargie and into the Gallery School in 1947, Clif persuaded Hayter to take him on. He found a studio in the Cité des Arts, a school for Dailan to learn French, and settled in to study etching and Hayter's viscosity colour technique.

In Mexico the family had lived in a village of austere adobe and stone. The light was harsh, the colours vivid, the issues absolute. There Clif painted the *Penitents* series, of Easter processions when the people crawl to the church, whipping themselves, scouring their bodies with cactus. These are paintings of noise and chaos, angular colours, slashed with black. When he spoke about that time it was about his disapproval of the church, encouraging the people to play out a manufactured guilt while sucking money from them.

In the soft frivolousness of Paris, where the very buildings are bedecked with flowers, where modernity itself is gilded, disapproval is more difficult. There had recently been riots, and passion; artists in the Cité studios and at Hayter's talked about them, but they seemed to have been absorbed by the society and by the stones. Clif and Dai had a domestic routine, eating as students ate in the local houses, where the housewife made one large meal and served it in her front room; in their apartment they cooked lentils with smoked ham hocks and ate delicious loaves from the local baker. Politics was around, the world was on the move again, but Clif was not concerned here with politics.

He didn't paint in Paris, but his imaginative energy was engaged, coming to terms with the ways of using a plate. He had to approach colour in an entirely new way. The viscosity technique involves a series of rollers, of varying degrees of softness, depositing inks, prepared to varying degrees of viscosity, onto a plate in one run. Each roller puts ink into a different level of the etched plate, so the line must be controlled as much vertically as horizontally. The plate is inked by each roller and then a print taken. Each ink of each viscosity resists, so that although the various inks mingle slightly, each prints as a separate colour.

His conversations in Paris with Hayter were about the techniques of etching, and of the international art world, mutual friends like the Americans Clement Greenberg, Harry Roskolenko and Kalman. But while he was again welcomed into a friendly sophisticated world that was focussed on the craft of art and the ideas that sprang from it, he was unable to work in his habitual medium. In that medium, in paint, in the galleries, he had different conversations: Bonnard, Matisse, Cezanne spoke to him through their work, about how you could ignore the rules, let the paint and the surface itself take you. He recognised that his training in tonal impressionism had constrained him. He saw that you could, while standing there, physically and intellectually engaged, enjoy yourself, invent, give up some conventions. And people would celebrate.

I can hear the excitement in his voice: 'The water runs up, the water runs uphill, and it *doesn't matter*.'

Hayter wanted him to stay on. Once the urgent blunt man was working in the atelier the mature commitment and ideas and the innate talent revealed themselves, and Hayter was impressed. But the tenant was leaving Dunmoochin, Parisians were leaving Paris for July. Dai was homesick. And Australia was nourishment, as well as the challenge. Home was where new ideas and techniques had to be used for his own images of his own culture. He came back to Melbourne in late winter, with money in the bank, to find Marlene settled with Ray Newell, raising a baby raven, renting the next-door property at Dunmoochin while they built nearby. He left Dai with them and drove to his beloved Australian desert, to Tibooburra, on the edge of the gibber plain in the far north-west of New South Wales. There, he was again in the dry heat and the desert colours, using gouache on paper to 'look and put', to record the observation of the moment. This was how he began consolidating the last few months of stimulation and revelation with his past work and image of Australia.

The only question was companionship on the journey forward. He had taken to Tibooburra a woman he'd known for some years, but with whom he'd never before slept. She was mature, ironic and loving, but she was married to one of his friends. They had an 'open' marriage, and she wanted the relationship with Clif to continue and deepen. Clif was unsure. He enjoyed her companionship but he wanted to keep her husband's friendship, so had not committed to the arrangement. He had organised to meet her and her husband to talk it over on the Saturday evening after the moratorium. I think he knew he wanted more than an affair; someone to live with, and really was uncertain how things with Ann would work out. Instead, he had explained over dinner that Saturday that he had met me the night before, left the dinner early, telephoned from two public phones, and collected me.

7

GUESTS, VISITORS, INHABITANTS

Banana or apple, black coffee, sorrel soup, maggots

Certain of Clif's friends never gave up the days of hanging out, making it clear they felt I was in the way of their relationship with him; the difficulty compounded because they tended to arrive unannounced and empty-handed at mealtimes and with several others, as if we were indulgent parents. The sign *Clifton Pugh – Did You Ring First?* on the gate had no effect on people who thought of themselves as important. Polite friends rang, and sensible people who wanted to be sure we would be home.

The distance from the city was just too far not to feed and water visitors. It meant that if someone had a bit too much to drink it was responsible to ask them to stay the night, so I had benches built around every window in order rapidly to accommodate quite a few extras. We could be very relaxed, and evenings would draw on into interesting breakfasts. We held open house for Sunday lunch, never sure who would turn up. We did learn, quite early on, to ask each other who was at table, to avoid the policy being exploited.

I remarked to Clif one day that I was concerned about the sheep in the car of one of our guests. I'd checked through the window that it had food and water, and I wasn't going to ask why it was there, but surely it must need to get out at some time? Clif said yes, he'd been thinking he must say something about it; perhaps he could approach it from the point of view that the creature wasn't indigenous. I pointed out that while he was raising the subject of local forms of behaviour perhaps he could see if the guy could pull his weight a bit. He'd arrived without an invitation and had stayed for several days; the least he could do was make his own bed.

'Well, he's your friend, why don't you ask him?'

'My friend?'

Most Dunmoochin residents were artists or potters, and they respected each other's need for quiet days in the studio, dropping in for a drink after work, or welcoming us on a stroll. Artist friends – John Perceval, Don Laycock, Fred Williams – were disciplined. When they came up to paint, which they did regularly, the house in the morning was a meeting place. They were off into the bush soon after they arrived, back at dusk for dinner.

Friends came to stay. Harry Roskolenko was a Russian Jewish poet from New York who had arrived with the army during the war. He had become part of Australia's literary scene, also publishing Australians in the United States, keeping up his contacts through repeated visits. Later, travellers ourselves, we dropped in to his New York apartment for a drink, the week after the American Bicentenary, and saw why he had urged us to be there on Fourth of July. Harry was one of the first people to live in a converted warehouse on the Hudson, and the Tall Ships were literally parked outside. It had been an all-day party; everyone in the literary and art and film world in New York for the day.

Writers and painters and family, friends returning after years overseas, politicians from interstate, clients and portrait subjects, dealers, critics, gallery directors, journalists, television crews; so interesting and such fun, especially as the house grew more convenient and we had more water tanks and I was able to use the kitchen that my carpenter-for-two-weeks birthday present built around me. To be the pale inconsequential girl meeting guests, making coffee and providing meals, clean sheets and towels, meant that people let down their guard. I met Clement Greenberg's train. He was regarded internationally as the most important American critic. I'd begun to form the view that the best judges of art, and the best writers about it, are those actually trained in it. People like to talk about themselves, so in the car I asked was Greenberg trained as an artist?

'Yes, I was absolutely brilliant, I was a prodigy, I could have had a career as an artist.'

I wondered: 'Why did you decide to be a critic?'

'Artists sound uneducated. I didn't want to sound like an uneducated man.'

I thought about the bluntness and concrete speech that I so enjoyed. Indeed, it could be described as uneducated, but the irony of remarking on it in blunt, concrete phrases in a Damon Runyon accent was amusing to contemplate. Greenberg's self-confidence was astonishing. He stayed overnight, giving no sign that he knew I was there, although he was not impolite, just very concentrated, talking and looking carefully through Clif's pictures.

Suddenly, he turned to me, and in the punchy New York accent: 'I came out here in 1968 and I said then that your husband is the artist in Australia with the most potential. I say it again now. But sometimes, Judith, it's your job to shoot him in the head when he's halfway through a painting.'

We became a destination for certain official visitors, sent by Foreign
Affairs. One such was the very tall Minister of Planning from Nigeria.
He arrived one afternoon when the emu chicks had recently hatched,
which happy event had coincided with Clif pulling down a section of
the kitchen wall. There was a pile of mud bricks at the door and a lot
of mud about when the minister arrived, and I was dealing with the
aftermath of the plumber letting the chicks through the gate.

The male emu sits on the nest, drumming a warning if you walk
nearby. He is camouflaged as a mound of leaves; you think 'someone is
making compost' until, as you walk up to inspect this phenomenon, a
snake hisses. Never is the reptilian ancestry of birds more obvious. The
snake is the emu's neck, flattened on the ground, writhing; its head is
his beak. The male emu was aggressively protective of his hatchlings,
who were, on the day when the Nigerian turned up, about seventy-five
centimetres high. In the way of birds they were spectacularly incontinent
when panicky. This didn't ordinarily affect us, as the emus' paddock was
fenced off from the garden, but when the plumber left the gate open,
they, naturally curious, wandered into the house. Rapidly followed by
their frantic father, six feet tall, very angry, using his feet as weapons.

The plumber refused an ambulance, although one could see the bone
where the talon had opened his tough plumber's thigh. The plumber's
mate, our housekeeper and I managed to get babies and father back
into the paddock. Mate and plumber left for the hospital, and the
housekeeper and I were restoring order to the kitchen when Clif came
back from collecting the minister at the turnoff. He was in a three-piece
pin-striped suit. He was a graduate of Sandhurst.

'Oh do come in, I must apologise for the mess, the emu chicks have
been running around.'

'Not at all, my people keep their chickens in their houses.'

'Well, I usually don't, as a matter of fact; but we are rebuilding, so
you see there is a hole in the wall, and they got in.'

'You need not apologise, my people live in mud huts.'

'Ah, well, you will understand the advantages of mud-brick buildings.'

'Not really, they seem primitive to me.'

'Really? We love them, so environmentally sound. Now do please sit down, I'll make some coffee.'

I picked up the wombat, who was asleep in the nearest chair.

'This by the way is a wombat, an Australian marsupial.'

'I understand. My people also keep their pigs in their huts.' And sat on his shooting stick.

I made the coffee, poured it, and turned to him with the sugar and cream on a tray. By this time I was a bit unsettled. Handing him the coffee and gesturing to the cream, 'Are you black or white?'

'What do you think?'

Fortunately not all our guests were as delicate about our living conditions as the Nigerian, and the advantage of wombats is that they are herbivores, who deposit neat droppings. They usually came to us as babies, their mothers killed by cars, the baby taken from the dead mother's pouch. We rarely had more than one, as they wandered off after a while. Once they were independent they spent the night and much of the day outside improving the intricate series of tunnels dug under the floor. Nocturnal means inactive in the deepest part of the night and the height of the day, and active at either end of the night. Although we all went to bed at about the same time, the wombat wanted to socialise again in the hour before dawn. Clif fenced an area in bluestone, concreting three or four feet below the wall, so we wouldn't be woken for a play and a cuddle at 4 am.

The commitment was to raise injured or dependent bush creatures and if possible return them to the bush, which meant allowing them as far as possible to be themselves, and having no exotic pets. Rats and mice were a problem, and we couldn't have cats, but I found the solution in time for Clif's first Christmas present. A python. The first poor love broke his neck, falling off the top of the roof where a flock of small birds was teasing him, but the next settled in happily. We'd see him sliding past occasionally where there was a gap in the ceiling.

One day I opened the liquor cupboard to find a bottle on its side, some glasses tipped over and one broken. Which drunken visitor had done this? I tidied the cupboard but a couple of days later the same thing had happened. I pressed Clif about it but no, he hadn't been drinking, and neither of us could think of anyone who had been so drunk they'd have made such a mess. That evening the cupboard began making its own noise. As we opened the door a startled brush-tail possum shot up into the ceiling, scattering glasses. The process of getting to know her was easy. A clear space and a bit of apple, which disappeared the next day. This was repeated for a few days, then Ms Possum looking down, waiting, then the entire possum when one opened the door, and eventually one handed her the banana or apple; guests too could visit this visitor and see the new baby.

When we had a guest staying I had friends to dinner to meet them, taking care to make connections for everyone. If one's guests are unfamiliar with each other, and especially if one of those guests knows no one else, it is important to ensure they are included in the conversation from the first. Useful for this purpose to know their background.

Stephen Murray-Smith rang to ask us to have Christina Stead. 'She's in a college at Monash and she's lonely at weekends.'

I'd read a number of her books, but Hazel Rowley's wonderful biography of Christina had not been written then, nor had we heard about Mary McCarthy's live television dismissal of Lillian Hellman, whose recently published *Pentimento* she regarded as a fiction. Hellman claimed to have suffered from the US House Un-American Activities Committee; both Mary McCarthy and Christina had in fact suffered during that awful time. I served the sorrel soup, made sure everyone had cream and bread and turned to Christina.

'I've just read *Pentimento*. Do you know Lillian Hellman?'

She looked up, waiting until everyone at the table, among them Bert and Barbara Tucker, Fred and Lyn Williams, David and Kristen

Christina and Clif

Williamson, was waiting for the answer. The bright black eyes looking into mine, and slowly, with emphasis on the second word, 'That Girl.'

Um . . .

'Barbara, would you like some wine?'

Christina stayed with us often, in a room with a desk for her to write, but I don't think she was using it. She was grieving for the husband she'd lost and for what should have been comfortable ageing among admirers and friends. The sense of isolation during the anti-communist years in the United States, and a lifetime's anxieties about money and reputation, had left her often bitter and angry in conversation. Alcohol didn't deaden the pain, just disseminated it. She drank thoroughly if she had the opportunity, and people saw this side of her too often in the Australian arts and academic scene, where wine drinking was a badge of difference for so many people in those days. I later came to love the confidence of the English host or hostess, who would simply remove the bottle from the table or refuse to serve Clif when he was drunk.

On the night Christina arrived for her first stay with us I woke up at about 2 am without Clif beside me. Downstairs in my nightgown. The two of them thoroughly pickled, an empty whisky bottle on the coffee table, another open. She was twenty-two years older than Clif, he was twenty older than me. Each had an international reputation and a history of political activism, each was conscious of the other's status. It must have been surprising for her when their deep political discussion was interrupted by a barefooted girl.

'Christina, you are more than welcome here, but there is a problem for me when Clif drinks. The rule will be that unless we have a lunch party you will have your first drink after dusk, and go to bed by midnight.'

Pause, two bright pairs of eyes watching in amusement; then she smiled. 'Yes.'

My problem was the effect on him of images of the jungle war. The letters to his mother described events, but their voice was that of a tough young man repeating propaganda. Clif, reading them, was amused at his constant requests for socks and interested that, even then, at that distance, he'd been talking about exhibitions of his own and other people's work. The letters may have started him reconsidering and remembering his war, but the images from Vietnam, in newspapers but particularly on the television set, night after night, were reminiscent of New Guinea and it was images, not words that mattered. An image reminds me of this. There is a photograph on the Australian War Memorial website: 'BUT area, New Guinea, 194–03–7. Members of the 2/2nd infantry battalion cross the swift flowing Ninahau river during their advance to BUT.' Among the identified personnel is sx29388 Private C.E. Pugh. Fully clothed, up to his chest in the river. Twenty-one years and four months old. You had to cross rivers on foot, trudge through mud, cut your way through slimy clinging vegetation, put up with mosquitoes and the diseases they bore, camp out in your damp clothes, eat appalling food, carry your wounded mates to safety, watch out for enemy soldiers, and fight and kill them, day after day.

Reflections on these conditions came into different contexts of our lives, not just late at night after a lot of wine with anger and despair. Blowflies were a constant presence in the house, which had no flyscreens.

'Just open a window and they'll go out' was frustrating, especially as mosquitoes love me, but we bring our experience of life to every situation.

'We all carried some maggots, it was useful to have maggots, scratches get infected in the tropics, and you bung your maggot on so the wound is cleaned.'

Australian War Memorial Negative Number 079797

8

VIOLENCE

Loaves and fishes from
roast chicken sandwiches,
oversized strawberries

We live with the narratives that form us, learned through family, school, religion, from books and newspapers we read and lectures we hear, from friends, from television and radio. And the narratives change; what seems normal or acceptable at one time is intolerable not so many years later. As I begin to write about Clif's anger and my fear, I think, 'How can I avoid the word *abuse*?' I was afraid, I did change, but I did not feel abused. I was apprehensive – indeed, afraid – once he had hit me, and he hit me first in the early weeks. But he was physically violent only intermittently. Mainly the anger was generalised, and even when it focussed on me he was threatening, or pushed me about rather than actually punching, slapping or kicking me. And one felt, below the anger, the waves of despair.

The word *abuse* seems modern, politically correct, and the common view these days, in this society, is that a woman tolerates violence because she *expects* it to be part of a relationship. But no one in my family condoned violence against women; indeed, the opposite was the case. My father offered shelter and protection to a housekeeper whose husband shouted at and hit her; he manhandled the husband from their apartment in our house. He never hit my mother. I had no model of such a relationship.

At first I wondered if I was somehow contributing to the dark mood. But no. It was a combination of personalities, history, and the coincidence of the time in which we'd met. His attitude to his work, not violence, had caused his separation from his other two wives. Marlene was an heroic drinker, fiercely combative when she had been drinking, whereas I simply went to sleep if I drank too much. So I sat and listened. I think it was this very passivity, that I accepted what he said without comment, which allowed him to go deeper through the images into his horror of the war.

He could be drunk and despairing but not get angry in this way. When Terry Whelan tried to take him to court to stop the second Mabel Brookes picture being shown at the Archibald, Clif was very upset. But the focus was on the fear of having to account in court as to how he painted, of having a breakdown as Dobell had, after giving evidence about his portrait of Joshua Smith. Upset, but the issue resolved by his lawyers, he was over it.

I think of a night in Glasgow, in the late seventies. We had arrived to stay with an artist. Was he a friend, or friend of a friend? Had he visited Dunmoochin, or Australia perhaps, before my time? I don't remember. We arrived before dinner, I can't even recall if we ate. The man began to shout at, then swear at, then hit his wife. I said we were leaving, we would go to a hotel and she could come. She said nothing, and we left. Perhaps it was the unnamed thing in the culture, known and ignored. Perhaps because twice in the century such a large proportion of young men – from every class, occupation and place – had joined the forces and gone to war, and then, on their return, dealt alone with the violent things they had seen and done. No one talked about the wars, neither war, except when men told funny stories. War films gave us images of heroes and very little horror.

Early on Clif hit me a couple of times, not beating me repeatedly, more striking out as expression of rage, so I learned not so much to expect physical violence as part of the mood but to be apprehensive of it. It was infrequent, but unpredictable. When it happened I would ask him not to hit me, and usually he went on to be morose, and I'd leave and go up to bed; often, as time went on, in a spare bed.

But this was only one strand in an increasingly interesting life. The anger was awful when it happened, and I hoped that if I could work out the trigger I could avoid it or divert Clif from it. It wasn't just about the war, his own in the 1940s or the Vietnam War. He could read the paper and talk about Vietnam, which he always related to his own experiences, without threatening me every time. He'd 'walked out' of the war, and a sensible doctor had certified him as unfit.

'I'd been near a grenade that blew so I had some shrapnel and I went back to base for treatment. When I stopped I had hookworm and dengue fever and two types of malaria. I was A1, but he made me B2. He gave me some stuff and I was out of it, raving, saying anything, they put you in the twilight sleep. Then the war ended and I thought, "Shit! I was late in, I'll be last out."

'I didn't want to sit around in some hospital so I went to him and said, "I want to go to Japan. Make me A1 again." And he said, "Okay. You're A1," and I went as an occupying troop.'

To Hiroshima, after the bomb. Shirley Hazzard's novel *The Great Fire* begins with her hero arriving in Kure, where Clif was stationed. Aldred Leith is a British officer, researching the effect of the bombing of Japan. His driver is an Australian soldier who later helps him by cheerfully and efficiently ignoring regulations. That character could have been Clif, whose anger and despair didn't seem to come from the time in Japan, although he'd seen the effects of the atom bomb.

'The bomb kills everything, including bacteria. So if you don't die straight away, and you're just badly burned, you don't get infected. Except that the people who come to help you bring the infection, they can't help it. People were lying there in silk hammocks, they were too burned to be in a bed, and they'd lost too much skin for grafts. So they just hung there, waiting to die from an infection. The radiation affected everything. The next year they had these huge strawberries.'

His stories from Japan, like the stories from his training days, were mostly Boy's Own adventures told from the point of view of the petty criminal. Lawless, but with an internal moral code. Sometimes dramatic, and often funny or farcical, few had the feeling of tragedy.

Australian culture before the 1960s is characterised by sociologists, novelists, historians, as bland and ordered. Workplaces, institutions, cafés, the very streets are pictured as uniform and boring, their inhabitants conformist. Is this the childhood memory of people who grew up in particularly rigid households? Or of those arriving from cultures that in expression and dress were more colourful than the basic British that was Australia then? Or is it an unsophisticated analysis of the superficial signs of the hierarchical management systems that prevailed in most western industrialised countries?

The men who joined up with Clif in 1942 don't appear to have been institutionalised or cowed. Indeed, they seem to have had no notion of army regulations, or a concept of the camp as a school, or even of a boarding house, which might have rules.

'On the first day we left the camp at 5 pm and went into a pub in town for a beer. We'd done a day's work and that's what you did at the end of a day's work. We were very pissed off when the MPs arrived and arrested us.'

Clif would spend his twenty-first birthday in gaol for insubordination, a disagreement with his commanding officer leading to his temporary departure from the base, to which he returned in handcuffs. In the tales there were always casual references to being AWOL.

'We were interested in fighting, not in regulations.'

Which was, no doubt, why his attempt to become a communist was rejected by the party. That, and the fact that when his unit was sent to cut cane in a period that straddled two union financial years, he refused to pay the two annual fees demanded by the union. Logic, a desire to see justice done, his need for independence, would always determine his decisions and actions.

If the trigger for his aggressive mood was not the memory of military life, it was certainly to do with the war. I encouraged him to chair the Arts Policy Committee, thinking that if he felt he could help get the Labor Party elected and end the Vietnam War, this would help him deal with his anger. And besides, Lyn had said that Fred wanted him active; Fred Williams was his closest friend, maybe he knew about the problem. I could hardly ask; that would be a betrayal. Fred was astute, but not sophisticated; it would be some time before a sophisticated man was to try to help.

In the meantime, on with life. A group around the historian Ian Turner met during the football season at his house in Richmond, when Richmond was playing at home.

Ian explained to me that sport, and in particular football, was a very important influence in Melbourne culture and that if I came with them to the football I would be expected to join the working class in the outer and put up with the conditions there. I didn't enquire where he got the idea that I didn't know about Melbourne, or football, but I never went to the game with the group.

En route to the Turners, we had driven past the grand Richmond house in which I'd spent the early part of my childhood. My father and my grandfather had practised medicine there. I'd grown up barracking for Richmond. In that backyard, my father and my uncles, all of whom played cricket, football and tennis and some of whom rowed for the university and represented it in athletics, had, with my tennis-playing athletic mother, taught me to throw and hit a ball. One year I'd been with our fanatic housekeeper to every Richmond home-and-away game, sitting on the shoulders of the nearest tall man she could find, yelling 'Carn the Tig-ers' at the top of my voice in the outer.

Not all men on the left leapt to conclusions about me. Harry Stein came to stay, sent by Tom Uren, who had appeared in the house one day as the star of a hair-raising event that nearly went extremely wrong. I'd offered to host a weekend lunchtime meeting at which Tom, as ALP spokesman on the environment, could speak. A limited number of tickets was supposed to be sold, and I was expecting about a hundred people, but hundreds turned up, having paid, and expected lunch. I'd planned to give them a quarter of a chicken each, but that wasn't possible.

'Loaves and fishes,' Tom pointed out. When one of the helpers returned from a speedy trip to the local store, Tom got to, buttering the sliced bread on the hastily formed sandwich production line. His rousing speech dealt with the residual resentment caused by the need to keep the crowd outside the house, and over dinner and breakfast he and Clif began a long friendship.

Harry, whom we didn't know, had left hospital after serious surgery and taken himself to a motel in Melbourne. Tom rang and told me, and I went in the ute to collect him; Harry was rescued from a comfortable motel and bounced up to a cold house where the wombat leapt into his bed at night. But he had company and distraction, which Tom recognised are so important when one faces terminal illness. During his convalescence with us Harry talked about the relationship between jazz and the left, and why men like him, funny and wise, joined the Communist Party.

'It was a way of expressing dissent.'

So not everyone left-wing expected the masses to rise up. A member of the Eureka Youth League, Harry had taken Graeme Bell's jazz band on a tour of Eastern Europe during the Cold War, and later became a journalist. He would join Tom Uren's staff when Tom became Minister of Urban and Regional Development.

Tom often stayed with us, and remained close to Clif: his was an emotional as well as ideological connection. He found it easy to talk to Clif because they both shared the experience of being young, uneducated and idealistic in the army, and Clif gave Tom a way of actualising the environmental issues about which he was being briefed by scientists in the abstract. We were living in as committed an environmental way as possible, many years before it became common. I used no plastic bags and few products made from petrochemicals. No insecticides, no detergents, only soap. The area was not connected to the main water supply, nor was it sewered. In common with all rural households we were very careful with water in our own self-interest as much as that of the environment; the septic tank runoff was directed to the vegetable garden. We had herbs, but no other exotic flowers.

Clif's commitment to the environment had developed from his observations of the destructive power of his cat over the indigenous birds and animals. And I think now, as I make these connections, that perhaps Jock Marshall's early death in 1967, while *Involvement* and the London retrospective were being organised and Marlene and he were separating, was another reason the war began to haunt Clif at this time. From engineer father to physicist grandfather, to an exuberant confident zoologist who took him under his wing in the army. With Marshall's death he had again lost another scientist companion and mentor, one who was able to give voice to the growing urgency Clif felt about the environment.

Jock Marshall had lost an arm in a shooting accident when he was a teenager. A naturalist with experience of the tropics, he had managed to argue his way into the AIF and then into the intelligence corps. Superbly confident despite his disability, he wanted to see action and eventually persuaded the army brass. In 1945, in Wewak, New Guinea, he recruited eight marksmen volunteers who could also draw, and set up *Jockforce*. Clif was one of them. Marshall had authority, and his men admired him for his tenacity, intelligence and his larrikin independence. He was the perfect model for the young soldier determined to be an artist. If you were shrewd and had a bit of luck, if you played the rebel but with some bluster, within the structure, it was possible to turn a colossal organisation to your own ends.

'Jock said, "We'll work for the army in the morning and for science and posterity in the afternoon." So that's what we did. We penetrated enemy territory, to observe their strength and position and report back. And behind the enemy lines, in the afternoon, we sat down with our guns beside us and we drew the Bird of Paradise.'

After post-war training at Oxford and work in the United States, Marshall returned to set up what became the Zoology Department at Monash University. A man of broad interests, he was the best kind of networker, bringing together his colleagues and friends so they could enjoy each other and inform each other. It was about ideas and action and good living, wherever he was. When he came to Melbourne he contacted Clif and drew him into the circle of scientists and artists: Vince Serventy, Eric Worrell and Russell (Tas) Drysdale, in whose company he revelled. They travelled together to the outback and the desert. Clif's talk when we were in the desert was of, and from, those heady argumentative times.

As a man becomes independent he has to separate from his authority figures, and Clif's stories about Marshall were a mixture of admiration and cynicism.

'He came up one day and I was telling the story about the emu, that I had to stay out of the paddock when we realised he was male, and he was fixed on me. I had to get him a mate and wait until he'd settled for her. Before that he kept dancing at me, then his penis would appear. Jock said, "Pugh, emus don't have penises, birds just have two holes." So I went into the paddock and Chick came up and began his dance and sure enough out came his penis and Jock had to ring his secretary and stop publication of a paper.'

But Marshall, for all that his crown was slightly tarnished by this incident, had been a boisterous link with the good times in the army, and perhaps a way of ignoring the bad. Jim Warren, a quiet American paleontologist, took over as head of the department when Jock died. Jim had been Marlene's lover; she had taken the boys and lived for a time with Jim, so the Monash relationship was muted at the time I arrived. I was invited by zoologist Tim Ealey to an environment conference for secondary-school science teachers run by the Monash department. Tim came up quite often, so we still had access to science and to the developing body of information about the effect of the settler way of life on Australia, and the larger global issues that were revealing themselves to those would look and listen. Not too many listened at that time.

Jock Marshall had been one of the first members of the Australian Conservation Foundation, which was formed in Canberra in 1964 by a number of scientists to give a national focus to the Australian environment movement. Its first meeting included non-scientists such as the poet Judith Wright. So absolutely mainstream now. Artists, writers and performers have always carried the message in partnership with scientists, and the issues have always been based on sound research.

It took from 1964 to 1971. An issue can attract learned comment, newspaper articles, a lobby group, questions in the house, and enquiry. But when it has its own ministry you know it has emerged. Billy McMahon was the first Prime Minister to appoint a Minister for the Environment. In 1970, as we became involved in the campaign, the arts belonged as an issue to the Coalition government. In retrospect, one can see arts policy as symbolic of the changes happening across the federal government. In areas of conventional arts activity there were rumblings of discontent. The long-in-office Prime Minister Robert Menzies had chaired the Historic Memorials Committee, which was the parliament's interface with the visual arts. To the outsider it appeared fixed in the 1950s, and this appearance was kept up by the shrewdness of its panel of experts, the CAAB, in particular Bill Dargie.

Dargie had managed the conservative anti-modernists on the board, and Robert Menzies and Harold Holt, collecting carefully for the putative National Gallery. By 1972, with Tas Drysdale, Len French and James Gleeson as members, the committee had credibility with all but the most radical visual artists. Under Will Ashton's chairmanship the committee had been very conservative, and Menzies had actively interfered in certain projects, notably the selection of artists to be represented when Australia was first invited to exhibit at the Venice Biennale. But Dargie's agenda was to build a collection of really good work, independent of the politics of the artist or the artwork. When the gallery opened, many years later, his veneer of respectability was seen to have concealed an eclectic and radical collection policy.

When I met Clif, John Gorton was Prime Minister and the agenda was lively nationalism. Gorton seemed pleased to take the advice of the CAAB, and under his prime ministership the Australian Film Development Corporation and the National Film and Television Training School were set up. Gorton's strategic mistake, from the point of view of the Coalition's alliance with the arts, was to set up the Australian Council for the Arts under the ownership of Herbert 'Nugget' Coombs, that archetypal controlling public servant, and hand to it all arts but the visual arts. A colonial Keynes without John Maynard Keynes' deep connections to the arts, Coombs saw himself and his sidekick as more capable at managing or distributing funds than anyone actually working in the arts. He constituted himself patron, and made funding decisions based on an outdated ideology that valorised High Culture, and meant traditional. This situation was intolerable for professionals who had struggled for years to develop an Australian voice, especially in the theatre.

There is a curious resonance now, as our actors leave to work in Los Angeles and our television ads are made in America, with the issues that were so important to artists in Australia in the 1970s. Perhaps this is how capitalism works, the peripheral culture struggling always with the centre, more or less publicly, more or less effectively. Perhaps *negotiating* is a better way of articulating it; perhaps struggle is how it feels to the peripheral participant, and negotiation is a better word for what takes place. The field of culture that was so contested had grown economically while the conservatives had been in power, but the very nature of the field is that it will develop uncontrollably in style and content, if not quantity, of production. One can see, in retrospect, the coalescence of intention that allowed Nugget so much control, but had by the 1970s earned him such hatred from the playwrights and theatre companies who were shaping the culture.

Robert Menzies was very engaged with the arts, with 'higher' culture, so it wasn't hard for shrewd advocates of the various arts to approach his government for subsidy. In the performing arts he was managed successfully by Coombs, who, with Charles Moses from the ABC and newspaperman John Pringle, had set up the Elizabethan Theatre Trust in 1954. Nugget was a centralist, whose idea of the role of government patronage was to bring culture to the masses, to educate the population rather than develop local voice. The Trust was the only way in which a tax deductible donation could be made at the time to the performing arts, and a donor could not even specify that the donation be for a specific project or theatre company. In general, apart from *The One Day of the Year* and *Summer of the Seventeenth Doll*, the subsidised theatres reproduced British, and on rare occasions European or American, drama.

Theatre happens in time. It is dependent for development on considerable capital, whether it is the investment of their time by writer, director, actors, musicians, crew and designers, or investment by a producer, or public subsidy. The concept of subsidising High Culture, as opposed to Australian culture, affected playwrights, composers, and film-makers who wanted to produce work with an original Australian voice.

Between them, Menzies and Coombs continued a fantasy of cultural colonialism. The Trust and its beneficiary companies had direct links with the ABC, where these operas and plays were broadcast, often live, and the broadcaster was careful to tread a middle road.

The 1970s were heady, idealistic times in the performing arts. The issues were made more complex by energetic newcomers to the scene, who translated the concept of good drama to mean that if theatre made audiences laugh, or if it attracted middle-class audiences, it was by definition corrupt. And also because jazz, blues and Sinatra had not amalgamated with 'classical' music, to be taught and studied in schools and universities; it was a time before they were officially taught or studied in Australia except by a kind of apprentice system.

Variety theatre – cheap, cheerful, 'for the masses' entertainment, that mixture of slapstick, magic, acrobatics, stand-up comics, singing and music – had not so much been killed by television as translated itself across to it, so that we who watched television did hear Australian voices speaking in variety shows, which in turn spawned satire. Commercial television gave work to actors and writers, in dramas and soap operas, but in what was regarded as formulaic undemanding ways. Pretentious elites or radicals claimed to watch only the ABC.

In 1970 the film initiatives, and indeed Gorton himself, made the Coalition look relevant, as though it were loosening up in the right direction. When Gorton was dumped by his party in 1971, the Coalition lost the populist edge that went with his larrikin image. Despite its record on arts funding, under his successor Billy McMahon the Coalition would seem mired in the past.

Clif had agreed to chair the Arts Policy Committee for the Victorian branch of the Labor Party, a committee set up on the initiative of Clyde Holding, then Leader of the Opposition in the state parliament. An amusing, very bright lawyer, Clyde suffered from the rigidity of the left, but really was too gentle to tackle the entangled post-DLP loyalties. The Victorian Premier Henry Bolte seemed invincible in a way that Gorton, who had already faced one leadership challenge, did not.

Clif had never been much of a committee man. He'd left the

committee of the CAS, the Contemporary Art Society, when he saw the sainted Sunday and John Reed ensure that their view prevailed over that of working artists. We talked about the CAS experience when he was deciding whether to work with the Arts Policy Committee. I encouraged him to take it on, because it involved working with professionals, not amateurs like the Reeds, and because I thought it might be a way to focus politics away from the war and its images. Clif was worried, because all politics requires compromise, and art does not.

Clyde dealt with this question. 'All the ALP members who even think about the arts are on the committee and have the same views. No one in the ALP at the state level will oppose the policy; your committee can send whatever it likes to the conference and it will become federal ALP policy.'

The federal member for our electorate of Casey was Peter Howson, whose ministerial portfolios were described by the journalist Mungo MacCallum in those politically incorrect days as 'boongs, pongs, and poofters'. Aboriginals, Environment and the Arts. Indigenous affairs and the environment are crucial departments now, and the arts, or their management, on every political party's agenda. But in those heady days, the two issues on which we would have an impact, the arts and the environment, were in our own backyard. Whatever our personal strains, we approached those issues together, just as we worked together on portraits and the business of our lives.

9

TO BE THE NUDE

Champagne, paté and salad

The model didn't arrive. It was to be Lilith, she'd posed for Clif and his friends for years. Fred Williams, Frank Hodgkinson, John Olsen, Bert Tucker, John Perceval had all arrived and were setting up in the main room when Clif came back from the station, quite bemused. He told often of the time that he went to Hurstbridge Station and she fell off the train, blood caked on her face, nose broken after a difficult night, but still on time. She hadn't come this morning, he'd even searched the train. I think, in the end, there'd been a mix-up.

Perhaps it was raining, or they'd have gone into plein-air. But how can it have been? I know it wasn't cold. Clif came into the kitchen. Would I model?

My first instinct was to say no. I can't remember if he'd already begun to paint me, that series of paintings that should have taught me about the way he felt, but even so, in the first one I know I posed in a lacy *kebaya*, all pink and pale, but ladylike. But then I thought, after all, it's part of a great tradition, so what? And took off my clothes and lay down on the rug.

They were very used to drawing and every now and again I could move to be comfortable: I'd done a lot of ballet training, so keeping still was not hard. After about forty minutes Fred Williams asked if I should have a break, and Clif asked if I'd make a cup of tea. So I headed for the kitchen.

'Don't you want to put your clothes on?'

'I thought you'd want me to pose again?'

Fred remarked that professional models usually dressed between poses. I pointed out that they were paid, not usually modelling in their own homes, and certainly not expected to make the tea. It seemed quite silly to be naked one minute and dressed the next.

Perhaps because they were artists, and in conversation concise and concrete, they couldn't articulate the problem; perhaps because they were blokes. From my point of view the issue of nudity arose at the time I was asked to pose, and, resolved, the question *should one be naked in front of people*, whether I was moving about or staying still, was irrelevant.

Once it became possible, there were other reasons for going naked. Aesthetics, convenience and budget had driven Clif's building process: the house had a roof, but no ceiling; lovely spaces, but the picturesque quality celebrated by visitors had less charm for me. I was bred for icy climates, and the house heated fast. The inconvenience in winter, when water and wind came through the holes, was nothing to the unmitigated beat of sun on iron.

The financial discipline and austerity that had underpinned Clif's success had welded onto the worries of the Depression, the time he lost his father. It takes a while to enjoy life when anxiety is a habit, and it was not until years later that we finally bought a big concrete tank and captured the run-off from all our roofs.

At this time we had only two small corrugated-iron tanks. The fine pale clay dust came through the unsealed doors and windows with the mosquitoes. We had people staying at least once a week, with three, sometimes four, of us living there all the time for that first year or so, and dinner parties or lunches at least once every week. I had not quite 7000 litres of water, we were in a rainshadow, 43 centimetres each year. Nudity saves washing, saves water. I don't want to sound as if I suffered: apart from the mosquitoes life was wonderful in those early days, and the house had silence and space. But the fewer clothes I wore the more comfortable I was, and the less water we used.

The designer of David Williamson's *What if You Died Tomorrow?* came up to see Dunmoochin. After the premiere, David surprised me by remarking that the actress had refused to take off her clothes. When would she have? And it transpired that, unable to make himself heard at the front door when he arrived for the first time at Dunmoochin, David came into the house. I'd found him in the main room and shown him through to the studio. I was naked, and he'd incorporated the scene in the play. If I had noticed I was naked it wouldn't have bothered me with someone my own age in the arts scene; if it had, I would have remained calm, made an excuse, got into a dress.

The artists got used to it, but I suppose they gossiped; I look back and realise that there must have been talk. I was new on the scene, much younger than Clif, but I was no hippy. No one remarked on it to me at first, and therefore I never had the opportunity to explain about the heat and the washing. I suppose everyone must have thought it was some ideological feminist position and been too afraid to ask.

Nudity became amalgamated with the first political stance I took publicly without Clif, which was to argue that there should not be laws controlling abortion. Naked flesh in paint has a sexual element, for all one's body may be a series of abstract planes and an exercise in colour; the question of our age difference, the paintings as an advertisement for Clif's masculinity, was unspoken. Unspoken, but not unstated. In 1974 he was to do a series he called *Copulations*, which had my body, together with deconstructed elements of it, and some bits of his, floating about the board as if in ecstasy; but when my face is visible I seem disengaged and the man's skin is not the colour of Clif's. The question of the sexual partner as nude, and their exposure, is an unavoidable question of power.

It happens that I was genetically extremely pale, without any angles to my body. I had very thick pale gold/red hair. If it had been curly I'd have looked like the complete bimbo. One could long for black hair, colouring associated with intelligence, and the sort of shape that carries fabulous clothes, but one must make do with what one has, or fund a plastic surgeon's lifestyle. In London, walking past a particularly wonderful dress in a shop window, I remarked that I'd love to be thought of as elegant. Clif could not stop laughing, trying to explain that it didn't matter. Being strawberry blonde gave extra height to the barrier to being taken seriously, and so did nudity. But I expected to scale it.

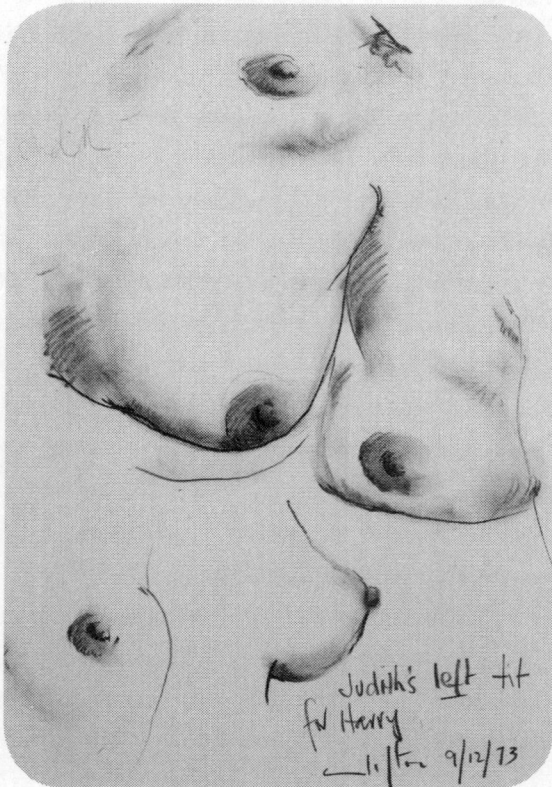

As fame grew, television crews would arrive to film for documentaries and for interviews about particular issues. And one day in the mid-seventies, as they were filming, there I was on the easel: sprawled across a nearly finished board. Muttering among crew, interviewer, and director. Then, trying to sound ingenuous, 'Would Judith pose as if she was modelling for this picture?'

I suppose they thought I'd refuse. But once an issue becomes one's own issue, somehow it stays that way. So, as Clif pretended to paint, I pretended, naked, to model.

The cameraman was frantic. When the first nude live models appeared on stage, the compromise reached with the censor was as follows: nudity is unobjectionable in art galleries, so of itself, when art, it is acceptable. The distinguishing factor between fine and performing art is movement. On stage, in order to be art, a nude had to be still. The question of what constituted acceptable on television had yet to be settled. Our cameraman was going to get his scoop, a few short seconds of the first nude woman on television in Australia, if not the world, and there was no question: it had to be art, it was a film of an artist talking about his work. But what if the model moved?

Umm . . . this wasn't live television . . . edit? Oh, well. It must have been a commercial station, the ABC were far more likely just to shoot a lot of film. He got his shot and I earned some more notoriety.

A panicky Joe Brown rang.

'Judith, you have to have this young painter and his family.'

Joe was taking on Rick Amor, and Rick wanted to paint full-time. I knew Clif would want to encourage Joe to move into more contemporary work, but I didn't think any of our studios were free.

'Can't they stay with you until there's somewhere free? You'll like his wife.'

So I told Clif they were coming up for a while.

'Where will he paint?'

'He'll have to share your studio. Ring Joe if you want to say no.'

Much later I was to understand how private studios could be. Bert Tucker and his wife Barbara had returned from New York in the 1960s and lived nearby, in Hurstbridge. He and Clif were close, and Barbara and I became very good friends. One day she telephoned to ask a favour. I was familiar with native animals: could I come down to help get a possum out of Bert's studio? Of course. Brush-tailed possums are very clumsy and it was obviously important to reduce the likelihood of damage that would be caused if it ran about the studio.

When I arrived things were slightly more complex than I had expected. They explained that the possum was living in the cavity above the ceiling, and they had very sensibly sealed off the entrance it had found, so that it was now hungry and thirsty. There was a manhole in the ceiling, and Bert's plan was that I would climb a ladder and, standing on top of it, slide open the manhole cover, while sliding the open section of a cardboard box along the ceiling across the manhole. A piece of fresh apple in the box would cause the hungry possum to jump into it, and I would then lower the box from the ceiling while closing it to keep in the possum, and climb down the ladder.

I was about to mention that I am not good with heights when Barbara added that as Bert's studio was a place of unfinished work it was not possible for anyone but Bert to look at anything in it, and that he would like me to wear a blindfold while carrying out this operation. Somehow the unlikelihood of this suggestion made the alternative – that Bert could empty his studio and then in some way reconsecrate it once we'd removed the possum – seem impolite.

So on with the blindfold and, box in hand, up to the ceiling. All went well and I felt efficient. But we had underestimated the enthusiasm of the possum. It leapt into the box and, despite its recent diet, it was quite a solid lump. The box unbalanced, so that I could not get the top pieces of cardboard folded in. I lost my grip momentarily, recovering it as the box, with the possum grasping its apple, dropped below my waist height.

Possums have few predators in the natural environment, and they instinctively climb when frightened. This one climbed up onto my head, dislodging the blindfold. Fortunately I was too high to see any unfinished paintings. Possums have quite sharp claws even when they are only using them to grip. They also have an effective defence system; they urinate on the animal that is threatening them. Even when sitting on the head of that animal and carrying a piece of apple provided by that animal.

I'd begun to climb down the ladder when I realised: not only that once my head arrived below the level of the top of the ladder I might be able to see some pictures, but also that the possum would then jump onto the top of the ladder and probably try to get back into the ceiling. Was it Bert's inspired suggestion or some reflex of my own that provided a simultaneous solution to the problems of the blindfold and the moving possum? I don't recall. I inverted the box over the possum and my head, and descended. Bert led me out of the studio and he and Barbara were able to close the box on the possum, who had nearly finished his apple.

Clif did ring Joe Brown, and was reluctantly persuaded to let Rick and Tina Amor come. Which they did, with an entire household of goods and a small son, Liam. The backdrop for a production of *Macbeth* that Clif had painted for Peter O'Shaughnessy formed a useful screen behind which the Amors' lives were stored, and we settled in. Rick was a vulnerable and shy man and I was worried Clif would be tough about the space, but it was summer and the studio doors were open frequently, and Clif's discipline was such that he was able to focus despite the intrusion. Rick painted a head of Chick the emu on an offcut of a painting of Clif's, and I bought it with my housekeeping money.

Clif was tough enough not to buy work he didn't yet respect.

He only rarely bought pictures. We met the artist John Wolseley because we bought a painting of his, but in the main Clif and his friends swapped with each other or with dealers. Fred Williams had made for Clif's *David Tolley and Family* as soon as it was painted, and in exchange Clif had chosen Fred's lovely picture that I'd rescued from above the couch. There was an Olsen painting of a local girl, and a John Howley, a Don Laycock and a Lawrie Daws (the 'Group of Four' had exhibited together in 1954), and a Dickerson and an Arthur Boyd: Clif and Arthur had shown together in the Antipodeans exhibition of 1959.

None of the Dunmoochin studios became available, but the Amors were easy company, and the house elastic enough to accommodate an extra family. They were with us for several months before moving to a cottage on Joan and Daryl Lindsay's property Mulberry Hill, on the Mornington Peninsula. Artists help each other.

Annual parties, buying presents, making puddings, the streets full of mothers with children home from school in early December, all the anticipation of Christmas. Hard to convey how the activity peaked and then altogether stopped, giving way to long hot aimless Januarys, when the city seemed asleep, universities were empty, and country towns looked as if a neutron bomb had been dropped in the main street.

One January, a long heatwave left several visitors stranded for several days; it was simply too hot to drive. Under these circumstances the nudity spread. In addition to the Amors, Bill Hartley, the ex-secretary of the Victorian ALP, Jan and Penny were there. We were lounging about, everyone completely naked, hardly able to talk, the air still under the unceilinged roof, spraying each other on occasion with water from my ironing bottles. The living room reflected the level of our commitment to normal social forms: glasses everywhere, clothes strewn about, together with towels from our evening dips in the clayey dam.

The entrance to the house was by a small curved hall. Immediately visible through a sliding glass door was the main room, with long walls for paintings, a big table always with a vase of flowers, eventually an elevated fireplace with a figured copper hood we'd found in a junkyard. Opposite, the door to the room in which we lived and ate, and at the end a garden through which one reached the studio.

The straggly house party was scattered about the living room. Suddenly, from the main room, Tina rushed in with a dress of mine. Luckily we wore long voluminous cotton dresses a lot in the 1970s.

'Men! Men in suits!'

'Oh shit, I forgot, a new portrait client,' said the naked Clif.

I threw the dress over my head and closed the door to the main room behind me, as Sir Andrew Grimwade, a trustee of the National Gallery of Victoria, walked in with Sir Lindsay Clark, Chairman of Western Mining. Andrew was carrying some chilled champagne. Sir Lindesay, who suffered badly from arthritis and needed warmth all the time, was wearing a three-piece suit.

All the bedrooms in the house were upstairs. Everyone's clothes were upstairs. The staircase was in the main room with us and the champagne. There was a permanent ladder leading from the garden to the upstairs deck, but the others would have to step down from the back door into the garden, go through two sets of gates, climb up the ladder, get dressed, get down, return to the living room, and, ideally, tidy it. Andrew looked expectant: the obvious thing to do was to call Clif and get some glasses. But I could rely on Andrew's manners and those of his companion.

'Oh how lovely, thank you, Andrew. I'll get Clif, but first Sir Lindesay, let me show you round, you'll be wanting to know about these pictures.'

The history of every painting, the type of flower and the potter who'd thrown the vase, the story of the fireplace, the writing on it, its symbols. That Clif had made the table from railway sleepers. I began to feel like a guide in a stately home.

Then Clif appeared from the living area, looking crisply ironed despite the heat, and said hello. He'd been 'out the back' as, it was clear, had everyone. The room was tidy, Penny in the kitchen laying out some paté and salad, Bill getting the glasses. Rick began to open the champagne. All was delightful, everyone fully dressed. Clif suggested that as it was so hot our latest visitors should take off their jackets.

Tina called out from the walk-in pantry that she couldn't find the flour.

'In the bin at the end.'

'It's not here.'

'Yes, Tina, the mouse-proof built-in bin at the end of the pantry.'

'I can't find it.'

I am very obsessive, and everything was very much in its place in that house in those days.

'Please come and show me, Judith.'

The Amors had been living with us for some time, and I was surprised at her memory failure. I went to the pantry. And there, of course, she was. The member of the party who'd stayed behind to tidy the room: still completely naked.

10

POWER

Home-baked bread, muffins

Food, my cooking, is essential to the story of our life together. My cooking and baking skills developed on the wood stove my father installed in the garden for me when we moved from Richmond to a magic house and grounds south of the city, and the kitchen there was modernised. The experience proved useful in the early days at Dunmoochin, because the electricity supply to the area was erratic. Gas bottles supplied two gas fittings as an alternative illumination in one room, kerosene lamps and candles the rest. Romantic – the pools of light and the shadows beyond – but someone has to clean the glass in order to maintain the pools. Running the house demanded a great deal of time and energy, even though I had help, and my housekeepers and I were hampered by our long skirts.

Supermarkets were being introduced as the norm in the seventies, but at the same time people who chose to live on the outskirts of the city, near the bush, were revelling in the pleasures of home-baked bread and muffins, of fresh wholesome food, of vegetable gardens. Pursuit of the 'natural' was in the air. Puzzling symbolism, that fashion for flowing dresses, long hair, home-baked bread, just as we began to articulate ideas about equality and liberty. But we wanted men to change, as well as women, for us all to be less defined by suit and lipstick.

That first summer, life seemed to be simple. I was physically fit again, nourished by the clear Dunmoochin air, and by trailing on horseback through bush and beside pasture, sometimes startling the local herd of kangaroos. The only worry was Clif's anger. But that was separate from everything else, it was infrequent and unpredictable and, I thought, manageable. Perhaps it was having some effect on the delicious intimacy we'd started with, but that might also have been the surgery or the initial lack of communication about the pain. Not that I blamed him for doubting me, the idea didn't occur.

When he talked about the way we would live he had surprised me by suggesting, when he brought up the subject of marriage, that I would not be faithful to him.

'You'll have affairs. But this is the core relationship, remember they won't matter.'

Should I have protested? Would that have made him secure? But surely this is the sort of remark to ponder. Perhaps he was suggesting that he might do so, but no, he was very hungry for me, that was unlikely. Perhaps already he was thinking he would age before me; but he was forty-five, fit and golden-tanned, and a happy abandoned lover. And he had what he wanted in me: someone to talk to who did not have a view about his painting, who provided a comfortable house, and with whom he had that intuitive connection which provides an intimacy that is not only physical.

Perhaps he was thinking of his own experience. We'd met in that extraordinary decade after the contraceptive pill became available, when sexually transmitted diseases were readily cured with antibiotics, before HIV/AIDS. Neither Clif's first wife, June, nor Marlene had this advantage. Contraception then was mechanical and unreliable. Technology meant that I had different expectations in a relationship.

The myth, his myth, was that he had sacrificed a loving wife, June, for his painting, because she wanted children and he did not; and that Marlene and the children had been sacrificed on the same altar.

Clif's mother had talked to June about contraception on his behalf, and June made the decision to leave rather than to live without children, and had left him and married again. I heard them both, June and Clif, talk about this when years later they met up again. But I suspect it was not just the question of children, but more that June was not engaged with the idea of art as part of the intellectual milieu. June was gentle and feminine, and I think that the idea of Clif letting his mother involve herself in such an intimate area made June aware of the time ahead, of what it actually meant, that Clif would commit himself to becoming an artist in post-war Melbourne.

He understood Marlene's great qualities, and saw how the issue of the unexpected pregnancy had distorted their relationship. She minded his resentment of the financial responsibility the boys brought, his distress that he had to focus on things other than painting, and the immature and impolite assumption that he could have a sexual relationship and ignore the consequences. This was not the cause of their break-up, but it allowed other issues to fester, and it was no surprise that Marlene had responded to Jim Warren's sensitive attention and later to the quiet support of Ray Newell.

One could expect such sexism in any man of his age at the time, but there was a particular reason for this dislocation in Clif's ordinarily intelligent and logical approach to life. We learn so much from our first experience of anything, but especially when we participate in sex. For most of us this happens in our own culture and society, so that we understand the articulated taboos and constraints. But Clif's first sexual experiences were with a Japanese woman he owned, in a brothel he owned, when he was part of the occupying force in Japan. This woman spoke no English, and contraception was entirely her responsibility. It made him a very relaxed lover, but it did mean that his experience, his bodily understanding, was not integrated into the commonsense of his own culture, which was that sex and marriage together meant children.

'June was younger than me, not old enough to consent to marry me, and her father refused his consent, so I had to become her guardian and then give myself permission to marry her.'

They had met when he was innocent of love and war, and the hardness he learned in New Guinea made it possible for him to harden his heart and let his mother interfere. The divorce was sordid, he and June both unhappy; the little house in the Dandenongs was sold.

But perhaps it gave him freedom, from the mortgage on the war-service loan, from the need to think about anyone but himself. He was able to enjoy a sort of adolescence, that timeless dreaming, lost when he'd joined the army. And perhaps all the activity of bohemia, the drinking, arguing about politics, sharing ideas, and partying, the very irregularity, meant he could bury the memories that troubled him so much.

We seek the same things in each partner, but they come in different degrees. Each relationship is different, and power differentials can change as circumstances change. I was a confident young woman and everything in my class background and experience of life confirmed that anything was possible for me. I had never thought money mattered, or wanted security, in the way many of my friends wanted it; I expected to experience life. I knew that it was destructive for me not to follow my intuition. So I accepted the physical reality of the house and the place and left the planning and articulation of our life to Clif.

A pity perhaps that I didn't see that I could help him feel content by making demands, so that he could share the burden of happiness. It can be hard to adjust to ease and comfort after years of stress and hardship, particularly if the hardship is self-imposed, and perhaps harder if the goal has been achieved so thoroughly. I thought of Clif as an experienced competent man, my expectations of relationship were fulfilled, and I did not attempt, until it was too late, to negotiate. All the power in our relationship – that is, all that derived from money: the convenience and comfort of the house, the size of the housekeeping allowance, the location in which we lived or bought other property, ownership of cars, of everything – was Clif's. He did not even think about discussing it, and I did not question that. Changes to the house, a more generous housekeeping allowance, less alcohol, an attempt at a room of my own, all these were negotiated by others – Alastair Knox, Phyllida Hodgkinson, Marlene, Clyde Cameron – negotiated, unbidden, on my behalf.

It did not even occur to me to worry about power or dependence. Because Clif was much older than me, most of his friends' wives were also older, so that around the dinner table we shared expectations that women just a few years younger than me did not. It was possible for us to think in such a way because the culture itself had, throughout our childhood and adolescence, systematically limited our opportunities. The ways in which this happened were as absolute as employment awards that deprived married women of permanent employment, and as unfocussed as the status of women as 'associate' members of sporting clubs, or the expectation that men on a crowded bus would give up their seats to women.

It is so hard to look back and understand this of myself, but, after all, I had no reason to doubt. Life was filling up and there was much to do. Dunmoochin itself sustained me. On the drive into Melbourne you could see the level of the polluted air enveloping the city. Our air was clean, the light clear, the bush subtle, its detail endlessly intriguing. In the wing of the house expanded by Alastair Knox we slept and woke in the treetops, surrounded by birds and in the rustle of leaves.

Downstairs, Clif had built rooms to accommodate, for example, a set of French windows. Over the years, when another room seemed like a good idea, mud-brick walls had extended the original wattle and daub, with a door or window from a junkyard. Conceived from the inside out, the house did not really embrace its surrounds, and was a series of rooms which, although charming, were not integrated. But that didn't matter, it was reality. Until Phyllida Hodgkinson came to stay.

Frank Hodgkinson and Clif had known each other for many years, and in early 1971 Frank had returned from some years in Majorca with Phyllida and their son Leon. We met them in Sydney on our way to Queensland, to Dunk and Timana Islands. We all got on, so we suggested they come and stay when we returned. Clif was to paint the ebullient businessman Eric McIlree on Dunk, the island owned by his company.

Frank, me, Clif, Phyllida, Barbara holding Leon, Patricia Hoppe

It was on this trip to Dunk that I came to understand why the green of the paddocks superphosphated for European-style farming so upset Clif. It was not just infuriating to see the environment stressed and destroyed by extravagant exploitation, reminding him of the crisis his scientist friends and his own observations anticipated. Clif's marginal colour blindness meant he saw red and yellow last, so that whatever he looked at 'warmed up' over time. His love of the desert and the Cottlesbridge summer was partly in response to this physical characteristic, I think; and green reminded him of the jungle war.

Eric McIlree had appeared to be inappropriately patronising on the evening before we began to paint him, but in fact was courteous, managing a rampagingly drunken Clif with grace and aplomb. Both men were successful and sensitive; neither, but particularly Clif, wanted to show it. When the next day on Dunk Clif produced an initial painting of vivid red and purple flowers surrounding an equally bright Eric, I made one of the few comments I ever made on the painting. Eric *was* a bit over the top, but surely Clif wanted to show the other side of his character as well? Clif was puzzled, until we realised that the dreadful hangover in the bright sunlight meant he had begun to paint while still wearing his dark glasses.

Eric's colour was restored to normal on the board, and he and Janice dropped us on nearby Timana Island for a couple of days to stay with Bruce Arthur, who had left wrestling in the 1960s to take up weaving. Bruce brought the confidence and power of an Olympian to his very physical craft. Timana was a peaceful place, precisely a tropical island: utterly white sand, jungle beyond, the waves' hypnotic rhythm. The only incongruous element feral hens. When they'd arrived, as egg producers, they'd been normally sized, but had more than doubled as the generations fed on the rich tropical undergrowth.

I sat on the beach in the morning and read, looking up occasionally to see Clif's snorkel travelling back and forth as he explored the underwater landscape. After a while the snorkel was joined by a dorsal fin, making its way in the opposite direction, rhythmically crossing a little way apart. I went to the studio to remark on this to Bruce. He wasn't alarmed; there was plenty for the shark to eat in those waters, but it seemed sensible to collect Clif so they could plan to make a tapestry together. *Make* actually meant *design*, but Clif's physicality demanded that he get involved, and soon he was adding three-dimensional objects to exploit the possibilities of texture.

We flew back to Sydney with Eric for another couple of sittings, but Clif and Bruce were planning a series of tapestries, so we booked our return to Dunk on a commercial flight. On the tarmac I had a sudden deep sense of foreboding, and told Clif I couldn't fly north, but had to get back to Melbourne.

'No, it's not about the plane crashing. I just know I shouldn't go.'

It didn't occur to me that he might think I was leaving him, and as the plane was waiting he, poor thing, decided not to argue. I got on the plane to Melbourne and, sure enough, began to bleed as soon as I got in the truck, which we'd left in the airport carpark. I drove to my gynaecologist, who was away; his locum told me I was pregnant, and that I should go home and lie down.

Penny came up from the studio she and Jan were sharing just below us at Dunmoochin, stayed with me and tried to contact Clif while I lay flat. I wanted to make the decision to get up and walk, because I thought the baby was not okay, but I wanted to make it with Clif. No Timana telephone. To be in touch meant waiting for Bruce to take the catamaran to Dunk for supplies, and if Clif weren't with him, another day or more, depending on the weather, while he sailed across to tell Clif I wanted to contact him, and then sailed back. After a few days I made the decision alone, walked about, and lost the baby. Kind neighbours drove me to hospital.

Clif was sympathetic but relieved I was okay, and confident we'd have another. When he came back it was with the Hodgkinsons, whose marriage, it was obvious, was ending. They must have been a terrific couple at one time, but the issue was cultural, and the marriage could not sustain it. Phyllida was a very bright and lively Englishwoman, but everything was difficult. They'd left a small village on Majorca where they lived among a lively sophisticated group of international painters and writers, to arrive in North Queensland with a child who spoke no English. Leon was used to the affectionate attention of familiar people, to being welcome in pubs and cafés. Not in North Queensland in 1971, nor even in Sydney.

Before she bravely left with Leon, and hardly any money, telling me she knew it was over (as Frank told me and Clif, although together he and Phyllida talked of his return to Europe), Phyllida one day asked Clif and me to walk around the house with her. She'd renovated old houses on Majorca and her sense of the possibilities of the spaces was exciting. It was just a matter of removing some walls. We did so, and suddenly the house opened out, inviting us from one area to another: some quite private where I could tuck a bed or a desk, some spacious, for a group to eat or chat. Each set of windows offered a different experience of bush or pasture.

When Phyllida left, Frank stayed on with us, a sophisticated presence, so that we had a period without anger to consolidate our life together. He managed the problem of John Olsen arriving with wine for lunch, and his laconic stories of the war and of post-war Europe began to teach me about the larger art world and to appreciate its inter-connections. When the press and rollers Clif had ordered through Hayter arrived, Clif and Frank prepared an etching studio in one of the outbuildings, and began to work together. John Olsen came in most evenings before dinner, and often stayed to eat.

Frank helped Clif with the house changes; very useful. For Clif, building was rather like making a sculpture: the material and the space suggesting the form as it developed. He experimented with walls, windows and entrances, and when it looked right he left it. Frank was more interested in planning, consultation and detail than Clif, building shelves and cupboards with doors that shut. He went to the bother of filling in gaps, so that the domestic supply of flies and mosquitoes was greatly reduced.

Frank found some tiles Marlene and Clif had brought from Mexico and laid them behind the sink so I'd have a splashback, but Clif urged him back to the etching studio and I was left to stain wood and paint walls myself. Until, one evening, I was toiling at a large mud-brick wall with a tin of white paint while Frank, John Olsen and Clif watched, glasses of wine in hand after a day's drinking.

John announced, 'No, I can't stand it any longer,' and the three of them grabbed brushes and finished the whole room, spilling not a drop. Of course! They were painters, they prepared their canvases or boards every day.

What power I had in the relationship was unarticulated. But I wasn't thinking in those terms. I didn't need to. The work I did, on the campaign, meeting clients or dealers, talking to portrait clients, running the house, was enjoyable and was absolutely in tandem with Clif. Life in an increasingly beautiful, comfortable and convenient space was full of intelligent interesting people. I loved cooking and extending friendships over meals.

The house and the parties began to be a sort of mud-brick salon. From which it is traditional that influence derives.

11

INFLUENCE

*Beer at the pub, dinner on a lake,
tea and consolation*

'Tom Uren. FMA 437. Telephone your friends in Darwin.'

And dropping his suitcase on the floor as he arranged for the driver
to come up the next morning, the sprawling energetic figure strode into
our life. The federal member's authority number allowed him, or anyone
quoting it, to telephone anywhere in Australia. Useful for people who
wanted to co-ordinate publicity and consult about issues across the
country, and Tom knew that it cost money to make such calls. All Labor
Party politicians were very conscious of the value of the resources they
had, and that they relied on a network of voluntary support to develop
policies and tell the community about those policies.

Parliamentarians had free travel on electorate business, but no allowance for non-electorate travel, so they needed accommodation when
they were away from home. We had plenty of bedrooms, and room
for meetings or fundraising events. Dunmoochin, on the edge of a crucial marginal electorate, thus became a hotel for itinerant politicians.

I made sure that while they stayed, Labor politicians met as many people of influence as possible. So much of our time in those early years was involved with the Labor Party: my work on the campaign committees, my door knocking, Clif's donations, our fundraising, his policy development. Work can bring its own reward, at least in politics. Our influence came about through the working conditions of federal politicians before the Whitlam government, as much as our commitment.

In 1970 no backbencher of any political persuasion had the support of even one salaried researcher or speech writer. Each member of parliament had one secretary in the office in his electorate. In Canberra Gough Whitlam, as Leader of the Opposition, had, in addition, a press secretary, two policy researcher/speechwriters, and three secretaries; the Deputy Leader, Lance Barnard, had three extra staff, the Senate Leader Lionel Murphy a press secretary and a secretary; Sam Cohen, Deputy Leader in the Senate, a secretary. Backbench parliamentarians had to be capable and resourceful to get media or other attention.

This was not a deliberate policy to deprive the opposition of resources, any more than the sexist division of labour (all administrative support female, all other positions male) was conscious. The hardest fights, because they must be the most subtle, are against *the way things are*. The way things were, in those days, derived from systems put in place at Federation. Many on the government benches and those in opposition had first been elected before the Second World War. The frugal administrative systems of the federal government meant policy development was minimal, and largely administrative rather than ideological; that is, it involved industry restructure, trade negotiations and response to changes in international conditions. Many of these policy responses were overseen by unpaid industry committees serviced by a few public servants. This structure went unquestioned, a habit, the taken-for-granted of the political culture. Where a consensus of the educated elite demanded a change in policy – for example as the White Australia policy fell from favour – that change was managed over time.

The political class – of media advisers, researchers, policymakers and speechwriters, who nowadays morph from party headquarters to members' and ministerial staff to the bureaucracy or unions or employer organisations and later reappear as politicians – was then extremely small. The hierarchical nature of the public service, and the strict understanding that its advice should be seen to be impartial, restricted employment opportunities. This advice was perceived by the left as not impartial. But it was, in a sense. Although entry was by public examination, staff recruited into the public service were selected by officials who, by definition, looked for people like themselves, those who rose slowly through the ranks (essentially acting as word processors) became images of the culture that created them. And that culture had served one government, through one structure, for so long that the interests of senior public servants and the government had coalesced; the public service developed policies that suited the Coalition and would not upset the applecart.

There was no superannuation scheme, although there was a parliamentary pension with some travel benefits. In the public service and universities there was permanent employment, so for those with a theoretical interest in public affairs and administration, or practical experience of these, leaving a secure job to stand for parliament was a risk, unless it was for a very safe seat. The ALP being a creature of factions, it was possible to lose endorsement even in such a safe seat. In a marginal electorate, if you had only one term, your financial situation and that of your dependents might be compromised. Politicians in the 1960s and 1970s had much in common with small businesspeople; the occupation could not be regarded as a career. This meant that the kind of person who took it up usually did so from conviction or because of a natural empathy with ordinary people.

Without official researchers, ALP policymakers formed relationships in academia and the professions. These advisors were franker and tougher for not being paid. Effective policy change, not money or career, was the desired outcome for both advisor and advised. When a carefully developed policy was altered on impulse by the politician, those same independent advisors could complain in public.

Powerful men in the ALP were in the main intelligent, but few had a tertiary education, and many had not completed secondary school. Most of these had developed an interest in politics through the union, and they were used to making speeches to people familiar with issues under discussion and uninterested in being patronised. They were used to defending their ideas and policies, indeed their own character, in raucous public meetings, not polite university tutorials. Focussed and resilient, the best of them were like inspiring stand-up comics.

Politics in so many ways was more personal. With fewer researchers and staff there were fewer formal meetings. New issues were being confronted – heritage, urban renewal, the environment, wage equality, no-fault divorce, broader arts funding – and these were areas where the ALP had to look for expertise and ideas beyond the party. Our dinner table was a place for everyone to make connections, and for issues to be raised and discussed informally. So for Labor politicians Dunmoochin became a comfortable and interesting place, not too far from the city, with connections to the party and an understanding of the electorate, not affiliated to any faction but connected to all. A place to relax, meet colleagues and advisors and potential staff.

By 1974, when he resigned from the Australia Council and left arts politics altogether, Clif had won three Archibald prizes, and ours were household names. Although the route to such fame was grounded in commitment to the ALP's election, to changing the political landscape and saving the environment, it sprang also from other connections. One of these was with Commander Michael Parker. Clif knew Michael through the art world, and one evening after an opening we went to dinner at the Parkers'. Parker had become a friend of Prince Philip when they were in the Royal Navy, and been appointed equerry when the Prince and Princess Elizabeth married and began their official duties.

When the Princess succeeded to the throne Parker became Prince Philip's private secretary. He'd returned to Melbourne when his first marriage ended; he was a businessman. I don't remember who was there, that evening in 1971. The group of mainly men was relaxed and talkative after the opening. I was used to watching quietly, the assumed bimbo. However, I do remember a moment when someone asked Clif with whom he was going to win the Archibald that year.

He replied, 'You can't just win the Archibald.'

He was right, but I said, 'Well, this year it might be possible.' The terms of the bequest were widely known. 'The prize is judged by the Trustees of the Art Gallery of New South Wales. The subject has to have made a contribution to the arts, letters, or public life. I think that to narrow the odds you have to paint someone who is well known to the Trustees, so they can respond to the portrait, and that you narrow them even further if you paint the man of the moment. Sir John McEwen has said he will retire at this year's election. He is the symbol of the stability of the Coalition, of the pastoral industries. I think this year a good portrait of Sir John McEwen would be most likely to win.'

The table was quiet as my bimbo status dropped away. Michael excused himself and returned to say Sir John would be delighted to sit.

Thus we found ourselves driving to McEwen's property, near Stanhope. On road bitumen-topped to the gate of the property: startling at a time when country roads across Victoria were surfaced with gravel. The bitumen surface was of itself a symbol of the certainties of the times; indeed, perhaps a universal symbol of local government. I remarked, as he stood for his portrait, on the convenience of this arrangement, and quite without irony Sir John said that the local council had thought it would be helpful for him to have a comfortable journey from home. One couldn't argue, he'd been in Cabinet for twenty-one years. Besides, Clif had his own arrangements for the grading of our private drive, which involved buying beers for the council roadworkers at the local pub – and no public scrutiny.

We began the portrait the next morning. Clif set up his easel. McEwen chose to stand, and I sat opposite a man who had been a figure of authority and power, whose answers at parliamentary question time, whose confident speeches had accompanied on the radio my homework, cooking, washing up, my reading, all my life.

I never planned my conversations with Clif's subjects. My role was not interviewer, in the sense that I had a goal to get information or insight; it was simply to distract the sitter so that they would let Clif see them as they were. I was trained in research but, without ever discussing it with Clif, I knew that what was important was to let his subjects emerge from their own point of view, so it helped not to have studied them. I began the usual politenesses with the Deputy Prime Minister; perhaps commenting on the pasture, or asking about stock, crops, the house, the time it took to Canberra; I don't remember the detail, they were just the sort of remarks one makes to break the ice. Clif often had to adjust the angle of his easel as he began, make sure the table with his paints was the right distance from the board, that sort of thing.

As McEwen responded to my remarks, I realised that something was rattling, an odd irregular sound, something chinking, perhaps a tin outside in the wind, or a piece of glass jangling. No, it was more a clinking, this persistent sound, and I looked to Clif to see if it was irritating him, and it was. As I opened my mouth to ask if we could deal with it I realised what always chinks, and I saw from the corner of my eye that Clif had realised too, and I must not ask. McEwen, 183 centimetres tall, a broad ex-soldier who'd worked as a farmer, a tough experienced politician, was shaking so hard that the coins in his pockets were rattling.

It is one thing to announce your retirement, quite another to face it. How often the portrait must be the first reality of retirement, and how poignant to have to chat with what very easily might be a young woman with no interest in or understanding of your achievements. I worked very hard for a while, until McEwen forgot Clif. As he realised that I did have a sense of what he'd lived for, of the war, the struggles of the farmers on soldier settlement blocks, he relaxed. I had no desire to take him on about the country's role in Vietnam, or any current issue, and wasn't there to lobby him. There was an obvious question, though. I had become involved in politics because of the parlous position of the state schools in which I was teaching, Clif because the government had gone to war again and because arts funds were controlled by non-arts bureaucrats. I was interested in McEwen's motives for seeking election and the processes by which he made decisions, especially since he'd been in government for so long.

The answer to *Why choose politics?* was no surprise: he'd been approached by locals who needed a voice. Well, even if he'd manipulated that, he was unlikely to say so, and as he told me he'd been in the Commonwealth Public Service in Melbourne before joining the army in World War I, and that he came to the area as a soldier settler, it must have been a logical step. He'd made his luck, and seen lesser men fail in the bad years of drought and rabbit plague; like my tough resourceful cousins on the land, he respected hard work and determination, but he knew, had seen, that Australian country resists European settlement. His solution, like my cousins', like so many in those days, was not to understand the land, but to fight and face it down. I asked what were his policies, had his ideas changed over all those years? And he surprised me by saying he had no policies, except that he said to his senior public servants that if they could give him three reasons for signing something, he'd sign it. Such was the understanding of the skill and detachment of public servants in those days, and the identification of these men with each other's values and systems.

The other question arose from listening to his account of the Australia he'd been born into and, since 1934 in federal parliament, had helped to form. This was a pragmatic man, a negotiator, a realist and, one could see, a shrewd judge of other men. In December 1967 Prime Minister Harold Holt had drowned and it was well known that McEwen, then Deputy Prime Minister, had refused to serve under Billy McMahon, who had been the Deputy Leader of the Liberal Party and a logical candidate to become Prime Minister. It was public knowledge that there had been many issues on which they disagreed, but I wondered why McEwen had taken the step of publicly repudiating McMahon.

'Because he was a pansy.'

There are moments in life when the reaction to a remark is entirely unexpected, and I could see that McEwen, seeing mine, abruptly saw himself, his values, through my eyes. But this was about portraiture, not about consciousness raising; and anyway it is in quiet reflection on such moments that people sometimes see their views as products of culture, rather than logic. Help him.

'I suppose, because it's a crime, you thought he might be subject to blackmail?'

'Yes, blackmail.'

No need to point out that the man had been and remained a Cabinet minister; we each knew the other was being polite. We turned the talk from politics for a while.

The next morning, he was enthusiastic to begin. He had thought overnight of a piece of advice he wanted to give me. I would need it. It was about negotiation. And in his unpretentious house on the flat plain which, when he was born in 1900, had been at the end of the British Empire, he described a style of living that derived from that Empire. In the telling, we saw the way things were done, how very personal the official world had been, when he flew to London so long ago.

'I knew the negotiations were going to be difficult. We went by flying boat, and the journey was in stages, it took several days. You dressed for dinner, white tie and tails; everything was very formal then. I'd had a wonderful meal, and we were staying on a houseboat on a beautiful lake, in the tropics. I was perfectly well, the night was very quiet, but I couldn't sleep. I began to walk. I was still wearing my tails. There were little boats on the lake with lights, it was very peaceful. I'd read my briefing papers carefully, I knew all the arguments, I went over them all. But I couldn't sleep. And then I thought, "What do *I* say if they say 'No'?" When I thought that, I could go to sleep. That's what you have to think before you begin negotiating. "What do I say, if they say 'No'?"'

We drove back to Dunmoochin with the unfinished portrait in the car. The public image of McEwen was suited and formal, but he'd sat in a shirt, and Clif hadn't dressed him up, because he was after all the leader of the Country Party, very direct and down to earth, and he worked physically on the farm for relaxation. The painting wasn't right, though, and Clif kept changing details: the way the hands sat, the angle of the head. But I could see the formality, the suits that had made McEwen's image. When he'd been young, artists and artisans wore suits; men of substance wore frockcoats and carried top hats. It was *suit* that had taken him through years of negotiation, the black suits that meant he had to be taken seriously. Nor should he be seated, or indoors. The Country Party, he, saw European settlers fighting the land, trying to empty it and tame it. Nor would he fit on the three-foot by four-foot board.

'I don't have a bigger board.'

'Yes you do, there's that painting of John Olsen you haven't finished. Use that.'

Oops. He was ropeable that I'd interfered. I had better leave. This was not the despairing anger at night after drinking. I drove to Marie Davison, the widow of writer Frank Dalby Davison, on her nearby farm, and that wise woman consoled me with tea.

Clif rang. 'I thought you'd go to Marie. You can come home, it's okay.'

There in the studio was the finished painting; Black Jack himself, formal, suited, powerful; emerging from a black shadow, against an abstracted landscape that could be natural and bare, or might be logged and eroded. We'd forgotten the Archibald, but Marie had come back to see what the fight had been about.

'This,' she said, 'will be hard to beat.'

12

GRASS ROOTS

Rhubarb punch, biscuits, mutton, tinned peas

Frank Dalby Davison had died in 1970, before Clif and I met. Marie still lived nearby, on their small picturesque farm, and when I arrived at Dunmoochin she was grieving for the long marriage and for the husband she idolised. Clif was worried about her, and so were other neighbours. Her grief was a bit dramatic, and they thought the usually centred and sensible woman might tip over into melodrama and try to follow Frank. She was refusing invitations in a way that didn't seem right, so I plotted with Marlene. With the courage of youth I arrived at Marie's door just before a dinner party to which Clif had asked Tim Burstall, whom Marlene disliked. I introduced myself to Marie, said I'd made an error in asking them both and that I urgently needed Marie's tact and discretion at the table in thirty minutes.

She came, and was the life of the party, and from that time on was a constant guest, always bringing her homemade non-alcoholic rhubarb punch. Frank had begun his writing life a conservative, and

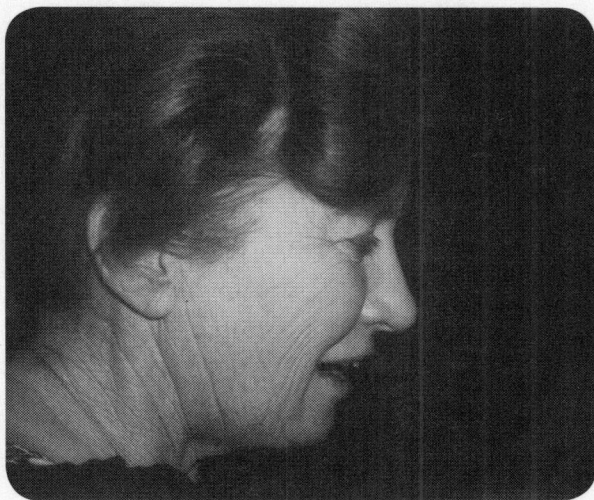

Marie

become an environmentalist and a political activist when he saw the degradation wrought by development in Queensland. He had developed the Fellowship of Australian Writers with Marjorie Barnard and Flora Eldershaw, ensuring it was left-wing.

Marie was a symbol of commitment: to husband, his work and his ideas. They'd struggled for years, had never become rich. Her stories were a reminder of the time when lives were lived in boarding houses in which the character of the owner, rigid or eccentric, could change those lives, when bohemian meant dressing up, not jeans and Indian cotton. She and Frank had lived their lives dedicated to his work and to issues of freedom of speech, of liberty. Marie had standards of dress and manner: she always went out in a broad-brimmed hat, driving in her Holden utility as if it were a carriage. She had lovely skin, explaining to dinner guests that she never took her make-up off at night; a man wanted a woman to look her best even after they were in bed.

When the time is right, and when new ideas are introduced without confrontation, people can contemplate those ideas. The community divisions along lines of religion, class and ethnicity were argued to mirror the political divide, although things were far subtler than that. This is why Dunmoochin and our parties were so important. The house was a place where men of commerce could feel comfortable; they saw Clif as a practical man and obviously a businessman himself. It was eccentric but beautiful, full of fascinating objects. The meals were interesting, so their wives enjoyed themselves; the very cuteness of the wombat making it cosy. Race Mathews was a frequent guest at dinner, educated, and apparently not a Trotskyist. One could see that our business friends were beginning to think, as they chatted to Marie, Race, and other obviously civilised 'left-wing' friends, that what had seemed, before intervention, to be a motley chaotic party was now a possible government.

This possibility was affecting the ALP members, too. The campaign meetings were becoming more practical. Well, in a sense. I had gone to Clif for money for the campaign, and he'd agreed to donate a painting to be raffled, and together we'd asked Frank Hodgkinson and other artists such as Charles Blackman and the potter Peter Laycock for a piece of work. Ticket sales went well; money was mounting up in the bank account I'd opened for the campaign committee.

The men on the committee and in the branches always talked about grass roots; indeed, so did Tom Uren and Clyde Holding. Maureen O'Brien, a committee member from Warrandyte and I realised that our grass roots, in Casey, were housebound women with small children.

The question was how to focus their minds on the election, the issues, and our candidate. We could invite them to morning talks on issues of concern, sponsored by the ALP but not by an ALP speaker. If they asked about policy, well, women from the branch would be there to answer questions. To start, we could buy a cheap set of crockery, tea, instant coffee, a tin of biscuits and a pint of milk. We would ask one of the women members in the electorate's most suburban suburb to door knock the block around her house and invite the neighbours. If it worked there, it would work in the apparently less conservative areas. We would offer to look after the kids in the garden or another part of the house while they were at the meeting. We carefully budgeted our two dozen cups and saucers, biscuits, beverages. We expected that we could take up a collection that would cover the cost of the next morning tea's consumables. There were eight thousand dollars in the bank account.

We explained our project to a campaign meeting, and said we'd need fifty-six dollars to start up. The men stalled, and began to question the cost, and the project itself. Maureen was very upset, I was at first astonished and then furious.

I asked politely, 'Just a few questions before we go on to the next item on the agenda. What plans do *you* have for the money?'

A newspaper, written by them, and distributed across the electorate.

'How often and what expense is involved for each issue?'

Costing incomplete.

'By whom will this newspaper be distributed?'

Branch members at weekends.

Well, fine, and quite possibly effective, if they could write interesting articles. But expensive and at present speculative. Besides, our little domestic campaign would hardly cost a thing; indeed, it could possibly pay for itself. After about an hour of argument it occurred to me: the money was in an account in my name. I explained their situation: I controlled their funds; I was not making a request, I was reporting a *fait accompli*.

Faye Dumont, a musician and teacher and the secretary of Clif's Arts Policy Committee, was our first speaker, about the importance of music education. All the women who came to the meeting made donations to cover the food, and some offered their houses for more gatherings. We had found a thirst to share ideas and for information, for company, to understand politics. By the time the campaign ended in December 1972, Race himself was doing several meetings a day. Faye suggested, as the second speaker, a woman she'd recently heard talking about tuckshops.

That second meeting, with more than twice as many women as the first, was addressed by Joan Kirner, then president of the Federation of State School Mothers' Clubs, which she was developing into a lobby group for education. I suggested she join the ALP, pointing out that she'd make a wonderful candidate. But at that time Joan was focussed on education, and she couldn't contemplate the notion of herself in parliament.

As winter closed around us and the colours became cold, Clif wanted to get up to Tibooburra. He rang Barney Davis at the Family Hotel to say we were coming. He told Barney he'd be bringing me, and Barney asked if I liked barramundi. It was supposed to be the most delicious fish. I said yes, but I didn't expect any in Tibooburra. Barramundi was caught in the Gulf of Carpentaria; Tibooburra is in the north-west corner of New South Wales. Think no more about it. We put the car on the wonderful Edwardian train, all polished wood and brass and copper, for an overnight journey to Mildura, whence the road led to Broken Hill and on to Tibooburra.

That straight and scrubby road is boring, made even less pleasurable because Clif had drunk his way overnight to Mildura. Displaying melancholy and anger at home was one thing, there I had the opportunity to get away. In a double berth, however, it was different. I was exhausted and unhappy. We stopped for lunch in Broken Hill, where a cheering incident occurred, reminding me of a different set of strains for an artist in Australia. We went to a pub, the ladies' lounge. In Melbourne I didn't front the bar, and in Broken Hill it would have been out of the question. That mining city is the national epicentre of testosterone.

The bloke next to Clif, looking at his paint-splattered army shirt, asked, 'What do you do, mate?'

'I'm a painter.'

'Houses or pictures?'

To my surprise, Clif ducked as he answered, 'Pictures.'

Under the swinging punch, coming up, fists ready to fight. His questioner backed off, and we were able to have our pies in peace.

In the early 1970s, beyond the outskirts of Melbourne, Sydney and Adelaide, there was no point in thinking about food. There were of course regional variations; it wasn't uniform. Every pub and café in Victoria and New South Wales had a bottle of tomato sauce on the table, whereas in Queensland one found Worcestershire sauce. I had anticipated nothing but tinned food in Tibooburra, but to my astonishment that evening we did have fresh barramundi. No lemons and no mayonnaise: ground white pepper, salt, tomato sauce. But barramundi. Knowing Clif was on his way, Barney had driven up to the Gulf, caught a huge barramundi, popped it on a block of ice, and driven back. One thought of Burke and Wills, the Dig Tree, the distance from the nineteenth century.

In Tibooburra, Clif was happy. And so was I. There were cultural differences to deal with, but when in Rome . . . The food was astonishing. After the barramundi, meat. At breakfast the question was 'chops or sausages?' Um . . . sausages.

My plate arrived with twelve midsize sausages and four eggs, six pieces of toast. 'Chops' meant eight lamb chops and eggs. Dinner was roast mutton or roast lamb; lunch, provided so we could stay out for Clif to paint, consisted of thick slices of bread sandwiching hunks of meat. Tinned peas were provided to me as an acknowledgement of my soft urban identity.

And there were marvels of a different kind. No wonder the 'red recessive' painter loved this place. It was as if God were experimenting to see what could be done with the colour. The orange red of the tracks, the myriad rose and russets of the rocks, flashes of scarlet, pale pinks . . . By contrast with the lacy detail of Dunmoochin, the height of the sky, its endless blue.

Where else is the immensity of the sky so linked with space and distance and time? On the ocean, even in calm, one is conscious of the vessel, boat or ship. I think the challenge of space on space, of making meaning in the abstraction of this desert, was why it was so wonderful for Clif. On our first day we went to Mount Stuart, one of the old properties, stations leased out by the New South Wales Government for ninety-nine years in the 1870s. The leaseholder telling Clif about his racehorses, with the homestead and outbuildings behind us, the vast plain before.

I wondered, 'How far does your place go?'

'See the mountain range?'

No, not really. I looked to see he was pointing to the horizon. There was a shape to it, a movement in the long flat line, which could be a range.

'She's just inside the border.'

He took us around a bit, and I asked about patches of ground, flattened, smoothed, designed, with rocks around.

'The blacks have their dances there. We sometimes do, too. Could tonight, if you like.' Something about the overwriting; I can't say I thought about culture as colonisation, but it seemed distasteful, although the night sky, the dry cold night air, was tempting.

'Actually I get bitten by every sort of insect.'

'The verandah, then.'

And so to racism, in a picturesque, a charming setting. The dance was on the screened verandah, a fiddle, an accordion, a mouth organ. Two women, the leaseholder's wife and I. I danced with the owner, Clif with his wife, we swapped. Not a great deal of light, men grouped against the screens, some from the town, and the stockmen. Who were black. Not that the others were fair; in that place the sun browned everyone. In the bar at the pub there had been Aboriginal men, perfectly welcome, it seemed. Not distinguishable by talk – hardly anyone spoke; nor by hat – each was uniquely battered; nor degree of drunkenness – everyone had had a lot by the end of the night. I'd noticed the wonderful gaudy shirts before I'd noticed their skin. The musicians started up again, and suddenly in front of me was a black man, hair carefully combed, shirt ironed, and sweat running down his face.

'Would you like to dance?'

'Yes, thank you.'

But he just stood there, and I realised that the sweat was fear. So I took his hand, which was shaking, and we walked onto the floor. The musicians stopped.

'Oh do play, please, I am so enjoying your music.'

Nothing.

Clif engrossed in a conversation with one of the town men.

'Clif, we can't dance alone.'

He summed up the situation and took the leaseholder's wife in his arms and nodded at the band. Who looked at the leaseholder. Who looked at Clif. Who was suddenly the soldier and the man of parts.

'Play.'

As we began to dance I wondered if I was a bet, or a dare; if, once the gesture wore off, my partner would relax. But he shook more, not less, I had to make him move me around the floor; he kept glancing not at his friends, but at the boss. This was serious. Would he pay for this gesture when we left?

The phrase is *making conversation*. The art is to ask simple questions that can be answered with a nod or shake of the head, but are without double meaning and do not refer to contentious issues. I thought, 'I have to make this our fault,' and looked across at Clif, who was thinking the same thing, and he danced across to us, saying firmly, 'Swap.'

He put his partner into the arms of the stockman, who stood there, appalled, and as we circled them I explained to her that I'd had to show him the steps, would she continue? And reluctantly, she did. Then we danced over to her husband and Clif gave me to him.

There we were, the four of us, circling their verandah.

'Do all the stockmen come in for the dances?'

'Yes, but they don't dance.'

'Really? That must be one of the ways things have changed in the city; these days if you have a company dance then everyone expects to dance with everyone, otherwise you might lose your staff.'

He looked straight at me. 'It's okay. It hasn't happened before, but he's the head stockman. He's a good black.'

Clif cut in on the stockman and told him to cut in on us, and I told him his boss said it was the first time he'd danced here.

'Worth it.'

I never cared about being beautiful when I was painted by the masters of their time, but that was a compliment to remember.

That first desert visit was a brief couple of weeks. We stayed near the town, spending nights in Barney's Family Hotel. I had books, Clif his paints, and we had the space, the silence, the sun. I'd had to prove to him, as I had to prove to everyone in those days, how easily and badly I sunburned. Early in our first summer, I'd begun to pose just as the shade moved off me, and he'd asked that I stay still. When I got up, deep red and blistered, he was embarrassed and sympathetic, so he'd attempted a solution for the desert. A happily surreal scene: Barney's ute, the figure at the easel, and a little way off, a gaudy beach umbrella; a thousand kilometres from the sea. I still had to wear long sleeves, because on the gibber plain the stones of iron reflect the light, so we took to going out together in the morning, coming back to a cooked lunch – 'Chops or steak?' – after which I would spend the afternoon in the hotel, trying to hide from the heat.

From the single-storied corrugated iron-roofed Family Hotel, with a primitive bathroom, holes punched in the walls, and vivid public notices – *I don't sleep in your toilet, don't you piss in my bed* – I did cast a longing gaze at the two storied air-conditioned Tibooburra Hotel across the street. But Clif was loyal to Barney, who'd looked after him and Eric Worrell and Tas Drysdale when a vehicle had broken down on a Monash expedition years earlier. Besides, the Family had a white cockatoo that imitated the dinner gong whenever anyone walked past its cage.

We were living in a pub; the bar was the place where everyone sat after the evening meat. Clif had a drink in front of him all night. But in isolation from the world of politics and from television, in the dry heat and the red country, his moods were even. He was cheerful during the day, and happy with the gouaches he packed with the beach umbrella for the trip home. Perhaps that was all he'd needed.

There was a portrait waiting, of a pretty older woman. A gentle solicitor had asked Clif to paint his wife, but we found when we got home that, in the way of solicitors, he'd sent a formal letter confirming the arrangement, and used the word 'commission'. This triggered a bout of drinking and despair.

'I'll be in court. Look what happened to Dobell.'

I offered to reply on Clif's behalf, outlining the way in which Clif approached a portrait that he had been invited to paint. Clif did not accept commissions. He would ask the sitter to co-operate fully, giving as much time as he needed so that he could get to know his subject, but he could not guarantee that he could make a painting. If he were satisfied with the product of their sessions together, the picture would be available for sale, and the person who had asked for the picture would have first option to purchase it, but was under no obligation to buy. Copyright would stay with Clif. Mr Lonie replied, agreeing to these terms, and complimenting me on the way they were drafted, so they became the written form with which Clif responded to putative commissions.

Copyright was an issue of moment for Clif. On several occasions he'd looked in a bookshop window to see one of his portraits on the front cover of a book, used without his permission. So impolite, let alone illegitimate. Copyright in a work of art was, and still is, owned by the maker of that work, except when the work is commissioned, or when it is produced by an employee in the course of the employee's employment. These exceptions were designed to protect employers who paid researchers, such as in a university environment, and envisaged a commission for, say, the design of a logo. Clif's problem with the De L'Isle commission had been that although he had been unhappy with the painting, the CAAB insisted on buying it. That issue was not about reproduction. But after that incident he had refused to sign contracts, and had always used the formula I describe, telling people he did not take commissions.

The understanding of myself as partner on every level anchored me to Clif. I had the opportunity to negotiate deals, to relate to his portrait and other clients on an equal footing. This was very unusual for a woman in those times, but it was how I had been brought up. It had been eccentric socialising for a female child in the late 1950s, but my uncles and father all behaved to me as if I were a male. I had been trained to throw and catch, to be direct and decisive in conversation, to care about ideas, not about underclothes or make-up. My role with Clif fitted my experience – that like my mother I would run a large house and entertain – and my expectations, that I would be treated as an equal by anyone I met, and if I wanted to talk or do business with them, I could.

13

WAR STORIES

Sugar, the smell of burning flesh,
fish and chips

Upset and anger were more and more on my mind. After the awful train trip to Mildura I was anxious about the return of Clif's evening demons, but the Olsens had left for Watsons Bay, and Frank Hodgkinson was renovating Olsen's old studio to live in and work, so while he repaired and built he had dinner with us most nights. Seeing the talk was of war, he made sure he and Clif shared the lighter moments.

The ship taking Clif's new unit to occupied Japan had arrived in port and begun unloading. Clif was posted on a particular street corner directing the trucks to the next man.

'A Japanese came up to me. He was beautifully dressed, he had a camel-hair coat, and he spoke perfect English. He had a wad of real pound notes. He said, "If you send every third truck up that street instead of that one, I'll pay you with these."

'I asked him what was on the trucks.

'"Sugar."

'"I'll have to square it with my mate," I said. He was on the next corner.

'"Fair enough" and it was on. That started us in the black market.'

Frank's stories mirrored the eerie objectivity of Clif's, although his were more ironic; perhaps because he had joined up as an older man, as a trained working artist, without the anxieties Clif had had as a boy. Frank had fought on the Kokoda Trail, before becoming a war artist. He remembered seeing a Japanese soldier dead in a particularly interesting pose, and scrambled down a bank to draw the image, his gun beside him, becoming so absorbed that he forgot his gun until he got back to the road. He had especially funny stories about the very gay Donald Friend getting into people's tents, and arriving for dinner in a particularly formal officers' mess, not only out of uniform, but in bits of enemy uniform and a civilian silk scarf.

Clif's urgency to get on with life while still in the army meant that he ran a two-up school, and with his black-market money bought the brothel where he had his first sexual encounter.

'The army was very practical about sex. We had lectures about venereal disease with pictures, lectures about protection. They knew everyone would go into town and get girls or pay for sex. You have to understand. The women, the Japanese, they were starving. We all went AWOL at night, the army didn't care, but when you went back in the gate you got gentian violet up your penis. My mate and I didn't want VD so we bought this house and had two second-class geishas, trained to have sex, the first-class ones don't have sex, we got two second-class girls. We said, "Okay, you can have sex with Japanese businessmen but not with any other Australian soldiers." When we left we gave them the house.'

I learned odd things about unarmed combat.

'If the other bloke has a gun and you haven't got a gun, you have the advantage. He is focussed on the gun, and you can think about everything else.'

'If you can touch the gun, then you can get it from the person who is holding it before they can fire it.'

And I learned about cars.

'I got out my distributor cap.'

'Distributor cap?'

'In Kure everyone carried a distributor cap. Officers had jeeps. It was easy to start a jeep without a key, so they'd disable them by taking the distributor cap. They were all the same, you just put in your distributor cap and off you went.'

He had known the things he did in Japan were illegal and risky and exploitative, some even outside his own moral order. His letters to his mother describe an incident in which he cut a painting from its frame in a Shinto shrine; when he told me about it he added that he'd terrified a priest who disturbed him. He wrote to his mother: 'We are now Despoilers of temples.'

He and his cheerfully criminal entrepreneur mate told themselves they were committed to fighting for causes, but the older Clif saw that they were simply looking for adventure, in the boredom of occupation duties.

'The Japs had intended to fight to the last person, all of them; no surrender, that was the code. Then the Emperor surrendered and that was that. But there were caches of weapons all over the place, and our job was to get them. So my mate and I decided to join Ho Chi Minh. It was all very romantic in those days. We bought a boat and started loading it with weapons and supplies. Then one night I was on security duty. One of my mates was supposed to be with me, but he'd asked me to cover for him because he wanted to see his girl in town. A message came through from the Yanks. There were two Australian soldiers who'd been collecting guns and had them on a boat. I asked for further details. They had no names, they hadn't identified the soldiers, but they were setting up a watch.

'"Fair enough. I'll pass it on."

'Which I didn't. So we gave up that idea.'

'Then we decided to fight with Mao. There was a plane that went out regularly, every night, making weather observations over China. We persuaded the pilot to drop us. We got a couple of parachutes, we were armed anyway, and we had a couple of extra guns. We stashed them in the plane with our gear. The idea was, he had to taxi the plane to the end of the runway and turn, that was near our hut, and we'd leave the barracks and when he turned, he'd wait, and we'd get in. We hadn't been trained to jump, but we'd read a manual and talked to a couple of blokes who had. We were fit, and we thought that Mao would be really pleased to have a couple of trained fighting soldiers.'

I asked whether, looking back, he thought they'd have been shot as enemy agents. 'After all, Clif, the Communist Party had already refused to have you as a member.'

The likely lad looked out from the mature man: 'We thought we'd talk our way round.'

In English, wearing Australian Army uniforms.

'We were ready to go, packed our kit, everyone in the barracks asleep. We couldn't turn on the light. My mate was checking his pistol, and it went off. People woke up.

'"It's okay. It's okay. Go back to sleep. The light bulb popped."

'Then my mate said, "Clif! I shot meself!"

'"What?"

'"I think it's okay, it's just a flesh wound, it went through the calf." So we went outside.

'"Let's have a look." And I ran some water from the tap through the hole, and there wasn't much blood, but the tap was near a light, and I saw a gleam, and there was a bit of metal stuck on the bone. "Mate, we can't go, you've got a bit of bullet in you."

'So we watched the plane come, and wait before it turned, then wait again. Then it took off, and that was over.'

Clif's attitude to wounds and their effect had developed through years of experience: the culture of masculinity made tougher by exposure to absolutes of injury. It meant he simply ignored or tried to tough out the symptoms of heart attack. I learned to keep calm.

At a dinner party in Eltham in 1977: 'Excuse me, darling, are you having a heart attack?'

'I'm having a conversation.'

'Yes, I do apologise, but I think you are having a heart attack, and Dad said to ring him next time you had one.'

'Okay, yes, I'm having a heart attack. Now, what was I saying?'

In the jungle most of the tales were about survival, and Clif believed survival had to do with attitude rather than luck. They left one of the unit with the RAP man, after he'd been shot, just a flesh wound in the knee. They went on to attack a Japanese position, where Clif shot a couple of rounds into the chest of a Japanese gunner, who played dead until Clif came up, then, despite his mortal wounds, began to fight back, so that Clif had to stab him and, when he still refused to die, to cut his throat. They returned to their superficially injured comrade and found him dead.

Frank moved up to his studio, Dailan to live with Marlene in St Andrews; near, but not next door. We were alone.

I hoped that things would get back to the quiet rhythm of the Tibooburra days, but it was getting on for the end of the gallery year, lots of openings and parties. The hour's drive from Melbourne meant if Clif had drunk too much before we headed home he became morose as we travelled, and that meant trouble when we arrived.

On these occasions it wasn't about the evil of war. The mood was not despair; it might be anger at some argument at a party, or disapproval of behaviour he disliked. This was the 1970s. People did argue and act out in public rather more than ever before or since; perhaps in extension of some of the more radical psychotherapies then in fashion. On a memorable occasion at South Yarra Galleries, the beautifully dressed Ellen, wife of the erudite and respected critic Alan McCulloch (they were both in their seventies), irritated a young art writer. He pushed her, chiffon, coiffure and all, into the swimming pool.

When we were alone there would be days of peace, and quiet evenings. But when the Vietnam news was bad, and if there were pictures, and because he was still reading his wartime letters to his mother, I would hear the stories of his and other horrors. I was beginning to realise that there were two types of drunkenness: the one about the war, the other about the way people in society behaved, their values, attitudes, ideas. It would be silly to say I didn't mind the mood that war triggered, but it was so apparently full of confusion and grief that, rather than feel indignant, my response was to sympathise and try to understand, although I was afraid. The other mood was only frightening. They intersected, but I kept thinking that if I steered one into the other, or if I could work out what particular incident was so upsetting, then this deep misery might be resolved. So when we were alone I encouraged him to talk about the war.

The stories from Japan had three moral dimensions, as it were; with concomitant drunkenness and degree of emotion. They were about the ethical dilemma of Hiroshima, which led to wider discussions of politics and war, about the casual larrikin behaviour of him and his friends, and about his own corrupt behaviour in Japan, together with his excesses in the jungle. He disapproved in retrospect of all but the *Boy's Own* category: using tent flaps for canvas to paint on, going AWOL and replacing distributor caps, going off to fight for freedom. The stories about what it was like actually fighting gave meaning to his anti-war position, and he understood the evil they illustrated: the inherent corruption, what happens when you take young men and teach them to kill, how they come to behave.

The cold efficiency with which they will make decisions:

'We got an officer straight from Duntroon. He had tickets on himself.

Now the Japs had orders to kill officers first, so the officers didn't wear pips in the field. They didn't order us about, we all knew what to do, it was small groups working together, it was hand-to-hand combat. This idiot turns up, never been in action, expects to give orders and be obeyed. He was a danger to us. So we decided to get rid of him, and we began saluting him all the time. He ordered us not to salute him. So we stood to attention whenever he spoke to us.

'"Sir. *Yes*, sir." Loudly. He got himself transferred.'

The dehumanising of their opponents:

'We got a flame thrower, and we had a couple of Jap corpses, we were disgusted by the Japs, we thought they were degraded, so I burned the bodies, I used the flame thrower to set fire to them to see if they would burn easily, if human flesh smelled like meat. They did. It does.'

That the rules of war will come to mean nothing:

'This unit had orders to stop at the side of a gully, await further orders. They knew that there were Japanese on the other side of the gully. The Japs were starving, you've got to understand that. They had no supplies, we'd cut off their supplies. They'd become cannibals. We'd seen bodies with bits of flesh cut off. There were planes going over every day, dropping leaflets on the Japanese, telling them they were losing the war, that if they surrendered they'd be looked after. These Japs surrendered to this unit. They shot them.'

And what happens when they begin to understand what all this implies.

When he was blown up by the grenade and got to the hospital:

'The doctor let me rave, he just let me rave. I had had enough. I said, "No more, I won't fight any more, that's it." It was treason, I suppose, I didn't care. No more.'

I used to wonder whether the doctor had been through this before; how many young men came in with physical wounds and then went to pieces.

I was hoping that telling the stories might dissipate their force, and he could come to terms with what he and others had done. That if the ALP won, if Australia pulled out of Vietnam, it would not be so immediate an issue. That the effect of reading his wartime letters would diminish. Most of all I hoped that when he felt he had absorbed all the delight of the Paris images, he would relax and be content.

Even as the stories became more detailed and frequent, we had some lovely nights alone. The days in the studio were work and relaxation for him, there was much purposeful activity for me, we had plenty to talk about by the fire. I had learned a great deal about local campaigning, and I had begun to focus on the wider obstacles to the ALP being elected.

There was an obvious problem that would affect the message across Melbourne: the talkback radio shows. Ormsby Wilkins and Norman Banks were the John Laws and Alan Jones of their day, masters of talkback. So I asked Clyde Holding to call a meeting of a disparate group: of commercial travellers, women at home with small children, and people housebound because they were disabled or were caring for someone.

'Well, okay, Judith, but why this group?'

They were the grass roots for a plan that I thought might deliver us the talkback shows. The scheme, its simplicity, derived from the mechanics of communication technology at the time.

Radio stations, like most businesses, had switchboard operators. These operators had manually to connect outside callers to the person they wanted. No direct lines through an automated system, no mobile telephones then. And no faxes, no email or internet, no text messaging. But plenty of public phone boxes. And the crucial technological distinction was that *a call having been connected, only the caller could disconnect the line.* That is what the commercial travellers were for. They knew receptionists with switchboards, and they drove past phone boxes. So they and the receptionists could ring in to the radio station and, simply by leaving the telephone line open, by not hanging up, they could reduce the number of lines available to talkback callers. Then the group of people at home, those who wanted to be part of the campaign but couldn't attend meetings or door knock or distribute leaflets or put up posters, could step in. There would be a reduced number of lines, we could saturate the stations with calls.

ALP candidates simply did not get onto talkback radio at the time, so the first problem was to overcome this. Invective, I had decided, was the way to go. The group was to ring in and say the most outrageous things they could think of about the ALP, its policies, and its candidates. The concept was a bit stretched for the meeting, but I thought that if we sounded even more outrageous than Banks and Wilkins, then we could tip the issue. I'd written out a series of questions to ask David Kennedy, the member for Bendigo and Shadow Minister for Education. I'd decided to go for education first.

With some misgivings the meeting agreed to try the idea.

'The ALP doesn't care about education, Mr Banks, they think kids shouldn't go to school beyond the age of twelve . . . that universities are only for private school children . . . that working class suburbs only need tech schools . . . that tech schools shouldn't have sporting fields . . . the ALP are all communists . . . they're criminals . . . you wouldn't want them on your program . . . they wouldn't be able to answer your questions . . . they wouldn't dare to come on . . .'

'Oh, now, I think that's going a bit far, I could ask them and see.'

And I held my breath to hear a wondrous pensioner reply, 'You'd show them up, about education.'

She'd really got into her act.

When David Kennedy left the station the next week he rang me, astonished and very amused. The apparently hostile callers had given him the opportunity to set out in a clear and detailed fashion the whole of the ALP federal education policy, and the last caller had contrived to sound reluctantly interested in the party's other policies. The strength of the campaign was the enthusiasm and commitment of the participants, and it became very successful. *Always remember the grass roots.* At first I spent a lot of time planning which issue to raise, and how; but with experience, the group became more sophisticated and clever as the campaign went on. After that election, when journalists travelling with Whitlam identified the scheme and wrote about its effectiveness as part of the overall campaign, the talkback stations in Melbourne asked callers to identify themselves and to provide their contact details.

Early in the summer of 1971, at Clyde Holding's beach house, Clif had a very bad night, shouting not only at me but at Clyde. Seeing the behaviour objectively, someone else a target, seeing how ill-mannered, arrogant and unkind it was, I saw briefly what was happening to me. I told Clif I wanted to leave. I hadn't realised how very unhappy this anger was making me, and 'It isn't to do with you, Judith' didn't wash.

Clif went to Clyde, the politician. Who took me to collect the fish and chips for dinner that night, and had a chat. How good I was for Clif. How the campaign in Casey was going well and that after the election might be the time to go, that he, Clyde, realised that the Arts Policy Committee was a strain for Clif; that things would be better after the election was over and Clif could give up its chairmanship. His arguments were persuasive, perhaps the most persuasive being the implication – because Clyde himself had been the target of abuse the night before and was suggesting I stay – that one had to expect such behaviour of a man of genius. And after all, Clyde knew Clif and he thought this was a temporary phenomenon.

When we got back with the fish and chips Clif said, 'Look, you've said you wanted to go to the Adelaide Festival. Why don't I try to get a portrait over there and we go? You can leave after that if you want to.' Clyde said he thought that was a good idea.

It hadn't been a plan to leave, more an expression of a feeling. I didn't know what else I'd do: train as a teacher? Finish the law degree abandoned for arts? And it was January 1972, nothing happened in Victoria in January. Okay, I would stay at present, and we would go to Adelaide in March. And maybe things would settle down after the election, maybe it was just about the war, and financial uncertainty as he settled with Marlene and wondered how his painting would change. I didn't want to walk out on the work I'd done on the campaign, nor was it right to leave someone who was wrestling with such memories and emotions.

Clyde Holding suggested that he contact Don Dunstan, the Premier of South Australia, then the only ALP premier in Australia, and ask him to sit for Clif while we were at the Festival. That would be good, painting the most charismatic man in the country, a truly visionary intellectual, at an international arts festival. And I could use the time to decide what to do if things didn't get better.

Then, on 10 February 1972, everything changed. Our public life, and fame, began.

14

DUNSTAN

Champagne, marijuana, ratatouille

On 10 February 1972 a journalist from Sydney, a woman, rang. Black Jack McEwen had won the Archibald Prize. Clif was pleased, and so was I; not so much that the strategy had succeeded, but because McEwen had his due.

Clif understood what would happen next. 'Journalists will come, television and from the papers. They'll want a drink, I'll get some beer and some champagne. When they've finished with me they'll want to talk to you. Now listen. Don't be shy, and don't be indignant, whatever they ask you. Think about an interview as if you are paying for advertising. Especially on television, but on radio or with a magazine or newspaper reporter. Stop before you answer, and think, "How do I use this question to say what I want?" They just want a story, something to film or record or write about. Just keep thinking, "What would it cost to buy this much time or space?" Think about issues. Always remember, you may not like what the interviewer asks or says, but you are not talking to the interviewer. You are talking to the audience. Use the question to say what you want.'

When he came back from the pub with beer and champagne
I suggested I should ring Race. 'If you want to use this for the ALP,
you should link McEwen, whom everyone respects, with Whitlam.
McEwen's resigning anyway, and you can remind them of this and say
you're going to paint the next Prime Minister, Gough Whitlam. Race
can warn Whitlam in advance; he can ask him. You can link him with
environment and the war.'

Clif agreed. While I handed out drinks he spoke to camera in his
studio about art and the Vietnam War, and then walked into the bush to
talk about the environment. He was filmed, recorded and photographed
repeating the mantra over and over: 'Next Prime Minister, Gough
Whitlam; next Prime Minister, Gough Whitlam.'

After a while Kevin Childs from *The Age* took me aside and said,
'This is terrific, but I think it will get lost soon, they'll have too much
information. Can you think of a way of redirecting it?'

Kevin, me and Clif

It was a hot day, and I suggested that we all have a swim in the dam. Some of the journalists went back to town, others came with us, and we went for our swim. One of the photographers suggested a celebratory photograph in the dam, but there was no more champagne, so we dipped our glasses in the muddy water. *The Age* photographer was snapping away. We were, as usual, swimming in the nude, which inadvertently helped our future access to journalists. I knew the paper wouldn't publish photographs unless they were respectable, but what I didn't think about was that they'd be circulated in the newsroom. I didn't care at all, but it did add a frisson when later, for instance, I was co-ordinating media liaison for the party, and wanted to arrange an interview for the Minister for Minerals and Energy.

Some days later I had a call from Mary Montague, a lively woman who, like most others of her sex, was condemned to the social pages and other 'women's' issues. She asked me to come into the *Herald Sun* building, and proceeded to introduce me to the Chief of Staff and every journalist who might be of interest. The message had got round that we could be a good source, we were focussed and knew how to tell a story, indeed, to sell the story. And we were prepared not only to acknowledge our association with the ALP but, in our polite accents, our spacious rooms, to be proud of it.

Now that Bob Santamaria is eulogised, and 'left' means latte, I want to emphasise how 'the split' affected the ALP and people's perception of the party through the 1960s, because it helps explain the publicity that later attended our lives.

Clif was a suitable subject to write about because it would have been laughable to call him a communist, and journalists valued that. He'd painted Daniel Mannix, Santamaria's master. He was obviously an entrepreneur, he was picturesque, he was an ex-soldier against the Vietnam War, and he talked about the environment. His language was without the clichés of the left. Political rhetoric had been bogged down in the language of the 1940s for too long, the journalists wanted something new. 'Terror' is used by governments now in the manner that 'communist' had been used to consolidate the failing image of conservative governments in Australia. The Communist Party had briefly been made illegal by an Act of Parliament, and when the courts threw out that Act, Menzies tried to change the Constitution so he could legitimately make being a communist against the law. The citizens of Australia, who had attended civics classes in primary school and who understood the principles on which the democracy was based, rejected the idea.

Bob Santamaria set up a secret organisation, which, he would argue, was opposing communist influence in the ALP and the union movement. But he also wanted to eliminate the progressive tradition of the Catholic labour movement. Such weapons as secrecy corrupt those who use them, however pure their motives. And what is worse, they destroy the organisations they are meant to save.

The split from the ALP of the faction which became the Democratic Labor Party gave control of the Senate and indeed the country to the Coalition parties, and slowed down even their progressive agendas. It weighted the power base of both the ALP and DLP toward their most extreme positions.

How unsophisticated those times seem now. Totalitarian communism was a dreadful system, but the likelihood of it taking over any established western democracy was remote even in the nineteenth and early twentieth centuries, when industrialisation was cruellest. The Communist Party and its ideas attracted well-intentioned idealists even in liberal democracies, but given that the principles of sharing production and power, of the state as a source of nurture and care, accords with Christian principles, this is no surprise. Both Russia and China were virtually feudal when the communist parties in those countries came to power; they'd not gone through a humanist renaissance, nor had their religious systems been reformed from within or without. The cultures of Britain and Australia, their systems and laws, derive from centuries of negotiations of power, and from their flexible social structures in which money gives possibility. Such cultures resist absolutes.

Anyone involved in ALP politics had to acknowledge and deal with the reality of the split. Clif was not engaged with any faction, and just as he dealt in the wider world with people of all political persuasions, so he moved in the ALP. He knew the very hard left Bill Hartley from Eltham, and he was great friends with Clyde Holding and Ian Turner. He met Bob Hawke at the races. He had no interest in gaining personal power; power struggles in politics and industry interested him as an observer of humans, a portraitist. His innate capacity to sum up a person's character had been refined by the urgency of war, when understanding the character of your fellow soldiers meant you knew who to rely on, who might get you killed. He had the country boy's shrewdness in the matter of judging men. He was trained to observe, he'd had years of practice as a portrait painter; he was prepared to use his instinct and to acknowledge his intuition.

Clif knew what he was doing when he dealt with the media. He had worked with stage and television performers – two of his close friends were Barry Humphries and Peter O'Shaughnessy – and Tim Burstall had made a documentary on his life and work for the Commonwealth Film Unit. He'd been photographed by Mark Strizic and understood how to talk to camera, and to pose. He was at ease with the television medium, clever at choosing the right light, at picking up a wombat or a kangaroo. His language for all this was blunt and to the point. The more concise, the more focussed you were, the less you would be edited.

Whitlam sent a message of congratulation, agreeing to sit. The Archibald Prize was very prestigious at that time – in the art schools portraiture was uncontested as part of normal practice – and of the few national art prizes it was the richest. Everywhere we went Clif was fêted, congratulated. But curiously, the admiration, congratulations, even the Archibald money didn't seem to settle him down. He was just as likely to drink at home and become morose, and just as combative in public. As we drove across to the Festival I was wondering what to do.

Don Dunstan had taken office as Premier of South Australia in 1967, on the retirement of Frank Walsh, and had lost an election in 1968, although his party had fifty-three per cent of the vote. The new Liberal Premier, Steele Hall, then introduced an electoral redistribution which ended the gerrymander, and Dunstan was elected again in 1970.

In the federal election year of 1972, he had made South Australia the Australian centre of technology, arts and design. Under his leadership, land rights and policies of self-determination were introduced for Aborigines, legislation for consumer protection and the ending of discrimination against race, colour, women and homosexuals were passed. Liquor licensing reforms meant that South Australia was the first state to have hotels, restaurants and cafés resembling those in Europe, alcohol could be served after 6 pm and outdoor eating was permitted. His government was one of substance as well as style, concentrating on practical reforms in education, health, housing and transport, opening trade offices in Tokyo and Singapore, and establishing the South Australian Film Corporation, the State Opera and an Industrial Development Advisory Committee. The most capable and visionary state premier in the country, he distilled all the possibilities of progressive, decent and exciting government.

Clyde had arranged for us to meet Dunstan after he'd opened Writers' Week, which event took place in the open air on a lovely slow summer afternoon. Made the slower, one felt, by the drifting fumes of marijuana which could be seen, head height, in the still air, a thin layer above the lounging crowd. One walked with one's head in the cloud.

Len French was there and pointed out the Premier to me.

'There's your quarry.'

Such an odd word to use, but to ask would somehow be to solidify whatever feelings it reflected. Indeed there he was, still on the elevated dais. It would be his wife beside him. I was very conscious that I looked bohemian. All the women in Adelaide appeared to wear tailored linen suits with hems at calf level, and I had on a long knitted cotton dress, common enough at Melbourne openings, perhaps out of place here. I could feel Clif behind me, hanging back, going into observation mode. So I walked up to the dais as Dunstan shook hands with an admirer, and watched him, with professional charm, ending the conversation.

'Mr Dunstan, I'm Judith Pugh.' He looked at me. I thought, *He's fallen in love with me.* Oops, the marijuana must be stronger than I thought. He stood silent, gazing.

'Clyde Holding said to come up to you.'

Still no response. Try the wife.

'Mrs Dunstan, I'm Judith Pugh, I do hope Mr Dunstan is looking forward to being painted.'

She was glaring, not gazing. She said, 'Well I can tell what's happened even if you can't.'

My extensive social training hadn't prepared me for this, but one goes on. 'Mr Dunstan, this is Clifton Pugh, Mrs Dunstan, Clifton Pugh.' The Premier recovered and jumped down from the dais.

'Mr Dunstan, Clyde suggested we talk about arrangements when we met.'

'Call me Don, please. Would you like to have dinner with us tonight? I have to launch a book of poetry, if you wouldn't mind coming with us, then we can drive home. We're having ratatouille.'

'Well, that would be great. Clif likes as much time as possible to observe his subjects, and to have an informal evening would be very helpful.'

While the four of us walked to the hotel where the launch was to be held, he asked me how long I'd been in the ALP. As I explained, and talked about what I was doing, he offered to lend me books and give me advice. He could come over and door knock in Casey. Door knock!

'But you're the Premier of South Australia.'

'Casey is a crucial marginal seat, and you always have to remember the grass roots.'

We arrived at the hotel, where the launch was to be in the foyer.

Don stood on the stairs. Across the crowded room, he launched the book to me. Clif stood on a chair, watching. I felt rather uneasy; either I was delusional, or the most charismatic politician in Australia was mad about me.

Shake off these ideas, get a grip. The book launched, I would ask Clif to buy one. The author was Chief Justice of the Supreme Court of South Australia. I went across to Clif, who was chatting, so I spoke to the man beside me.

'I might get one of these, can John Bray write poetry?'

'I think so, but then I am John Bray.'

Oh.

We travelled home with the Dunstans, and had drinks in the lounge, where Clif and Gretel settled down. I went to the kitchen to see if I could help, as Don was making the ratatouille. Don asked if I'd like to see the house, and promptly took me to see 'my bedroom' which proved to be a small room that seemed to be part of the back verandah. Perhaps he was some kind of aesthete who meditated alone. Clif and Gretel drank away during the meal, as Don offered to take us with him to every show he was attending, and to make time in his schedule for sittings.

'And Judith, you said you will be . . . distracting me? I think that was the word you used?'

Clif seemed very pleased and not moody at all, despite the amount he'd drunk.

The round was more than hectic. Never had a busy man been more available. Every night, plenty of alcohol, Clif moody but contained. Then one evening the four of us went to dinner. Clif and Gretel were drinking, and beginning to argue; I did my best to calm things down, but Don was making it happen. He asked me to leave them alone, and so I did, he was the Premier, after all. They got up and left the restaurant.

He said, 'I want to say how much I love you. I can see you're unhappy. Gretel and I have been apart for some time. I want you to leave Clif. My strategy is to exhaust them so they ask to be left at home.'

At which point Clif and Gretel returned, having settled their dispute.

Gretel was not with us the next evening when we went to see Mikis Theodorakis perform. This was the time when the Generals had power in Greece, and, as many Australian Greeks were radical, Theodorakis in exile was a symbol of dissent; the auditorium was crowded. We arrived and the crowd yelled for Don, cheering us all the way to our seats in the front row. Theodorakis acknowledged Don and the crowd yelled at a more frantic pitch. Don, on my right, took my hand. Clif, on my left, in an unusual gesture of public affection, also took my hand. Theodorakis had a view of the front row. After the concert, a party for Theodorakis and the band. He was a very tall man, and powerfully built. He came over, picked me up, and sat me on his lap.

'My turn.'

Don asked for me to have lunch with him so we could discuss the terms of the state acquiring the portrait. I should come to Parliament House. Where he was waiting at the top of the steps and ran down took me in his arms and kissed me, in front of a startled policeman. This worried me; what would a reporter think if the Premier kissed a woman not his wife like this? Over lunch he told me his plans. He'd arranged somewhere for us to go, the house of a friend. All that was needed was for Clif to drop out of the ceaseless round.

I was swept off my feet, astonished. *Le Vainqueur du Vainqueur de la Terre.* He was attractive, it is wonderful to be the object of such a man's attention. Of all the men in the country, he was the one as capable and intelligent as Clif. He was interested in the things in which I was interested. He would show me what to read in economics. He was a lawyer, and I had begun university life at law school. He was gentle, he was not a bad drunk; in fact he seemed not to get drunk at all. I felt rescued. I was worried though about his judgement, his discretion. But he was a successful politician, he must know what he was doing, Clif calculated every public move, surely Don must, too.

South Australia was obviously different, after all. The bitter divides were not apparent, and the transition from the twenty-seven-year rule of Thomas Playford had been apparently smooth. Was that so? Yes, it had been. When Don became Premier, he told me, Playford telephoned. He congratulated Don and said they should meet the next day in the Premier's office. Don said he thought, 'Oh well, he was Premier for a long time.' But when he arrived, there at the head of a long table was Playford, and all the departmental heads on either side. Just as Don wondered how to approach the situation, Playford got up, and gestured to him to take the seat he'd vacated.

Playford reminded the assembled public servants of their duty to provide impartial advice to the government of the day, telling them that he would be dropping in to see Mr Dunstan and would be giving him advice if he asked for it. He told Don that their advice could be relied on.

And so it had proved. Before his first Premiers' Conference, the annual meeting at which the federal and state governments allocated funding, the premiers met to discuss their demands, and agreed to stand together. All except Don were conservatives, Liberals or Country Party politicians, and the Prime Minister, Harold Holt, bought them off one by one. No money at all for South Australia. Don was about to protest when his head of department, beside him, said, 'Say nothing.'

Remembering Playford's advice about advice, he said nothing.

When they left the meeting: 'Mr Premier, if a state gets nothing from the conference it is entitled to borrow on the market. You will be able to make your own plans.'

Don asked would I mind being the wife of a politician.

'Well, Adelaide seems lovely.'

Yes, indeed, Adelaide was lovely, but he and Bob Hawke had a deal; they would go to Canberra together, as Treasurer and Prime Minister, when Whitlam left. Would I be happy to live in Canberra? By the way, the Whitlams were coming to Adelaide for a couple of days, and wanted to meet us. Don had arranged for us to have a drink at their hotel that evening. We made plans for Gough to come and stay, and then went off, the four of us again, Gretel, Don, Clif and I, to another event. The next morning Clif asked if I would mind going alone that evening. I rang Don, who said good, that was fine, nothing formal was happening that night, just a quick reception before the concert.

I wore a plain white dress and Clif painted flowers as necklace directly on my skin and flowers on my bare feet.

When I arrived at Don's office he was very apologetic: it was a very formal evening, and the Governor would be there. I thought I'd better not go, but Don was certain. So we arrived together at the top of the stairs in a reception room and walked down together to the crowd below. Don introduced me to the official party. Adelaide matrons can be intimidating when they want to be, and this group wanted to be, because from their point of view not only was a complete stranger, but one without an understanding of protocol, being foisted on them. Don explained that he was being painted, that Clif was unable to come that evening. Silence and disapproval.

Then stepped forward a man I'd never met: 'Mr Premier, I see that although he wasn't able to come he has sent a painting,' and I had the opportunity to explain that I hadn't expected to be at a formal occasion, and all was sunny.

This was my first meeting with Clyde Cameron, who I was to discover was the wisest and most sophisticated of all the Labor politicians. When Don and I left the reception it was to go to the house of his friend. Don's strategy had taken effect just as the portrait was ready for Clif to take back to the studio and contemplate. We drove back to Melbourne. Dunmoochin would give me time to think. Meanwhile, Whitlam was coming.

15

1972

Cinnamon-flavoured cream,
cinnamon buns, homemade butter,
a chicken in every pot

If your wombat is feeling poorly and won't come out of the burrow, mix a packet of cinnamon with some whipped cream. Smear the cream onto the end of a piece of wood such as a broom handle, and poke it down the burrow. The wombat will soon emerge in pursuit of the cinnamon. I discovered the attraction of cinnamon for wombats when we were painting Gough Whitlam. During a break on the first morning I made some cinnamon buns; and put them hot, wrapped in a tea towel, in a basket on the studio floor. Gough and Clif went outside to stretch while I went back to the kitchen. Carrying coffee, cups, and accoutrements, I returned to the studio. Where Whooper, ecstatic, stretched flat on his tummy, a few crumbs on his whiskers and all the buns gone.

It was the first time Gough had come to stay. The previous evening we'd driven up from town together; his driver had delivered him to us at the Pram Factory for *The Sonia Leg and Thigh Show*, the revue named for the split-to-the hip dress worn earlier that year at the White House by Sonia McMahon, wife of the Prime Minister. We sat on tiered benches, with Gough's suitcase, briefcase and overcoat beside us at the edge of the in-the-round stage. Evelyn Krape, as a skimpily dressed tart, did a role-reversal sketch in which she sexually harassed male members of the audience. Naturally she picked on Clif and Gough, telling me she fancied the one with the glasses, offering to leave me the big one. They were unsettled by this.

'No! No!'

Each held firmly to one of my arms, to the great amusement of Krape and the rest of the audience. They were even more disturbed when, in a later sketch, Krape approached us wearing a grey dustcoat and carrying a clipboard and evicted us with our nearest neighbours to the other side of the stage. Whitlam particularly resisted when she made us go back to our seats to collect suitcase, briefcase and coat. Squashed into already crowded benches, we watched a long black-plastic freeway unroll over our seats. After the show Whitlam and I stood in the street – no minders, no security – while Clif went to get the car.

Politicians, especially Labor politicians, were regularly exposed to real life in those days. There had been terror attacks in Australia, IRA terrorism had begun in the United Kingdom, terror was a common tactic in the Middle East, but the Australian atmosphere was relaxed and easy. The McMahon government was too decent, or perhaps too complacent, to use terrorism to divide and rule.

We'd begun work in the studio after breakfast. Gough was expansive, relaxed. Race Mathews arrived through the garden at the studio door. Race, as Whitlam knew, had taken some days off to work in Casey, and he also knew that I'd been door knocking with him that week.

'Race, at last. Where have you been all week?' Glancing at me, he added, 'I've had to spend the week with nothing but women.'

I got up and left the studio. Clif came to get me.

'Yes, I am really happy to talk to sitters but not to be insulted by them. In particular, not to be insulted by one who wants to be elected prime minister and who is supposed to be on about equality.'

'Race says that Whitlam is joking, sending himself up.'

'Well, it didn't look like that to me. He looked at me just before he said it.'

I refused to make lunch but Clif insisted I come to the pub for it, where Whitlam concentrated on charming me. And as the local birds carolled, he told Race the party would have to change its policy from a chicken in every pot to a magpie in every garden. Oh all right, I'll talk to him. So the portrait proceeded. That evening Clif asked me to model in front of the fire, and in front of Whitlam, who was reading some papers. And who announced after a while, 'I'm getting used to it.'

Across the years I see myself as a tool, advertising Clif's masculinity: the nudity, the painted dress. But in the context it was simply what happened; we took risks in many ways, challenging the status quo.

For instance, soon after Whitlam had gone back to Canberra (he was scheduling days for us as he travelled, but he was always on the move in that election year), Marlene arrived with forms for us to enrol to be conscripted. This was one of the strategies adopted by Jean McLean's *Save Our Sons* movement against conscription. Young men of eighteen had to enrol and be balloted to serve in the army. So we enrolled our friends and ourselves at our own and fictitious addresses; we enrolled the Prime Minister and all the Cabinet; we enrolled Napoleon Bonaparte, 'State if you have a preference for a particular branch of the army' – *Commanding Officer*; and the wombat, *Whooper Algernon Pugh*, 'State if you have a preference for a particular branch of the army' – *Sapper*.

This was fun, but the risk was prosecution and imprisonment, and the attention of the crude, possibly sinister Australian Security Intelligence Organisation. Jean had been gaoled for distributing anti-conscription pamphlets on government property, Tom Uren had been arrested and gaoled for marching in a 'Right to March' demonstration.

In gaol, Tom told us, 'They all came to me with their problems. After a while I had to ask to be put in solitary.'

Young men who refused to enrol for the ballot or who ignored notices to report for duty were pursued and went into hiding or were gaoled. When the state overrides liberties, everything comes into question. When it gaols obviously good or naïve citizens and going to gaol seems normal, all boundaries become questionable.

These questions arose when the culture was becoming deinstitution-alised. Two generations of men had spent their youth in the army in the twentieth century. Through this experience men were acculturated to expect that an employing organisation would be large, authoritarian, inefficient, and slow. They left the army to work in organisations which met these expectations.

Patronising and inefficient attitudes to women derived from a culture in which there was unreliable birth control, in which marriage and families sustained the social fabric. The basic wage, set for certain national industries but filtered through to almost all, was calculated as an amount of money paid to a man supporting a wife and family. By 1970, women could control their fertility. A generation without the discipline of war and with fourteen years of television had large expectations of life.

But it was conscription for the Vietnam War that focussed examination of the social systems of the time. Despite the pill, there was discrimination against women in employment and in membership of many organisations. Discrimination extended to communists, even though membership of the Communist Party was legal, and to Aboriginals. Abortion was illegal. Condoms could not be advertised or displayed. The physical expression of homosexuality was prohibited even in private. Wonderful buildings, whole streets and precincts, places of natural beauty and crucial environments for species protection were being destroyed. There was an obvious need to plan development and, as the country's manufacturing base declined, to invest in education and technology. The country was ripe for change.

The parliamentary party, all male, looked like the 1950s. Every now and again one of the more obscure ALP figures mumbled something inarticulate for too long, sounding as if the party was committed to the past not only in costume but sobriety. Not entirely their fault. The systems that constituted the opposition to the conservative parties were if possible more rigid than those of the government and public service. Trade union officials and ALP politicians were constantly engaged in arcane struggles for control of those unions and the party, and were unused to communicating with the outside world.

One of the very amusing aspects of the harder left was that because virtually all its members had attended church when young, and were deeply committed to one or other ideology, they all sounded the same, evangelical in speech and determination, appropriating different formulae. Not great television. Clyde Holding called another meeting, and I did some coaching in television presentation.

How amenable they were; such an idea must have been so exotic. Years later Maximilian Walsh told me that at about the same time as I began trying to train spokesmen to speak to the community at large, he and Laurie Oakes sat Mick Young at a table and trained him to smile whenever one of them grabbed his knee. Then each asked him a question, and the other grabbed his knee, causing him to smile before he answered. Then they repeated the exercise in front of a television camera, and Mick became, on the news, the genial man he was in life.

Journalists were looking for stories but I needed to change the image of the party. Don had told me as we chatted in Adelaide that he'd support the arts policy at the federal conference; he said we needed the Treasurer or the Prime Minister to be Minister for the Arts.

'In pre-budget meetings a weak minister, an outer-Cabinet minister, or one whose area isn't strategic, will lose in the share-out of the cake. But no one will fight either the Prime Minister or the Treasurer for money, so you tuck the arts under their wings and you're okay.'

Maybe I could kill two birds with one stone. If I could add the glamour of the entertainment industry to the substance of ALP policies, that just might give the party a new image, while persuading them that the arts were the way to attract the attention of the swinging voter. Whitlam, fast on his feet, a barrister, educated, was the obvious choice. So I told him, on that first afternoon when we came back from the pub, that we wanted him to be Minister for the Arts.

'No, I can't. I'll be Prime Minister and Minister for Foreign Affairs, and I might have to be Treasurer. I can't do it.'

I changed the subject. I would come back to it, when I had planned and had in place a campaign to get him to agree. In every campaign you have to think about the grass roots, and I'd have to define them in this one. There was still time, and after all, I now had on hand the advice of an experienced arts minister.

The question of state and national image was a matter of concern, but in Casey we were getting a lot of press. The handsome and charming Premier of South Australia was door knocking the electorate.

The telephone had been ringing as we walked back into the house from Adelaide, Don rang me every night and often during the day until his auditor-general commented on the cost of the calls. He came over as often as he could, and we went out in the evenings with Clif to openings or the theatre. Don and I spent hours surprising suburban families at their front doors.

'Hello, I'm Don Dunstan. I'm just in the area and I am canvassing support for Race Mathews, your local federal ALP candidate.'

He had separated from Gretel, announced it with no apparent effect on his support base, and moved to an apartment. Clif finished the portrait, but did not appear to notice how much attention I was getting from Don. He was drinking steadily, but without angry outbursts. Life was busier with dinner parties and clients coming up to see gouaches, there was less chance for the really dramatic evenings. And there was huge success, with welcome financial reward.

The publisher Denis Wren asked Clif if he knew Ivan Smith's radio play, *Death of a Wombat*, about bushfire. Yes, he did. Would he illustrate it? No, Clif didn't illustrate. But, if he could have a recording, he could listen to it again and he would see what happened, if some of his paintings would work in the context of the book. Perhaps he could do some drawings that would work with the text. Perhaps, indeed.

A perfect marriage of interest and intention. The text evokes the coast, and there was a gouache that he'd done at Shoreham, a painting of a dingo that might be used. But *Death of a Wombat* gave Clif an opportunity to paint indigenous animals in a crisis of nature, part of an inevitable cycle that preceded European settlement, the drama of which was abstract, without moral implications.

The work seemed to absorb much of the emotion he carried. He'd wanted to paint portraits while the European pictures had time to settle in his mind. He'd anticipated long days in the studio, time to draw and etch, slowly to find a way of dealing with the ideas they generated. Instead there had been meetings and interviews, interruptions to routine. Now he had a reason to refuse interruptions.

His paintings before Europe were often narrative, with dramatic ensembles of forms across the foreground of the picture, distance implied, but without space. Their theme was conflict; death and domination of species over species and, by implication, over the delicate Australian bush. Violence was implied even when the paintings were not dealing with a moral issue.

Death of a Wombat begins before dawn, as creatures gradually wake and go about their lives, innocent that later in the day fire will destroy them and the bush in which they live. The paintings done as Clif listened to this part of the tape have a light play of pale on pale, are spacious, gentle, and still. He'd always apologised for little 'swamp bird' paintings he did when he was happy, but there was no need to apologise for these paintings, even though they spoke of contentment.

I think the *Death of a Wombat* morning paintings were the way in which the impressionist palette and celebration of life, its optimism, began to find its way into his work. He played the tape over and again, and gradually a series of pictures, etchings and drawings emerged from the story of the fire. In the latter paintings – crowded as ever with meaning, where it is logical for the painting that the foreground dominates the action, where claustrophobic smoke and heat eliminate distance and space – one could see that the memory of testing the flamethrower informed the images of burning kangaroos.

Another meeting at Michael Parker's. *The Age* would do a special book promotion, there would be an exhibition of the pictures at *The Age* gallery. The Duke of Edinburgh as President of the Australian Conservation Foundation was asked to contribute a foreword.

I'd found a local dairy farmer who would sell me a gallon of cream at a time, and I was not only making my own bread but I was using in it the buttermilk I got from churning my own butter. I got up, lit the fire, set the dough to rise, and when my guests came down for breakfast there was fresh bread, and bacon and eggs amid the bird calls. Margaret Whitlam came to stay with Gough and kindly pitched in.

The goals Clif had set were achieved. He had the comfortable house where people liked to come, enough reputation to ensure he'd be able to buy his two houses (he always bought houses for cash) and a housekeeper who could keep things going. All he'd wanted.

And what he'd predicted. Even though I had an IUD, I was going to have a child.

I rang Don. 'I'm pregnant.'

And immediately: 'I'm so sorry you won't be able to have the baby.'

So he did plan every move.

I hadn't thought much about abortion as an issue until I'd first fallen pregnant several years earlier, and I'd surprised myself at the time. I had thought of the foetus as a baby, and could imagine having it; but unless I could provide properly for it – a place in society, a home – I knew immediately I'd have an abortion. It had happened a second time a couple of years before I met Clif. I wasn't stupid or careless, just unable to take the pill – I was covered in bruises as soon as I took it – and despite other forms of contraception, I was extremely fertile.

This would be my third abortion. I made the arrangements, Don was to come over for the day. I was not worried about the abortion. I was worried that while appearing to take risks about people knowing he was having an affair, he had been so quick to respond to the news, without even asking what I wanted.

Clif and Marlene's divorce was approaching, and Clif wanted me to come to the hearing. Which was on the same day as the abortion.

'I'd rather not.'

'What do you mean? You know you're better with the law than me, I really want you to come.'

'No, really, I am having lunch with . . .' *pluck a name from the air.*

'Well, change it.'

'Look it's your divorce, you'll have Frank Galbally and Peter O'Bryan with you, you don't need me.'

He was looking suddenly very serious.

'You're having an affair with Dunstan, you're pregnant, and you don't know whose it is, so you're having an abortion. Judith, I know you've been unhappy, but this isn't good. I don't like it. You shouldn't be having an abortion, you don't need to, not this time. What's his telephone number?'

He rang Don. 'Get over here, straight away.' And he came.

While we waited Clif said he realised that having affairs was no good for a relationship and that I shouldn't have done so.

'You said that people have affairs.'

'I've changed my mind.'

'No, you've changed your policy, I agreed to your policy and you're trying to make a unilateral change to it. I don't agree.'

But I had realised that I was delighted to think I could have the baby.

When Don arrived, Clif, who remained quite calm and was not at all drunk or dangerous, argued his case. He said I was the sort of woman who should have children. He assumed that Don, in his position, could risk divorce – that was politically okay these days – but not remarriage to an unmarried mother? Yes, Don agreed that was so, the only reason that he had suggested I not have the baby. Okay. Here was the deal. Clif would get divorced, Clif and I would get married, I would have the baby, Clif and I would get divorced, Don and I would get married.

'Would there be a short interval in which I might have a life of my own?'

Clif: 'Judith, this isn't funny.'

Don: 'Darling, this will work for everyone, please don't be upset.'

And Clif went on: 'This might be my child, and I have always wanted a girl, but even if it's another boy I'll take joint responsibility for it. You're a lawyer, you can set up some sort of trust where we both pay expenses, and I want to be involved, I wasn't involved enough before, and that's a mistake, you'll have to agree to that.'

Don was delighted. 'This will work, it's a very good idea, mate.'

Clif: 'There is one thing, just one thing, this sort of thing will work only if everyone is frank all the time. There can't be any secrets. We have to be frank all the time.'

Then I knew there was a problem. My intuition had been battered out of the scene for a while, but I still had instinct.

'Actually, no. I think that this won't work. I think it would be better if I had an abortion.'

Don: 'Darling, I am a politician, I know what's possible.' And looking at Clif he added, 'I haven't got a daughter either.'

I went to get dinner, thinking to the baby, *It's you and me, kid, and we can't trust anyone.*

But I knew I could. I could trust Don to do what he said, and I could trust Clif to use anything and anyone to get what he wanted.

If only the intuition would come back.

16

LOSS

Barley sugar, hospital soup,
ground rice

Don's visits became more frequent and more politically risky. I wasn't in love with the party, it hadn't been my life, but I was very serious about having the ALP elected. One of my cousins had been conscripted, I thought war was bad and that this war in Vietnam was particularly bad for Australia; I thought of the illiterate state-school teenagers to whom I had tried to teach English without the benefit of books. And here was this man who was unnecessarily being seen with me in public, insisting I go to Adelaide for a few days to see the apartment, sending his driver to collect me at the airport, sleeping with me at the apartment and taking me to the markets in Adelaide to shop, sending me back to the airport in his car, coming to the market in Melbourne when I shopped for a dinner party, and reassuring me that Clif could be trusted, that all would be well if we were frank with each other.

And he was frank with Clif.

And I wasn't frank with anyone.

And Clif was frank with every journalist he met, for the next few months.

Kevin Childs, the journalist who'd advised me when Clif won the Archibald, and who was now a friend, met me at an opening.

'Don't tell me if this is true, but Clif is telling everyone that you're having an affair with Don Dunstan. We don't want to publish anything about this, but you should see if you can stop him talking.'

Lionel Murphy rang. We'd never met.

'This is Lionel Murphy. I've just come from South Australia, and there are rumours everywhere about Don. People don't mind that his marriage has broken up, but the rumours are that he's having an affair with you and you're pregnant. Do you realise what this could do to the party?'

'Did Clyde Cameron ask you to ring me?'

'No, it wasn't Clyde, look, we know that Don was unhappy, no one will mind if you marry Don, it's just that the rumours will affect the election.'

'I quite agree. Can you get Clyde Cameron to try to talk some sense into Don? I'll talk to Clyde Holding.'

Lionel seemed surprised. His tone had been tough when he rang, but he asked if I was okay, and said that he could see why I was good for Don. I saw Clyde Holding and he too was sympathetic. He would get Clif out of the country. They left for Israel and Italy the following week, and I looked forward to a quiet time in the bush to collect my thoughts.

Don arrived again. I organised to stay near the sea. We had a lovely few days, I could see that he would be a wonderful companion and a terrific father. Everything had happened so fast, I knew I cared for him, but I had lost my intuition and I knew that I was partly seeking shelter. Best to let life take its course, why shouldn't this work, the man was in love with me. But better not to provoke the fates. We had dinner with some of his staff members at a restaurant back in town, and he announced in front of them that we had tickets for *Carmina Burana* the next evening. Afterwards one of them asked me not to go.

'Exactly, but you'll have to persuade Don.'

Then Don explained to me that it might be better if I didn't go. Well, at least someone was getting through to him.

He was leaving for Adelaide the next morning, and I went back to Dunmoochin alone. Letters from Clif, telling me about Israel, telling me that he loved me. It was quiet and peaceful and I began to feel more myself, but it was curious that although I was very conscious of the baby and very happy about it, the intuition just didn't take me forward. I knew it had gone because of the anxiety about Clif's drinking; the threat of verbal and physical violence. All anxiety keeps you in the present and on guard.

Perhaps the anxiety derived from being pregnant. I had a niggling pain in my back, in a place I'd never had a pain before, and rang the obstetrician, who reassured me that I was quite okay. I pointed out that I was an hour from Melbourne, but he was quite authoritative, so I ignored my anxiety. And woke the next morning to realise I was losing amniotic fluid, in which the baby was supposed to float. Neighbours drove me to the hospital and left to contact Clif, who was in the air en route to Rome. I asked a friend to tell Don but to say I was quite okay, and that he was *not* to come across.

I lay on my back, reading. The baby was alive, and the best thing to do, said everyone, was to wait. A message from Clif, that he was coming back. Then my temperature started to rise. They had to induce labour, both the baby and I were in danger. Would I mind being in a trial of a new hormone? No, if they were certain it wouldn't hurt the baby. The young woman who put up the drip sniggered when I told her that it hadn't gone in properly, that I'd felt it go through the vein.

'Don't be silly.'

They'd arrived with some barley sugar because my blood sugar was low. Of course it was low. I hadn't been given anything to eat when I arrived as it was the evening, then I hadn't had anything in case I had to have an anaesthetic, and I'd been monitored on a drip in the delivery room for several hours. I wanted some soup, I wasn't having any barley sugar. Because this was a trial, someone came to take a blood sample every half hour and someone else to do a clotting time, so I was festooned with little bits of cotton when Clif arrived, exhausted; he and Clyde had been met at Rome by consular officials who'd simply put him on the next plane home. It was reassuring to have him there, as I was a bit worried about the capacity of these people to think scientifically, or even sensibly.

The obstetrician arrived and could still hear the baby's heart, but said he would have to use forceps to deliver it. He didn't ask if I could push it out so I didn't try, although I'd done so on command the year before when Clif was on Timana Island. Nor would they let me try the force of gravity, so I was trussed up in stirrups. An anaesthetist arrived, gave me an epidural anaesthetic, and took a newspaper to a chair at the side of the room. The obstetrician tapped my leg.

'Can you feel this?'

'Yes.' I could feel it.

And again.

'Yes.'

And again.

'Yes.'

The obstetrician looked across to the anaesthetist. 'If I don't get this baby out now it will definitely die.'

So of course, although at the time he wasn't touching me, I said, 'Well I can't feel anything now.'

The baby was dead. I put out my arms, of course I put out my arms, but the obstetrician said, 'No, you can't hold it.'

So I asked to be able to see it, and there just for a moment was the tiny pearly body, and then it was taken away.

I didn't care about the pain as the obstetrician pulled at bits of placenta that were stuck on me and looked for the Dalkon shield that was supposed to have stopped all this.

After a while Clif said, 'I can't stand the pain.'

Everyone looked at him, alarmed. Was he about to break down? But it was clear he was talking about me. He was holding my hand. I had inadvertently been squeezing it every time the obstetrician came anywhere near me.

'You said the epidural had taken effect.'

'Of course I did.' The anaesthetist had given up his paper and was grabbing a syringe.

'I'll put you to sleep,' and grabbed the drip, so I said, 'Not the drip, it's not in properly.'

'Don't be silly.' The pain as the sodium pentothal was forced under my skin was excruciating. The arm went black.

The anæsthetist panicked. 'Oh god, give her the mask.'

Before I could ask to be shown how to use it he slammed it onto my mouth, breaking several of my top teeth. I had been weeping, and my nose was blocked, and he'd jammed the mask into my mouth. After a while I thought, 'Better to die anyway.'

But Clif told me afterwards that he'd watched me stop struggling and begin to go blue, and had looked at the nurse, who was obviously alarmed and wondering what to do, and had decided to knock out the doctor. Which he did, the nurse later remarked, 'Very efficiently, with just one punch.'

So I was alive, and Clif was in charge again.

I wanted to bury the baby. I asked the nurses how I should make such arrangements, and they went very blank. I kept asking.

Clif didn't deal with death, but he said, 'You can do whatever you want.'

I couldn't get anywhere with the nurses. The obstetrician turned up.

'You keep asking about this baby.'

'Yes, I want to make funeral arrangements for it.'

'You must understand. It isn't your baby.'

I was still pretty shocked. I'd lost a lot of blood and the arm had been, still was, very painful. But surely this would have seemed surreal, even if I were fit and happy. I asked what he meant.

'The baby doesn't belong to you. It belongs to the hospital.'

'How can it belong to the hospital?'

'It's the law. If a baby is born under one kilo and alive, it belongs to the parents. If it is over one kilo and dead it belongs to the parents. But if it is under one kilo and dead it belongs to the hospital.'

These people are mad, what could they want with a tiny dead baby? Fight, but use practical arguments.

'That may be the law, but the hospital will be using public money to bury the baby, and we can save the expense and the administrative bother, just let me know who I have to deal with.'

He was standing at the end of my bed, just inside the door. He'd not bothered to come to my bedside.

'You have to understand, the baby was not yours. It has been taken away and cut up and used for scientific purposes.'

And left the room.

Clif came in late that afternoon and I said I wanted to go home. The nurses were worried, I'd lost a lot of blood and was still bleeding, but I made it clear I was leaving whatever the risk.

One of them remarked, 'Well, at least you've stopped crying.'

My uncle had been a prisoner of war of the Japanese, and he had lived with us on his return from Burma. I'd been a very small child; it may not have been the best policy to leave us together, as he'd told me a lot of things not necessary even for adults to know. But I was glad of his voice in my memory.

'There are times, Judith, when you just have to go on, when the things you do every day keep you going.'

So that is what I did. Just went on. One of my closest friends would be having a child at the time mine had been due, so it was easy to give away the things I'd got ready. Then I resumed the reality of door knocking, meetings, parties. While I was in hospital an article had been published claiming that Don had a pregnant mistress, but it named no names. And now no one was pregnant. Don had realised the danger of Clif now, and I was simply unable to argue.

I was never going to go through that again, so I decided to be sterilised. At first no one would do it, doctors just attempted to persuade me to 'try again'. I didn't tell them that my fear was the icy cold of the question of ownership. I spoke to no one at all about that, not Clif, not anyone. I found my way to Carl Wood, Professor of Obstetrics and Gynaecology at Monash University. I began to tell him about the delivery, just the incompetence and pain, not the conversation about ownership, and I began to cry.

'Go on telling me, but I will sterilise you, I don't expect you to want to have another baby.'

We made a date for the surgery but he rang up and said that he was a bit worried that he'd been very affected by my emotion, and would I see a psychiatrist? I said I was not mad, I was simply too afraid to risk putting myself through the pain again. Well, would I mind coming in to see him with Clif, and would I mind if he asked one of the psychiatrists about me? That would be fine.

When we arrived, he said that he had one question to ask me, and if I gave the wrong answer he'd like me to agree to see the psychiatrist. Oh well, I could always go elsewhere . . .

'What's the question?'

'You're twenty-seven. What will you do if you're thirty-seven and you want desperately to have children and I can't reverse this?'

'I suppose I'll kill myself.'

He turned to Clif.

'Is she always like this?'

And Clif, smiling: 'Yes.'

'Okay, I'll sterilise you.'

It occurred to me to ask, 'What was the wrong answer?'

That such a scenario would never happen. I knew I might regret it, it was simply that I had no other choice.

There didn't seem a way to feel less than bleak. People were kind, this was the time when Clif rang Bert and generous amusing Barbara Tucker took me about with her and helped me to keep going.

Then one night I answered the telephone and a voice said, 'Mrs Pugh, I have your baby.'

Clif saw my face, took the phone and identified himself.

'It's all right. It's a wombat.'

Wombalong arrived an hour later, to the horror of everyone but me. Hairless and blind, orphaned, they thought she would die. But I knew she wouldn't. I rang Tim Ealey at Monash to ask what to feed her.

'No one knows. Just write down everything you do.'

I put her in a sock, and wrapped it in an old jumper, and wore her in a cotton bag hanging from my neck. I had to unwrap it all to feed her, which I did not so much on demand as on impulse, with very thin ground rice. Wombats, like kangaroos, don't suck; you have to pump the milk into their mouths. Their teeth keep growing, like horses' teeth. They have powerful grinding jaws and, when they're young, very sharp teeth, so she went through several teats.

I took her to lunch with my mother at the Lyceum Club, and to dinner parties, to openings. She slept beside me in a box with an old pottery hot-water bottle. In the middle of the night I'd feed her, and one night I fell asleep cuddling her, only to wake up because she'd peed on me. I popped her on the sleeping Clif and went to wash.

Wombalong wandered down his sleeping body to find his pubic hair, wiry, just like a wombat mother's. Then an obstruction. Which with her sharp teeth and powerful wombat jaw, she bit.

He always complained that I came running back from the bathroom calling out, 'Don't throw her! Don't throw her!'

Thus through love she survived, and I survived.

17

STRATEGY

Sweet potato

Eventually I would give up Wombalong. Our commitment was to rear and release our wombats. It was about saving Australian fauna, not about domesticating them. Sometimes this meant taking them to the nearby state forest, where the wombat population could accommodate an extra, leaving them a huge sweet potato to munch on while we crept away. Sometimes they would burrow out, or a gate would be left open, there'd be one or two calls from neighbours who heard or saw them on their way. Whooper left us, a couple of days before his call-up papers came, allowing us enormous fun, as we were photographed for *The Age*.

'We just want him to know that we support him in his right to resist conscription. We think he may have gone underground.'

Two men came in plain clothes to ask where he was. I said we were distraught at his disappearance, so pleased to think they'd search for him, and asked, if they found him, to let us know. I gave them a description: Brown eyes, brown hair, button nose, short bandy legs.

'I actually don't think he'd have passed the medical.'

'Oh, but Clif, he's very strong.'

They asked if I'd enrolled him.

'I enrolled everyone I could think of, officer. I think we should all have a chance to serve our country, no matter who we are.'

'It has been suggested to us that Whooper is a wombat.'

So they read *The Age*.

'Yes, officer, he is. But he is like a son to us.'

They could have arrested me, but there beside me stood Clif, the famous ex-soldier, and it was apparent from their faces that they were not planning to act. Perhaps even in this ominous bureaucracy the concept of public relations was beginning to filter through.

To the Security Services, but not yet to the ALP. Whitlam seemed confident he could use parliamentary question time, and other parliamentary strategies such as personal explanations and the adjournment debate, to change the public image of the party, to communicate his message before the campaign proper began. He had what one might call a statistical point. There were very few radio licences at the time, and no FM band. There were places in the outback relying on short-wave radio, but in the main the ABC stations, national and local, served the nation, together with a few commercial stations. Community radio virtually did not exist, nor programs not in English.

The ABC's legal obligation to broadcast parliamentary proceedings focussed the nation's attention on politicians and politics. In many towns there was a choice between the ABC stations and one commercial station which concentrated on local news, this station usually having links to a commercial network that brought in serials, pop music, the races. Every farmer listened to the *ABC Country Hour* for the stock prices and the weather and the river levels. The ABC broadcast the Test Cricket; this as much as anything unified the nation. Even in the cities, despite a wider choice of commercial stations, one might walk along a summer street and hear the cricket through every open window.

The parliament was the national white noise, the background to household and workplace. It was mostly undemanding. We could concentrate on the task at hand as it rustled away like a gentle breeze while we cleaned, or cooked, or did the filing, or worked on cars, or painted, or studied. Then suddenly the breeze would become a gust, and someone would go across the workplace to the set, or you'd reach above the canisters and turn it up, and there would be Whitlam roaring away, or Fred Daly shaking some pompous minister from his complacent tree.

Passion had to be genuine and commitment thorough to withstand the assault of brilliant and hilarious interjections from either side of the house. Question time in the parliament was a marvellous game then, before political correctness, when wit was the weapon of choice.

Whitlam knew he had the advantage of McMahon in the parliament; that he would have the attention of the parliamentary press gallery and through them the opinion and news pages of the major city dailies, and the current affairs programs on the ABC. But there were the commercial stations to reckon with, and as television began to assimilate the daytime radio audience and intrude into every evening, the culture was changing. Besides, the parliament was not always sitting; something more was needed.

I could not have articulated this at the time. It was my taken-for-granted that the parliament was the national place of political focus. Rather, I thought in terms of popularity. How could I make the party popular? And it came to me. I had access to the grass roots of popular culture – the people in the arts.

Odd how the concept of the grass roots helps to focus one's attention. The plan was simple and strategic but, if I could execute it, would have effect in a number of pleasingly intersected ways. It would connect the ALP with popular culture, thus making it hip. It would connect it with dance bands and musicals, making it seem something you might enjoy after a game of golf, and with high culture, making it possible to get together with it over a glass of wine. It would confirm the policies and structure so carefully crafted by Clif's committee. It would put arts funding on the agenda. And it would make Whitlam agree to be Minister for the Arts.

It only required a little co-ordination. Whitlam would announce just one element of the arts policy. Across the nation, figures from the arts would be asked by a journalist who just happened to be standing next to them at the time what they thought of the idea. They would say, 'I think it's great! I'm going to vote for the ALP!'

Then another section would be announced, to more enthusiasm. Before trying it on Whitlam, I began to contact people in the arts to see if they planned to vote for the ALP and if they would agree to make their intentions public as part of the campaign. The initial response provided an insight into how things worked. For example Mary Hardy, whose brother Frank wrote *Power Without Glory* about the years in which John Wren exercised his questionable influence in Melbourne, was a broadcaster.

'Darl, I'd love to but I couldn't. I'd lose my job.'

Of course. *Begin with the self-employed.*

Now to persuade Whitlam.

One of my front teeth broken by the anaesthetist began to hurt, but I was through with medical procedures, and I ignored it. Soon the swelling was noticeable and Clif said I'd have to go to a dentist. I simply couldn't; I got to the door twice and that was it. Barbara Tucker intervened, and sat with me for a couple of hours while a specialist removed quite a lot of infected bone.

'Now I've had to put nineteen stitches in, and when the local anaesthetic wears off this will be very painful. I'm going to give you an injection of morphine, and then you must take these tablets and stay in bed.'

But there was no time for bed. I had to be alert and on my feet. That evening I had an opportunity to explain the policy and to get Whitlam's agreement to the campaign plan.

His schedule was more and more hectic, he could no longer give us a couple of days at a stretch, but we had organised a couple of hours at Clyde Holding's house in town. We needed the time because Clif was having difficulty with his portrait. Press comment, television coverage, everything that might affect election prospects affected Gough, and more than his demeanour. The self-image of a politician absorbs and responds to external forces; in this crucial time Whitlam's personality, his *self*, was fluid.

The Arts Policy Committee had briefed me about the structure they wanted: arms-length funding, a statutory body run by professionals, professionals making funding decisions, budgets set by a professional council. All the arts minister had to do was get the money in the budget. This evening would be my best opportunity. I needed to be alert. I was negotiating with a labile brilliant egocentric barrister and I had to succeed. If I had an injection of morphine I might not be alert enough.

'No injection thanks, just the tablets.'

That evening while I explained the policy, the effect of the morphine began to wear off. Focus.

I said that we wanted him to be Minister for the Arts.

'Judith, I can't. I have already explained. I'll be Foreign Minister and Prime Minister. I simply wouldn't have the time'.

I explained our position, and said that he would hardly have to do a thing. That the crucial issue in arts funding was that decisions must be made by professionals, that for too long funding had come through amateur first-nighters who liked lavish productions and who could not build an industry because they had no understanding of its workings. Funding big companies was simply following the commercial mode of extravagant overseas productions and grand tours; it did not develop Australian culture but simply repeated the European of yesteryear. Whitlam listened.

Then I asked him again to be Minister for the Arts. And he again refused. *What do I say, when they say no?*

I had gone over the arguments. I could promise he would not have to commit time, because once a statutory body had been set up all he had to do was appoint to it. I didn't want him to listen to the detailed strategy plan, how the arts would help him be elected, because he might get irritated and say something that would anchor his refusal in his ego. I had to speak in principle. Clif and I had agreed as we talked about his character that he was impulsive, too fast on his feet, enjoying his own jokes when he should be listening. So I spoke about the value of the arts, of the fact that he of all the potential front bench would be able to enjoy the people involved and promote their ideas. I could tell he was engaged with me, because he began to question me like a barrister, to enjoy provoking me. This time I was expecting it.

As the pain increased and my lip and gum swelled, I thought of Uncle John and Clif, talking about engaging the enemy, not letting him see your weakness. I felt a stitch in the flesh snap, and I could taste blood in my mouth. I smiled and went on talking, letting the blood drip down my chin. I said Margaret would enjoy the productions, the writers, the visual arts; he made a crack about women. He knew I knew he was teasing me, and as I smiled another stitch snapped and I made a decision to go for broke and expose my plan, and I asked, 'What if I show you it's worth your while?'

He looked sceptical. 'I doubt you can.'

'But if I can?'

'If you could, but it's unlikely, Judith.'

'All I ask is to let me co-ordinate with Race. When we are ready, you announce one part of the arts policy. We'll begin with that and I will show you that it will be worth your while. I don't ask that you agree here and now, but that you agree to contemplate it, while I show you what I mean.'

The blood was running quite freely now, dripping onto my shirt, which was a theatrical white.

He turned to Clif. 'If I agree, will she stop bleeding at me?'

'Yes, Gough, if that's a yes. If you agree to consider it, I'll stop bleeding. I'll get on to Race tomorrow.'

Clyde brought me a glass of water so I could take a tablet.

All across Australia the message went out, and the effect was astonishing. At first, we relied on friends, old acquaintances, self-employed artists, writers, and musicians, or people already connected with the left: Graeme Bell, David Williamson, Harry Bluck in Perth: 'I'm the Ballroom King of Western Australia.'

And artists like Frank Hodgkinson. Some artists would not support us. Fred Williams refused, saying he never declared his politics, and indeed Lyn asked why Clif was being so active.

'I thought you said he should be involved in politics?'

'I meant arts politics.'

Oh.

Those who were aboard suggested others, who then made further suggestions and contacts. These people were professional, they knew what publicity was, the need to provide a slow, steady drip of information. Not one person pre-empted the campaign, which developed from support for arts policies, to all the ALP initiatives. I would come home to a brief message from increasingly mainstream figures: the name, the contact details: 'I'd like to be involved. Just say where and when, and what you want me to say.' I had not thought it would work so quickly to break the respectability barrier.

There was at the time a variety host, Bobby Limb, with a popular daytime program on a commercial TV channel. His live audience was women beyond a certain age, the blue-rinse set. And the queen of the musicals, everyone's darling, was Jill Perryman. When they offered, I knew the ALP would win. And I waited. It was obvious to me, to us. Would Whitlam see the connection between endorsement by arts figures and popularity? Finally he rang.

'Okay, Judith, I get the point. If I announce I'll be Minister for the Arts, who will you give me?'

'I'll give you Bobby Limb.'

Bobby and Jill came up to lunch.

'What will I wear?'

'Do you have a red suit, Jill?'

'I'll be wearing one.'

And there they were, Whitlam beaming down on the three of them, Bobby and Jill beautifully dressed, Clif as ever in army shirt, Wombalong snuffling about, perfect images for the television crews and the photographers. We were becoming used to watching Clif, the animals, the house, on television.

That night I saw the portrait beside the set was still not working.

'I don't want another drama, but haven't you got the same problem with Gough that you had with McEwen? Can you get a six-by-four board for him?'

There was one in the studio, and Clif prepared it. I had no image in my mind this time, and I realise now with surprise that neither of us thought of him standing, although his figure dominated any room. Then, one evening as we watched television, he gestured in a particular way, apparently expansive but contained, and there, very quickly the next day was the portrait that would win the 1972 Archibald Prize: Whitlam seated, perhaps about to rise, both persuasive and threatening, absolutely confident. He moves against an abstracted background. It may be hindsight to make the remark, but it seems that with his usual prescience Clif painted the energetic figure against a background suggesting turmoil.

By the time the portrait of Whitlam was completed I was working with a broader marginal-electorates committee. On the outskirts of Melbourne people were actually joining the party or attending meetings, were welcoming door knockers, detaining them to ask questions. It seemed that the ALP would win the election. One could see that the difficulties Clif had had with the portrait were not only due to our putative leader's response to the changing public temper. His personality

itself was volatile, with the staginess of a barrister. But we thought, we remarked to each other, that it wouldn't matter; because the solid, formal public servants, the processes of government themselves, would provide structure and order when he became prime minister.

Across the country one could see people of all factions in the party working together in anticipation of an ALP victory; all the issues being brought together by so many people who had worked at every level for so many years. For me it was a matter, for the last couple of months, of treading carefully, keeping up the talkback pressure, co-ordinating the announcements of support, driving shadow spokesmen to meetings, amid the usual daily tasks of running the house and the end-of-year openings and parties.

The election campaign was to end in Melbourne, the last speech before the television and radio blackout from Thursday evening. We were asked to come to Whitlam's speech; it would be televised and they wanted us in the front row at the St Kilda Town Hall. Nothing more one could do now. McMahon had chosen Ormsby Wilkins' talkback segment for his last Melbourne radio appearance. So that morning, for the first time, I dialled in to join the now very sophisticated team.

The Coalition had given one-for-one grants to assist with science laboratories and libraries, mostly to private schools. I recognised the voice of a disabled boy who was taught at home.

'Mr McMahon, my parents had to take me out of a private school, but the state school they've sent me to is just as good, I don't know why people complain about education funding for state schools.'

'Thank you, my boy, my government has always been committed to education, and we will continue to fund educational facilities.'

'Oh well, then perhaps you can explain why my new school has no science laboratory and no library?'

'My boy, stay on the line, I'm going to ask the producer to get your name and address, then I'll ask my Minister for Education to ring you, and we'll see if we can help you.'

The phrase *pork barrel* rolled into the mind of every listener.

I repeatedly dialled the talkback number, to find it engaged, when suddenly the line was clear, ringing, and then answered. I was told I was next after the current caller. My god, what issue to choose? Well, the Deputy Prime Minister had told me McMahon was gay. Should I ask if he had married just to be prime minister? The focus for me would be hypocrisy, not ambition, the distinction a bit subtle for talkback radio. The eternal problem with such a question is how it affects the family, and his wife was heavily pregnant. But there was another issue; McMahon had raised it, probably too late, but I wanted to unsettle him about it.

Two days earlier, he'd announced that he supported laws that made abortion criminal. This question had not been raised during the campaign, nor should it have been, for the simple reason that the criminal law is the province of the states; for the Commonwealth, the question of abortion arises only in the Northern Territory and the Australian Capital Territory. It is not a national concern in the way fighting a war is a national concern. How to get the topic out of the water? I would have to think about the issues and treat the conversation as a sort of surreal negotiation, letting it have its own creative life, and treat pregnancy as if it was of no concern to me at all.

Meanwhile, the second caller was our lively pensioner. The economy had been good for McMahon, but inflation was beginning to be a concern.

'Mr McMahon, I've rung to thank you for the dollar on the pension in the budget.'

'My government looks after those who've contributed all their lives.'

'Well, it's just that it doesn't buy as much as it did.'

I don't recall the reply, because I was on.

Deep breath, and . . . McMahon had not yet faced an election as Prime Minister:

'Mr McMahon, I just want to say that I've voted Liberal all my life, and I'm looking forward to voting for you for the first time.'

'Thank you very much.'

'There's just one issue I'm concerned about.'

'What is that, dear?'

'Motherhood.'

'I made my position on motherhood perfectly clear on Tuesday.'

'Oh no, I don't care about abortion. I just didn't like the way Mrs McMahon was pregnant and was used during the campaign.'

He was silent. Use the silence. This silence is platinum. Breathe quietly, say nothing.

Talkback hosts abhor a vacuum. Ormsby Wilkins: 'I hope you're not suggesting that Mrs McMahon was made pregnant just for the campaign?'

It's not often in life one is handed such an opportunity, on the day of the broadcast media shutdown, by the Prime Minister and his host.

'Oh. Perhaps it wasn't Mr McMahon, perhaps it was one of his staff . . .'

McMahon still said nothing. The Prime Minister of the country, on live radio, a man who'd spent his life at microphones, and he had stopped.

Ormsby Wilkins thanked him and McMahon left the studio.

Alan Barnes, one of the Canberra press gallery, rang a little while later to ask if we'd be at the rally that evening, and could I stay on a bit?

'Well, Alan, we always love to see you, but we're driving home, it is an hour's drive.'

'Judith, it won't take long.'

Okay. We'd been asked to arrive early, with more than half an hour to spare. The hall was full, there was excitement, many of the faithful were there. The arts people in the front rows knew that the message was already either delivered or not, this probably would not close the deal if it wasn't closed already. I did not want to be there. I am not by nature a joiner – I've always lived on the margin of social groups – and I was not romantic about the ALP. But we all were prepared to go through the ritual. We'd been milling about a bit in our rows, and were slightly irritated when Bob Hawke was announced, obviously to warm us up. Oh well, be polite.

He walked to the microphone, and delivered an astonishing speech. It was a riveting account of the history of the struggle of the working class with capital, of the history of liberties. We'd been concentrating on strategy, detail, lobbying, organisation, planning, for years. Hawke took every member of his audience back to principle, reminding us of why we were there, how we had become caught up with each other and the flawed, chaotic, difficult political party.

We thought of all the draft resisters in gaol, the soldiers at risk in the pointless war, of kids without schoolbooks, of women and migrants underpaid, stranded in the suburbs without transport, of discrimination, of lakes and forests and precious terraces under threat, and we felt proud to have come this far. He reminded us that it was possible for ideas to change history. He brought us to our feet, and he introduced 'the next Prime Minister of Australia'.

Whitlam strode out, and began Graham Freudenberg's great speech with John Curtin's words.

'Men and Women of Australia . . .'

Afterwards, Alan Barnes took me to the press room, where the press gallery had assembled. They had heard about the talkback campaign, and wanted to congratulate me. They had a small presentation. They'd recognised my voice, and thought that this would be an appropriate memento. It was the tape of me and Billy McMahon.

18

VICTORY

Xmas ham and Xmas pudding, ballast

It's a new century and the State Library has been renovated since last we came here together, but my ghosts remain. By 1970, when I met Clif, the gallery, together with the school that produced so many of Australia's painters, had already moved to its modern building at the other end of the city. The new museum had not yet been built, and at the entrance to Melbourne's historic place of culture the taxidermied corpse of the champion racehorse Phar Lap stood as a reminder that the city hosted the richest horse race in the world; the dioramas of my childhood were still in place. In this building I feel so absolutely at home, embedded in Melbourne, in a culture handed on to me by generations of scholars, writers and artists. Here had sat people with whom I shared holidays and meals and houses; and others, too: seen at openings, across restaurants, to whom I listened and from whom I learned.

One hot day Clif and I climbed the stairs to the lovely studios, where he spent his post-war years. Briefly, as a schoolgirl, I had been there too, and he was amused when I told him about it. A friend of my mother's, Lesta O'Bryan, had arranged for me to go to the annual summer school.

Some years after this, Lesta was to open Australia's first gallery dedicated to sculpture, but when I was fifteen she was a student at the Gallery School and an assistant at South Yarra Gallery. Ebullient and forceful, she arrived suddenly in the room crowded with school children, followed by the painter Justin O'Brien, who was taking the adult summer school. Together they removed me to the grown-up class.

There I spent happy weeks being taught to use oil paint by the summer-school adults, and in the evenings listening to Mary Cecil-Allen, an Australian painter based for most of her life in New York, lecturing about American Art. Cecil-Allen had left Australia in 1926 and was living in Provincetown, Massachusetts. She talked about her friends William de Kooning and Jackson Pollock, showing enormous slides of their work and of other artists of the New York School. Later Frank Hodgkinson was to talk about Bill de Kooning in Italy, another reminder of how small and how international the art world is.

The grand architectural spaces of the Heritage Collections Reading Room and the huge bound folios of *The Age* on the wide tables emphasise the dignity and authority of the library. Researchers ruffle through boxes of nineteenth-century letters and diaries, earnest and purposeful. I feel at home, but a sort of fraud. Somehow researching one's own life seems a charge on the public purse. I have my own records – diaries, photographs, letters – but I am looking for a particular date, and to read again about the period of the 1972 election, because my memories are entangled, as if everything happened at once.

I handle carefully the weighty tomes that once were newspapers. And am amazed at what I had forgotten. I was there, this happened to me, but it still seems astonishing. Before the federal election in 1972, the ALP took out a double-page spread. 'Join Us!!' is the call, and there, on the left-hand page, are photographs of national figures from various walks of life, encouraging citizens to vote for the party. On the right, the lower half-page is text, and on the upper right a quarter-page photograph of Gough Whitlam. And upper left is Clif.

It is both reassuring and amazing to see, in the six months of this paper of record, that everything did happen at once, my memories are accurately entangled. Clif's fame, the morph into a person beyond himself, into a *public figure*, happens in these pages, in parallel to the political campaign, as all our issues came together in the last months of the year. The promotional campaign for *Death of a Wombat* began and resulted in huge sales for the book; Clif's first cheque after his advance was astonishing. The campaign also had the effect of committing *The Age* to the environment issue and to educating its journalists, from editor Graham Perkin down, in conservation values; and of making Clif into a spokesman on the environment for all media. It re-enforced his reputation as a landscape painter, in the year he'd won his second Archibald Prize, so he was not seen only as a portraitist. *The Age* had made prints for sale as well as promoting the book and the exhibition, and the gallery had thousands of visitors. The show sold out, the book became extraordinarily popular.

There was no celebrity cult nor were there professional managers then, but Clif was in command of and dealt with what would now be called celebrity. Melbourne, indeed Australia, was a provincial place, where recognition on the street or in shops was cheery, not awed. People talked to him about the environment, asked after the wombat, said they liked his work, but without excitement and not intrusively.

At this time, the latter part of 1972, there was less anger at night. When he was drinking Clif was realistically angry about the Vietnam War; that is, about its politics, about Australia as a vassal of the United States. Indignant but not maudlin, he could discuss politics more objectively without segueing to World War II. He was also more wary about his behaviour; there were still moments, but they were less frequent and less intense. He knew I had limits, he knew I'd wanted to leave, that this had lead to Dunstan.

There was much to make him happy. The mood of the country was pretty clear. Australia's involvement in Vietnam would end. The book and the show were making a lot of money, he could buy a house in Melbourne; Dunmoochin was becoming more comfortable and we were very contentedly entertaining friends and clients. I hoped that the happiness in the early *Death of a Wombat* paintings, the light palette, the celebration of delicacy, meant that he might be able to accept success.

And success was separate from politics and the ALP. His clients were industrialists, bankers, businessmen and their wives, academic institutions, conservative politicians as well as bohemians. The paintings were sold to a range of people in many occupations, and the photographic prints promoted by *The Age* brought his images, and his message, into households that were far from the art world.

Which was what he wanted. He thought about communicating with his buyers, he wanted his work on walls where it was seen as part of the culture of the intellectual and aesthetic life of his clients, rather than their investment strategy. He lived in the art world and among businessmen as much as artists, but his approach to art as business was to emphasise the content and not the value of his work. Here he was at odds with Fred Williams.

Clif and Fred Williams were very close, Fred coming up regularly to paint, going out with John Olsen and Frank Hodgkinson and John Perceval, coming back to a drink and, often, a meal. Fred was on the Commonwealth Art Advisory Board. He played art politics with principle, judging the work and never the artist; he was committed to collecting for the putative National Gallery in Canberra.

Fred was a prolific painter, Clif comparatively unproductive. Which made their respective attitudes to the price of their work very amusing. Clif was lucky to finish a painting in a month; Fred, working from the colour wheel, was far faster, but wanted to push his prices up: Clif wanted to keep his down. If a painting of Clif's came up in auction and sold above his current gallery prices, Clif would put pictures in the next auction to reduce his prices. It was part of an overall anti-investment approach to the market.

Money was for security through property. We could use the house in town overnight and for guests, but the aim was to own the two houses he'd talked about in our early days together. To own assumed to *own unencumbered by debt*, no loans for Clif; there was always the fear that he would lose the freedom to paint that he had lost once before, through his father's death, and then won again. Once he had two houses, if the bottom fell out of his market, he would have the rent and could go on painting.

'I live to paint, not for money. I want to sell each painting so I can paint the next.'

I read, often, that Clif was identified with the ALP. This is true, but insofar as he loaned it his reputation; he formed its arts policy and endorsed its anti-war, civil libertarian and environment policies, and its protection of the poor. But like all artists, he was a small businessman, a capitalist entrepreneur. It was clear that his industrialist and business clients respected him.

Therefore it was no surprise when, just before the end of the year, Michael Parker telephoned, inviting us to dinner with a couple of English businessmen who were visiting Australia and hoped to meet some people who were close to the Labor Party.

'ALP must be going to win,' said Clif.

Michael took us to Herman Schneider's Two Faces, where Clif had invited me on the night we met. The restaurant was in a basement, and on that late summer evening in Melbourne we arrived in daylight, to be introduced to Leopold de Rothschild and Tom Stonor.

British businessmen indeed. De Rothschild was a member of the great banking family and a governor of the Bank of England, Tom a director of the Rothschild bank and heir to Lord Camoys and the stately home Stonor Park. Not that they mentioned this, although I assumed Leo came from the banking family. At the end of a very pleasant meal I suggested that Leo and Tom come with us to the end-of-year party at Powell Street Gallery. They hesitated.

'It's a private party.'

'No, this is Australia. Of course you can come. It'll be fine.'

What better introduction to any city than a party at one of its most fashionable galleries?

When we arrived the street door to the gallery was closed, but in the warm summery twilight the crowd, mainly now of artists, was partying on in the rear courtyard and the back room. As we waited for Clif to find us a drink I introduced Leo to a young artist standing beside us. I was a bit surprised by the response.

'What have you brought him here for?'

Well, after all, it did look as if the ALP would win in a couple of weeks, this guy must fancy himself a revolutionary. And everyone had been drinking for a while. Never mind, there was Fred Williams in his suit.

'Fred, I'd like you to meet Leopold de Rothschild.'

'How do you do. You're not as good looking as your cousin Evelyn.'

Oops. Even Fred had been drinking for quite a while, enough to lower the official persona for a moment.

'Leo, perhaps you'd like to see the gallery?'

And in we went. He looked around for a while, asking who did which picture, about the Melbourne art world, inconsequential talk. He didn't ask for a catalogue and it simply didn't occur to me to get one. This wasn't about selling pictures, but about welcoming strangers, introducing them to the local pleasures, keeping them safe from enthusiastic radicals.

Then, 'Judith, this is a commercial gallery?'

'Yes, it is.'

'And do you have the same system as we have, the ones with red dots are sold?'

'Yes, we do.'

'Could I see the dealer?'

Of course. I found David Chapman.

'David, I'd like you to meet Leopold de Rothschild.'

David laughed. Best ignore that.

Leo asked, 'This is your gallery?'

'Yes.'

'And the paintings are for sale?

'Yes.'

'The ones with red dots are already sold?'

David turned to me and said, 'He's very good, Judith.'

'David, this really is Leopold de Rothschild.'

Leo, indicating, 'Then I'd like to buy this one and this one and this one and this one and this one.'

David, hooting with laughter: 'Judith, where did you get him? He's fantastic!' And heading outside he called, 'Everyone! Come and see what Judith's got!'

'Leo, would you excuse me for a moment?'

I found David's wife Bea, possibly the only other sober person in the place, and explained what had happened. We held David's head under the cold tap, but to no avail. Bea and I decided she should talk to Leo. As I introduced them I could hear David telling the slightly volatile crowd about my marvellous joke. Introducing Bea, I wondered if it would be possible for Leo to come and have a look at the pictures in daylight the next morning. And he, tactful, took up the idea about the light, to the considerable improvement of Powell Street's balance sheet.

Openings, dinner parties, meetings with the publisher, co-ordinating the arts campaign, travelling into town and out, going to the show, portraits; all this activity took us forward together. Clif and I never talked about what had happened with Don; the three of us simply took up a friendship as if nothing more dramatic had ever occurred. Our baby had been due in early December, and my friend Julie Shaw was to have hers around the same time. It had been sensible to give her my maternity clothes and things I'd bought for the baby, but I wanted to be away at the time hers was born, so we left for South Australia.

Life is work for a painter, and for a landscape painter so is travel. The parts of our lives were distinct: the pace of political meetings, parties, openings, negotiating, thinking fast and making decisions, contrasted with our journeys – slow, into silent country and space.

Where he was rarely drunk or angry. That summer trip of 1972–73 began lazily, drifting about the Coorong in their houseboat with Rosemary and Jim Ingoldby, who made wine in South Australia; they'd also invited Frank and Kate Hodgkinson, who came on with us to a cottage in Willunga. The Coorong is that region where the great Murray River meets the sea in a series of lakes and gentle sandhills, where evidence of ancient occupation is revealed in middens, great mounds of shells that emerge with wind and weather from the sand. We spent each night in a different cove, eating our way through Christmas ham and pudding, and drinking the ballast, which was thoughtfully stocked by Jim not only with wine he and his friends had made, but with plenty of spirits and liqueurs.

There are always moments from those journeys. Clif and I were alone on a walk, ahead of the party, when two startled emus ran up the sandhill in front of us. Graceful and clumsy at the same time, a leg lifted high, planted, sliding; the neck stretching jerkily for balance, while the opposite foot extricated itself; their comical slow-motion dance leaving its pattern momentarily on the land. On our return to Dunmoochin he made an etching of the image, and I began again to see the point of it all. Perhaps we could spend more time away from Melbourne, even get a permanent place nearer the dry hot country, and go there for longer periods, perhaps then we could be happy. At least, now that the ALP was in government, he would be able to concentrate on his own work again.

But I was wrong. Politics hadn't ended. Indeed, for us, each of us, *realpolitik* would now begin.

19

TONE

Wholemeal bread, soup from fresh peas and ham

The ALP had won government by a margin of less than four per cent, and 67 seats to the opposition's 58. The maths are not difficult. First you appoint the Speaker, then you have a majority of eight. But if you lose one seat, the opposition gains one. Effectively, thinking of it as a game with moves, the ALP had a majority of only six seats. And, if two per cent of the four per cent change sides . . . It was no landslide. The obvious course was to consolidate the position, initially introducing those reforms that would make substantial improvements to the wellbeing of the majority of Australians, but not to threaten any interest group that had not had fair policy warning. Medicare would obviously be very popular, but the doctors, for example, needed careful negotiation. Educational funding. Infrastructure projects. Regional development. In Victoria, for instance, the party had lost Bendigo, a very Catholic electorate, but it was on a knife edge. With work and stable solid government we might win it back. Obviously we had to keep up all the systems of contact and communication we'd established through Casey and the other sprawling outer suburban seats, especially those we'd just won.

One of the reasons Whitlam had appealed to swinging voters was that he conveyed authority and dignity in a manner reminiscent of Menzies. His bulk and eloquence gave continuity with Menzies' long incumbency, they were both barristers, both used historic and classical references to illustrate ideas and make points. Both had wit which they used to effect in the parliament. Like Menzies, Whitlam's manner was confident, even patronising.

There had been change during the Menzies years, but the very dignity and remoteness of the government, the apparent soporific order of the bureaucracy, had meant that when major restructuring such as decimalisation of measurement and currency took place, it was organised and presented to the citizens of Australia as if we were pupils in a very large school. Gorton had appeared to be a larrikin, McMahon seemed a duffer, veering from nice but ineffectual to pompous bumbling embarrassment. Holt's death and Gorton's scallwaggery, followed by McMahon's ineptitude, had removed the dignity and remoteness, and with it the awe of incumbency. As memories and experience of the war and rationing receded, and technology made events immediate, it became possible to experience the order of government as control, and its process as delay.

Inconsequential things can affect any relationship, but to have deep and lasting consequences they must trigger an underlying facet of the personality of one of the participants. In December 1972, several factors, each trivial, allowed the transfer of power from the conservative Coalition to the ALP to be far more dramatic than was desirable. Their effect on Whitlam set the frantic tone of the Whitlam years, turning what might have been a long contented marriage of party and population into a dramatic affair marked by love and bitterness. Conventions, practices, possibly the fact that the Governor-General, Paul Hasluck, was not a lawyer, and did not suggest alternative solutions to Whitlam's proposals for the transfer of power: all these intersected with other events and systems to delay the consummation of the election, and to shift the relationship from courting and happy honeymoon to romantic elopement.

The situation is complicated to explain even in retrospect. Among the mistakes made at this point was the assumption that everyone in the country understood all the complexities and thought that Whitlam's solution was the best on offer.

This was the position. The electoral office counted the votes in a particular order, *based on the previous result in each seat*, beginning with the party whose candidate won. This did not affect the result, but it slowed down counting where the voting pattern had substantially altered.

In addition, a number of sitting members of the Coalition government had retired at the 1972 election. When an electorate is vacant, the Coalition parties have a standing agreement that each party runs a candidate. This splits the conservative vote, preferences may leak; preference distribution can take longer.

It is the law that postal votes arriving up to ten days after the election must be counted if the number of outstanding postal votes might affect the result.

Also, in 1972 there were a number of close seats in which a recount was called. For all these reasons the Chief Electoral Officer advised that the Electoral Commission might not be able to declare a number of marginal seats until at least two weeks after the election.

The ALP had a policy that the caucus, the whole of the ALP parliamentary party, elected the ministry, and the prime minister then appointed ministers from that elected pool. So the ALP parliamentary party was unable, until these marginal seats were declared, formally to meet to elect the ministerial team.

And lastly, there is a convention that once an election is announced the incumbent government becomes a caretaker government, making no new decisions. McMahon conceded defeat. Invited by the Governor-General, Paul Hasluck, to form a government, Whitlam explained the dilemma. Hasluck had been a minister in Menzies' government, he could not be regarded as partisan in any way. He agreed with Whitlam that while it was constitutionally possible, it was inappropriate for McMahon to remain in office, either as caretaker or as proxy for Whitlam. Whitlam suggested that a temporary two-person ministry be formed to sit with Hasluck as the Executive Council and make urgent decisions that were administrative, that is, that did not require parliamentary authority. Hasluck agreed to this, and Whitlam and his deputy Lance Barnard were appointed as ministers of the various government departments and statutory authorities then in place.

These unusual arrangements were negotiated constitutionally, immediately announced, and explained. But they seem to have embedded in his prime ministerial persona Whitlam's tendency to behave impetuously and expect to be rewarded for it. Because the two men shared the portfolios of the previous ministries, continuity of administration was in place. But the excitement of being at last in power, and able to make effective decisions without even debating them in Cabinet, appeared to go to Whitlam's head and stay in it.

At first we all shared in the ebullience. There were indeed urgent things we'd worked for; to see them happen was very gratifying. The ALP had a clear mandate to end Australia's involvement in the Vietnam War: by arranging discharges for national servicemen, bringing home troops from Vietnam, releasing draft resisters from prison, and ending conscription, together with all the prosecutions and other processes underway as part of its administration. There were also foreign policy issues, which placed Australia in the postcolonial world; votes in the United Nations on which the ALP differed from the Coalition. These were well-publicised policies; action was appropriately urgent.

The processes for diplomatic recognition of China began without surprising anyone. Returning the equal pay case to the Arbitration Commission, and there supporting arguments for equal pay, was a solid workable symbol of the government's commitment to its policies and principles and would stimulate the economy. Referring the question of colour television to the Tariff Board might not now seem urgent, but we had been watching ourselves and the world in black and white; this would bring colour into our daily lives. Abolition of the huge excise duty on wine and the sales tax on contraceptives, and in particular on the contraceptive pill; even the simple one-off gesture of restoring his passport to the left-wing journalist Wilfred Burchett, who'd effectively been exiled by the conservative government; all these were clear actions based on well-canvassed policies that were guaranteed to put the Christmas spirit into everyone.

But Christmas was the point. The party and the country had been focussed on change for a time, the principles were in place. There was no need to behave as if there was a limited time in which to act. We had worked so carefully to change the perception of the party from a dead grey thing you would avoid if it had collapsed in the gutter. The Commonwealth government had previously moved at glacial pace, a gentle walking pace would have been an improvement, allowing the voters to take in and enjoy the very positive changes that were on view.

What appeared to be a disorganised melée of activity precipitated the conditions which shortened Whitlam's tenure – the revived thing in the gutter had become manic and multicoloured and a danger to traffic. The open-ended 'It's Time' theme had meant, to us, time to do what was necessary and then calmly to take stock and to plan, for supporters and party workers to have a rest, to use the long inert Australian summer to let everyone get used to the new order.

We hoped that things would settle down when the realities of government took over from the excitement of power. Whitlam would have appeared a decisive statesman if he had taken just a few urgent decisions, set some processes in motion, waited ten days for his ministerial team to be elected, and ensured that they move on in an orderly manner. It was only ten days. He knew, everyone knew, that there would be considerable upheaval for many sections of society when the ALP policies were implemented. Medibank would mean change for every doctor and every patient; every taxpayer would be paying a levy. Almost every schoolchild would be affected by educational funding changes. Equal pay would change the metaphor for women and have economic consequences. But Whitlam began in his very first week in office to take unexpected actions and to make the sort of unnecessary remarks that he'd made in the studio at Dunmoochin. One thing to tease a woman heavy-handedly in her husband's studio, but he was making flippant remarks as prime minister, in front of microphone and camera.

When, on 18 December 1972, one week before Christmas, the full ministry was elected and portfolios were allocated, some ministers – Clyde Cameron, Tom Uren, Bill Hayden – had all made plans and carried them forward without fuss. The tone had been set though, and Whitlam did not attempt to modify it; in fact he continued the drama.

When Tom rang to tell us about the Australia Council being on the Cabinet agenda it took only a few quick phone calls to get the item postponed until we found out what was going on. I made the calls. Each conversation confirmed the degree of competence and attitude to the job of federal minister that Clif had predicted. Clyde Cameron – cool, dry, and efficient as ever – was happy to help. He would enjoy claiming that they were too busy to worry about the arts, and he'd talk to Lionel. Tom said he would do whatever Clif wanted; he was having a wonderful time saving The Rocks, the picturesque historic area under the Sydney Harbour Bridge that had been under threat of development. I hadn't spoken to Jim Cairns for a while.

'How's it going, Jim?'

'Awful.'

'Awful?'

We knew that Tom and Clyde had carefully planned their teams, Tom to set up the new Urban and Regional Development Department, Clyde to work with the existing structure but to change its personnel. Bill Hayden had plans for structure and personnel. I wondered if the idealistic and academic Jim was having difficulty with his public servants.

'What's the problem?'

'Oh Judith, this is so boring, I hate it. Nothing but figures and reading papers.'

'Well, Jim, you are the Minister for Trade.'

'Yes. But I wish I was back on the streets leading a march.'

Which would have meant draft resisters in gaol and soldiers in Vietnam.

That is the problem with being in opposition for a long period. You will take with you into government some people who want to work off old scores, some adolescents, and very few people who have experience in administration. Some will have become acculturated to opposition; some will simply be too unsophisticated to make decisions and will be run by their staff or their departments.

While we drifted around the Coorong, getting the papers every other day, the Labor politicians began to reveal their abilities, and we and the country could see character interacting with ideology and circumstance.

As 1973 began, things between us were almost back to the beginning. Don stayed with us in Willunga, and without discussing it we all understood that neither Don nor I wanted to be more than friends. The Amors were still with us during January. Their presence meant we went to bed early; without the trigger of alcohol Clif was less likely to become angry. With a small child about, life is more domestic, and he therefore drank less.

The year's beginning consolidated Clif's reputation absolutely, with the announcement in January that he'd won the Archibald Prize for the

The Premier takes tea

second year running, with the Whitlam portrait. This third Archibald consolidated what was then fame and would now be called celebrity.

Beginning with a portrait prize, the month continued with an interesting portrait. The miner and businessman Sir Lindesay Clark, brought by Andrew Grimwade into our naked lunch, could not have been more charming. A poet in private, he was the sort of visionary that gives engineering a good name. His severe arthritis created a particular challenge; he moved constantly, shifting in his chair, because the pain became worse when he didn't move. It might have been a problem in a less straightforward man, but we were lucky; his intelligence and character were apparent. He was another of our sitters who surprised me with advice.

'Judith, always give the poem to the person for whom it's written.' And produced the one he'd written about the experience of talking to me.

Just when everything seemed on an even keel, as Clif was more sober, the ALP was less. Our troubles began again.

Before the election Gough had announced that Nugget Coombs would join his personal staff. That had seemed like a good thing: Nugget would be in his element and assist Gough in his way around the bureaucracy, leaving the arts to arts practitioners. That had been the deal, the understanding, indeed the party policy. Alas, no. In the arts, for which Whitlam had promised to take responsibility, not only the pace was too fast. It became apparent that Whitlam was extending Coombs' control, ignoring the very policies with which we'd so carefully gathered support for his election.

Clif's committee had been polite but unsophisticated. Everyone had assumed that the very important things – setting up systems for education and social security, administrative changes, complex and crucial alterations to funding – would have priority over the arts. No one had thought that personal staff meant Chairman of the Australian Council for the Arts.

But Nugget was on the loose and on the move. For a man who seeks control, the arts are a natural target, and it was an easy-to-get target in those early days of the government. Clif's policy committee had taken a businesslike approach to arts funding, because they were in business in the arts. In each arts industry there are similarities in the needs of professionals, but also differences. Each art form board was to be composed of professionals from that sector. The Council was intended to be made up of the chair of each board and people with extra expertise, legal and accounting, in the manner in which say, the dairy industry or Mining advisory councils consist of industry professionals and other experts in support. But Coombs had been left to nominate Council members, and the professionals were outnumbered; non-professionals were on the boards.

We came back to Dunmoochin in mid-January, to a message from Whitlam asking Clif to join the Council. No. Definitely not. He'd done his bit, we explained, and he wasn't a committee man. Whitlam rang several times and, more importantly, artists and other Arts Policy Committee members began to ring, worried. Clif reluctantly agreed to go on for a while, but he had to force Whitlam to put a dancer on the theatre board. And there was no community arts board. This was all precipitate, but we expected that over time things could be shaped differently.

The first sign of really bad judgement came on Australia Day 1973, less than six weeks after the full Cabinet had been sworn in. To our amazement, Whitlam decided to celebrate the day with an address to the nation in which he announced a competition for a new national anthem, to replace 'God Save the Queen'.

This single gesture sums up almost everything silly about his government. There was to be a competition process and consultation process, undecided at the time the announcement was made, which indecision of itself illustrated the ad hoc nature of the plan. When the process to decide on the anthem was announced in February it had a Maoist air about it: a selection of submitted texts would be made by an unnamed panel, and these texts would be published in a booklet to be made available to interested parties. Oh where is that booklet now?

After this, the competition for words and music would be held, the composers free to set their own, those of a collaborator, or any of the words in the booklet. Another judging panel would choose six finalist anthems, including two 'familiar or traditional' songs. The people would make a final choice on or before 26 January 1974, the method for the latter process to be determined by the Australia Council for the Arts, media representatives, the ABC and other interested organisations.

'God Save the Queen' was still played before every live performance in a mainstream theatre, commercial or subsidised, and some movie houses, and many if not most other formal events such as school or university assemblies. To change the anthem was to affect the daily lives of everyone.

Where to begin? National identity appears in so many ways to be the icing on the cake, but it is in fact the whole cake, icing included. People who take an interest in national identity are usually themselves very articulate, and they will often be conservative. Those who are conservative will have clear ideas about process. Conservatives with an idea about process in January 1973 were even more likely than usual to be edgy, as they had a new government to deal with, and many of the changes they'd voted against were already afoot. Now here was an idea that had not been mentioned in the election campaign, one that threatened their idea of continuity with the crown, the British tradition.

When you become prime minister, especially if your margin is small, your Cabinet team a little unruly, your backbench outspoken, it is best to give the appearance of being urged to make changes and to respond to the urging when it is clearly for the common good and supported by most of the community. You must seem steady, a little bit awkward about accepting ideas, but susceptible to argument.

If you want to change the national anthem, have a soldier suggest it. Have a bishop agree with him, and a cricketer. Let an actress say she likes things the way they are, and the mayor of a large regional town gently chide her. Make an announcement that you have grown up with things the way things are, but your children are telling you that you are old-fashioned. Ensure a surgeon laughs at you, and that a particularly unpleasant and aggressive club man supports you and insults your daughter. Defend your daughter and let her be seen smiling through trembling lips. Say this has all gone too far, and you want it to go away. Arrange a Royal Visit and ask a member of the royal family to say that they do enjoy a variety of anthems. See that an academic responds to this with an erudite article in the respectable press, and say that after the next election you will have a panel look at it. Wait. Most importantly, wait.

As I carefully turn the pages of the newspapers in the reading room, ensuring each settles in its place without creasing, my mind offers an image. Lunchtime. I'd be in the kitchen, Wombalong would have settled down after her morning's activities, back in her burrow perhaps, or on the couch. The scent of wholemeal bread cooling, and bowls from the local potters ready for soup from locally grown peas and stock I'd made from a fresh ham bone. I'd go to the studio to tell Clif lunch was nearly ready, and I'd hear the ute start up as he went to collect the mail and the papers from the box at the main road. We'd read them over lunch, the stories we'd heard on the morning's radio. Distance from town meant they were rarely surprising. Now, on these pages, en masse, they are: the astounding activity of the government, the number of things happening all at once. Patience is part of leadership, of maturity. But waiting seems to have been the only thing not on the federal ALP's agenda.

20

CHARACTER

Slow-cooked lamb necks,
clingstone peaches in marsala,
biscuits and cheese

The atmosphere in Canberra in early 1973 made Commonwealth government into a kind of action movie. But the plot was hard to follow, and there was no hero. To read about the early months of that year is to see goodwill thrown to the winds; to feel the tension, for journalists, between getting a good story and knowing the story was not good.

Gough Whitlam appeared magnificent. A charismatic, intelligent leader, who understood the magic of ideas and was unafraid to stand up for principle. But prime ministering is essentially management, negotiation and public relations. Understanding character is an essential requirement for success in the first element of the role; self-control in the second and third, whether in public or in private.

In the Whitlam government two men, Clyde Cameron and Tom Uren, stood out because they had brought into power a mature understanding of how people function, a sophisticated strategic plan and a capacity to manage policy. Others, such as Bill Hayden, were innovative policymakers and alert to organisational structure, but the sophisticated strategists were Clyde and Tom.

Tom Uren extrapolated socialist principles from his experience as a prisoner of war of the Japanese. He'd taken these ideas into his work as a Coles manager.

'I used our "satisfaction guaranteed" policy to help local organisations. You could take home enough crockery to provide afternoon tea for the cricket team, the mother's club, whatever fundraiser you were having, and then bring them back on the Monday morning. You just paid for the breakages.'

His awful war experiences had made Tom confident, not cynical; focussed and purposeful; like many ex-army men he was good at assessing people. He found effective competent people, appointed them, took their advice. He didn't interfere in process but brought his expansive goodwill to chairing meetings and ensuring everyone got on. Whitlam, however, was setting up problems for himself. Early on, Clif began to worry that Whitlam seemed intent on putting various shaped pegs into holes into which they wouldn't fit; not that these people were inept or incompetent, but there was a pattern of mismatching people to positions.

Ordinarily, character assessment is affected by class, culture, experience and even hope, but Clif seemed to have overcome these constraints. He couldn't always tell you what you wanted to know, but what he could tell you was always apposite. He offered, to no avail, to meet and advise Whitlam on particular appointments, because he was absolutely confident of his capacity to sum people up. I mean *absolutely* confident.

To illustrate. In 1976, after John Kerr in late 1975 had dismissed the Labor Government, I rang Ray and Betty Marginson and asked them to introduce us to someone new and interesting. Otherwise, when we left the country, which we were about to do, we would stay away. Someone who wouldn't care about our fame but see us as ourselves. We arrived a few nights later for dinner and to meet two strangers, Lois and Ted Woodward. What a coincidence, I thought. Ted Woodward is the name of the man that Whitlam had appointed, and Malcolm Fraser had then confirmed, as head of ASIO. Clif, cheerfully accepting a drink, hadn't reacted, and I thought well, that must be another Ted Woodward. After all, what would the head of the Australian Security and Intelligence Organisation be doing in the home of a small-l liberal jazz-loving university administrator and his politically active wife?

At the table, as the wine flowed and the conversation amused, it was clear that the Marginsons had met the challenge. This charming and interesting couple were typical of hundreds of intelligent pleasant Australians, the country was still itself in most of its particulars, what a lovely meal. The talk turned to recent events in Canberra. Ted remarked that he'd written to Fraser telling him he should not have acted in the way he did, so presumably he was indeed not that Ted Woodward. Clif said that Whitlam's greatest problem was that he was no judge of character.

'He always appointed the wrong person to the wrong job.' The Woodwards looked at each other. The Marginsons looked at each other. Oops.

'Always?' asked Ted.

Clif was absolute.

'Always.'

Now what to do? Ted was giving an impression of a man intrigued.

'Surely there must be one example of the right person in the right job?'

'No, not one.'

Should I set fire to my hair? Or is it more correct to set fire to one's hostess's hair? I tried to change the subject, but Ted firmly intervened.

'No, Judith, I really want to examine this.'

Well, on your own head be it, then. With the apparently casual technique of an experienced barrister, Ted proceeded to lead Clif gently down a corridor of examples of appointments, the weakness of each

explained, and Clif narrowing the corridor with instances of his own, until there was a blank wall. Ted pointed out the notice on it in black and white.

'Well, I hope you're not always right.' Clif suddenly understood. 'Oh. I see. Oh, right. Okay, okay. What has he appointed you to, then?'

'I'm the head of ASIO.'

'See what I mean?'

It was a good choice of dinner guest. If the head of the security service can roar with laughter under those circumstances, then a country can't be all bad. Not, of course, to comment on the security services or on Ted's capacity to reform them: how could one know, how can one, even in retrospect?

Encouraged by his lack of official distance, we asked Ted what ASIO thought of Lionel Murphy arriving unannounced at ASIO headquarters in March 1973. We knew from Lionel what had happened, and the background to his visit. The Commonwealth Police advised Lionel, whose ministerial responsibility as Attorney-General included ASIO, that a group of Balkan-born Australian terrorists were planning to assassinate the Yugoslav prime minister during his imminent visit to Australia. Taking with him a contingent of Commonwealth Police, Murphy flew on the instant from Canberra to ASIO's office in Melbourne, to search for the files he believed ASIO must have on this real terrorist threat, but be keeping from him. The police found none. He found that the issue was not concealment, but incompetence.

But the damage, in public perception, was done. This unannounced intervention would have been dramatic and newsworthy even if he had just ordered the Commonwealth Police to conduct a sudden search. Lionel was the least paranoid of people, but believing that the organisation was behaving unconstitutionally, he wanted to make the point by being present at the search in his capacity as Attorney-General.

ASIO lurked at the back of everyone's mind at that time. From the 1950s to the early 1970s the department was thought to be partisan, to have become part of the political process instead of offering impartial advice about threats against the state. Over the years of conservative government, the security organisations had indeed come to identify with the government they had served for so long. The process is easily understood, especially in the exaggerated atmosphere of secrecy that must prevail in such a group.

Identifying the Coalition incumbents with the nation, ASIO had begun to investigate and monitor anyone who opposed the government, including opposition members of parliament. They became unable to distinguish criminal threats to the social order not only from outspoken political disagreement, but from attendance at jazz or film festivals, or even membership of writers' groups. This made their super-efficiency seem ludicrous to anyone of any sophistication.

The communist threat had been so useful for so long to conservatives as a power tool, officially and in so many organisations, that it still divided the wider community and exacerbated the naivety of a sparsely populated nation. The ALP still assumed that ASIO was a dedicated if delusional group of people who investigated real threats from deranged individuals and from any political fringe. But no. They had been photographing the entire moratorium march, of more than 100,000 individuals who were busy declaring their views in the most public possible way, while failing to investigate a group of people secretly training in Australia for an armed uprising in Yugoslavia, and who had already been criminally violent in a number of attacks on people and property, including bombing the Yugoslav Consulate in Sydney in 1967.

Ted described Murphy's action as a decision taken after a long dinner, one that *seemed like a good idea at the time*. But as it was an abrupt decision, his staff didn't have time quietly to brief journalists, and the visit played entirely into the hands of the opposition. It was possible to describe what happened as a 'raid'; and the word *raid* gave the impression of chaos and political interference, rather than ministerial overview.

Lionel Murphy's creativity was such that the restrictions of office simply eluded him, and the portfolio he loved, that of Attorney-General, and through which he developed such far-reaching reforms, was really too constraining. His warmth and his ability to charm, his commitment and intelligence even now override for me the chaos that trailed after him, although I was very cross at the time. He loved men and women, one never felt patronised. Originally trained as a scientist, he was a brilliant dreamer, astonishingly creative, and in every way what you saw was what you got; the intelligence, the acute observation without rancour, the engagement. Lionel was not impulsive in the sense that Whitlam was impulsive, because like Clyde he valued ideas above his ego, so he wasn't trying to win. He did want more personal engagement than was useful for a politician, but the pleasure of knowing him was because he so lived in the moment, and enjoyed it, that he had no need to get on to the next thing, then the next.

More contemplative than most politicians, he retained an interest in science, reading about advances in research and wondering aloud about how they would affect society and the law. He loved to talk about ideas and explain or discuss the law; he had a commitment to education and, in those days of celebration of values through the arts, was always keen to remind us about the use and processes of scientific method.

When he was appointed to the High Court, Lionel remarked to me that he'd increased its workload, because he had announced that he would hear any application from any individual who was incarcerated and waiting trial; that is, that his view was that individual liberty was more important than an intra-state or corporate dispute.

Lionel's compassion was apparent, a presence in the room, and he was endlessly curious about people and facts. When we arrived in Sydney for him to sit for his portrait he was full of delight about his small son Cameron.

'I came into the corridor and he didn't see me. You don't often see them when they don't know you're there. He was looking in the mirror and he was practising saying, "No." He was trying all different ways, Judith. "No!" very firmly, and "No", gently, all different ways.'

This was the fastest portrait. Clif set up his paints. Lionel and he were having coffee, and I had to slip out just for an hour; as they were good friends and Lionel was quite unselfconscious about sitting, I thought Clif would be able to get started without me. Andrew Grimwade called his book on the portraits *Involvement* because that is the word Clif used all the time, what he wanted from his subjects, and with Lionel he had it. When I returned, the picture had indeed started, and was finished, Clif surprised but confident. No need to shoot him in the head this time.

Lionel's best friend in the parliament was that other intelligent compassionate visionary, Clyde Cameron. Clyde had been a shearer, and had become a force in the ALP through his work with the extremely tough Australian Workers' Union. He was de facto Minister for Labour when the two-man ministry of Gough and Lance Barnard took power while the 1972 election returns were finalised. The equal pay case was returned with Commonwealth Government support to the Conciliation and Arbitration Commission, at the time the central wage-fixing authority. It was Clyde's strategy to use the public service to move Australia to equality in employment. The most intelligent and subtlest of all the politicians in that government, his counsel and tactics steered the party through a number of crises.

Lionel had the barrister's habit of asking questions; Clyde was more direct. Time was never spent more interestingly than when we were with both of them, and like so many friends who appreciate each other they would often ring and report on each other's doings, so that we had a constant picture of what was happening in the Cabinet. Clyde had rescued me from the embarrassment of the formal evening with Don, and of course because his power base was in South Australia, he appreciated my restraint in wanting to minimise that affair. He'd given my name to his protégé Mick Young. Mick, in turn, had made me part of a small network of ALP members, mostly lawyers, around the country, with whom I could co-ordinate for publicity and on policy. Clyde stayed with us whenever he and Doris came through Melbourne, relaxing and meditating on life and the Labor party, the challenges of government, people. A brilliant strategist, he kept his ego out of the way of his plans. He was practical about daily life. When Clif and I were to go Europe together for the first time, he said, 'Judith, remember this. We spend a third of our lives asleep. When we sleep we're unconscious. You need to sleep well, you need a comfortable hotel. But you are not going to spend the other two-thirds of the time in the hotel, so you don't need an expensive one.'

All the elements that affect us, from the way we think to the weather, have the potential to affect our actions and our lives. And politics is life distilled. A politician needs to be aware of the potential effect of every technology. Just as the internet has changed communication, so the pill changed the status of women. ALP politicians had marched with people demanding an end to the Vietnam War and discrimination. But few of them contemplated the chaotic energy that would be released by the 1970s feminism that swept across the globe at this time, or anticipated the way in which it would claim the culture.

Clyde Cameron goes uncelebrated for his feminism, but he kept the noses of that sexist bunch of boys to the grindstone at all times and in every way he could. First initiating the equal pay case, he then turned to his own department, working on every level to put into practice the principle that the best person should get the job. Whitlam's response seemed more a gesture. His establishment of a post on his own staff of advisor on women's affairs had merit, but it lacked structural impact. When such issues as child care are isolated as women's issues, they became entangled with far more contentious emotive areas such as fertility and appearance. In this role the academic philosopher Elizabeth Reid made some positive administrative changes, arguing for example that all Cabinet submissions (effectively any proposed federal initiative) should include an assessment of their impact on women. But her naivety with the press and lack of ALP experience meant in the end that her appointment gave the impression of being a public relations strategy rather than a serious effort to address a serious issue.

Not her fault; she did manage a number of changes, for instance to make Commonwealth employment advertisements gender neutral. But she, in that position, was yet another of the increasingly worrying examples of Whitlam's failure to read people, always to put a round peg into a triangular hole.

In the meantime, Clyde encouraged Di Yerbury to apply for a position as a First Assistant Secretary in his Department of Labour, making her the most senior woman in any Commonwealth department. Bill Hayden had appointed Marie Coleman to set up the National Social Welfare Commission, but Di was within an established departmental structure and culture in a discipline – Industrial Relations – dominated by men. Even though the marriage bar (the rule that women who married or were married could only be employed on a temporary basis) had been removed in 1966, the culture of the public service, itself reflecting the endemic sexism of the society at the time, was such that even unmarried women had little hope of achieving senior roles. Clyde was practical about supporting Di, who had spent the first weeks of her appointment arriving at meetings at which she was the most senior officer to hear, 'Good. The minute secretary's here. Now we can start.'

Di's response to all this pressure was to work extremely hard, and Clyde saw she was unlikely to rest. So he rang me.

'Judith, are you going to be at Dunmoochin at the weekend? Good. I have a woman who needs support. She isn't taking time off, her marriage has broken up, it's a time of stress. This is the plan. I've told her she's coming to a weekend conference with me on Friday evening. She will walk out of the department with me at exactly 5 pm. You will be parked outside. She will be carrying her briefcase, and another member of my staff will be carrying her suitcase. He will open the back door and put in the case. I will take her briefcase, and open the passenger door. I will close the door, keeping the briefcase. You will drive off and you will deliver her to the department on Monday morning.'

And on the Friday there they were. Door open. Door closed. Foot on accelerator.

'Hello, I'm Judith Pugh. The minister wants you to have a weekend off, so I'm taking you to stay with us. I'm to return you on Monday.'

Clyde was as good a judge of character as Clif, and he'd realised that Di and I would become friends. She became the first senior Commonwealth public servant to model nude for Clif, prompting Race Mathews to remark that he could hardly wait till she made the cover of *Time*.

Clyde took every opportunity to recommend women to his colleagues, suggesting Mary Gaudron, for instance, as an Arbitration Commissioner. Clyde loved people and treated everyone as equal, but like Clif he made moral judgements and was tough. Similarly, his demeanour was that of a sensitive man who'd grown up with a bunch of toughs and had adopted their manners in order to manage them; in Clif's case the army had provided the shell, in Clyde's the shearing sheds. Both of them observed, quietly, guardedly. Clif when drunk became at times demonstrative, Clyde on only two occasions appeared at all emotional when he was with us, although he could be scathing and, of necessity over the years, ruthless.

I was in the way of a bad mood of his when he and Doris arrived one evening to stay. He'd had an infuriating day with a very inept Department of Immigration, and had missed lunch. I had decided on a slow-cooking casserole of lamb necks, and had a dish of clingstone peaches covered in marsala in the smaller of the ovens. Clyde had a headache and was very hungry; I could see he was containing his irritation. I said I'd just check the oven, but when I went over, its door, where the marsala had formed a cloud, blew off.

'Now we'll have to wait even longer,' came the anguished cry.

I was able to fix the door back on, got some biscuits and cheese, and suggested we go out onto the deck for a breath of country air.

'Look, Clyde, now isn't that lovely? That's what you come up here for.' There was a delicious possum, in the tree over the deck, and I stepped forward to point at it.

It promptly pissed on my upturned face.

'Well, Clif,' said Clyde turning to him, happy at last, 'that does make it all worthwhile.'

But in the end Clyde's commitment overcame his judgement. Realistic and depressed by the ineptitude of Whitlam's appointments, in particular of Kerr, Clyde became cynical about the chances of re-election, and tried to bed in advantages to the trade union movement that only assisted in rendering the government less electable.

Here is another issue you'll have to handle if you win government after a long period: the deep commitment to a particular portfolio of your ablest people. Your party will have developed policies with which they are identified, and they will have such command of the field, its personalities and its regulation, they will be effective. But then, initial changes made, they should move on to another, more senior position. Clyde was too long in labour and industrial relations, and his skills and sophistication ought to have been used elsewhere once he'd restructured the department and implemented the party's fundamental policies.

Clyde's portrait, painted in 1974, wasn't difficult, and we all were pleased with it at the time. But soon his hand, enlarged at the base of the painting, seemed clumsy, and Clyde wondered about it; Clif kept meaning to have another look at it, but somehow, while I was with Clif, it was never done. Clif kept worrying about the puzzle of Clyde's relationship to power, what the image meant, and he did a series of paintings in which Clyde is a figure threatened and threatening. The paintings were prescient. When Whitlam finally moved him to the Science portfolio Clyde was passionately angry, and his failure to toe the public relations line helped bring Whitlam down.

Clyde went further than giving me advice during the portrait process. I came downstairs one evening at Dunmoochin to have Clyde tell me that Clif had decided to swap his portrait for a block of land that Clyde owned in Adelaide, and to put that block in my name. To Clyde's chagrin, I refused. Long before I could, he saw how my options were being limited, how powerless I was. After this he kept looking for paid work for me. Registry offices were then virtually the only places to marry, except for buildings dedicated to religious worship. Lionel, intending to reduce the power of the church, expanded the ceremonial options for marriage in place and style by introducing marriage celebrants. Clyde thought this would be good for me.

A telephone call: 'Judith, Lionel's had a wonderful idea. He's going to arrange it so you can get your friends drunk at parties and marry them. It's called marriage celebrant and you could be one.'

And although things were beginning to get rough, and sad, it was wonderful to think that the man on the other end of the telephone was a Cabinet minister who retained his sense of humour.

21

ABORTION

Roasted drunk

The immense goodwill that focussed on the federal election was still in place early in 1973. The Coalition under Henry Bolte was firmly in control of the Victorian Parliament, but if there were a run-on of votes and enthusiasm for change then Clyde Holding might pick up some seats, and begin the way forward to an ALP government in Victoria. Clif had not yet had to begin a public campaign to rein in Coombs on the Australia Council, and no one really worried about the ASIO raid: that organisation was still tarnished by its anti-left stance. Besides, these issues were federal, they didn't intersect with state issues, so prospects for the forthcoming state election were hopeful.

Imagine my surprise, therefore, when one evening in March Beatrice Faust rang me to ask if I'd write to the papers saying I'd had an abortion. I was in the pantry. I knew Beatrice from my time at Melbourne University; she was the most consistent and thorough opponent of abortion laws. But I was interested in strategy, and although abortion laws were indeed bad, this was an issue guaranteed to derail the plan. It wasn't a federal issue. As far as I knew the police had control of the situation in Victoria; that is, they allowed competent if black-market professionals, doctors, to perform the service and stopped backyard operators. Beatrice had started Women's Electoral Lobby, WEL, a non-party political group that canvassed candidates for their attitude to 'women's issues'. I thought it was for nice middle-class women who wanted to have equal pay and child care and legal abortion, without having to bother with fighting conscription or addressing issues such as the environment or wider economic and infrastructure questions.

'Now, Beatrice, why would I do that?'

'Well, without warning us, so we haven't had the opportunity even to start a campaign, David McKenzie and Tony Lamb have announced they will table a bill to remove the abortion laws in the ACT. We are really a bit annoyed. Because you're involved with the ALP I thought you might want to be involved. As a start I'm asking as many women as possible to write to the papers and say they've had an abortion.'

'Beatrice, may I have your number so I can ring you back?'

I rang Race. No, he knew nothing about this and was as concerned as I was. So I rang David, who told me that in Canberra Moss Cass, the member for Maribyrnong and federal Minister for the Environment, had bumped into him and Tony in Parliament House and asked them what they were going to do about abortion. To which the correct answer was 'Nothing'. *Nothing*, because it is a State Issue. *Nothing*, because if the ACT electors want to press the government on this they can. *Nothing*, because it will not benefit the voters in my marginal seat. *Nothing*, because my marginal seat is in Victoria. *Nothing*, because I am a very inexperienced politician. *Nothing*, because the Bill will not have the support even of my colleagues in the ALP. *Nothing*, because I have to spend all my time looking like a helpful ordinary bloke, so that I can convince the electors in my marginal seat to re-elect me. *Nothing*, because even the party platform may unsettle some people, and this issue will attract the opposition of the Catholic Church, which is the best organised and most influential lobby group in the country, and we have only just neutralised their opposition by promising state aid to schools. *Nothing*, because there is a state election coming up in Victoria, I am a Victorian Labor Party politician, and this will have the added effect of embedding this divisive issue in the middle of that campaign.

The *Medical Practice Clarification Bill*, which was not a piece of government legislation, but a private members' Bill (and thus had the added effect of allowing conservatives in the ACT to claim that the issue was no business of Victorians and was patronising to citizens of the ACT), was set down for Thursday 10 May.

We'd hoped for a calm and sober government; that Whitlam, winning, would curb his tongue; that responsibility would cloak the new ministers with sense, if not wisdom. That after a period of settling down the Australia Council, Clif and I could retire from politics. Apparently not. I went outside into the cool night and thought. All that effort might be worthless, all those meetings and the driving and the cakes and tickets and phone calls. I had never wanted personal publicity, everything had been about promoting Clif and the party, and carefully calculated, so that where the ALP was concerned, Clif's commitment to landscape painting linked in to the main issues, to the environment and the expression of Australian culture. We'd wanted people to see the ALP as stodgy with a contemporary edge, not radical and threatening. The very last thing I wanted was to revisit the question of fertility, of pregnancy, of foetuses. It hadn't even been a year. I did not want to write a letter.

But I must. There were three years to the next election, and the only way forward was to make abortion a non-issue by making it middle-class. The argument would have to be legal and political, and yes, Beatrice was right, to have effect, someone had to own up to having an abortion. I would write a letter. I rang Beatrice and told her that as it was obvious it was too late for the Bill to be withdrawn, the local electoral damage was already done. So I would write to the newspapers in order to try to contain that damage. I also rang my youngest sister, Rosemary, who was at a Catholic school, to warn her. She said that she agreed with me about the law, not to worry, she'd deal with it. I sent off the letter.

Graham Perkin telephoned. 'Judith, I think if I publish this it will change the whole debate, I think it will change the law. I'm sure you can carry it through, but I wanted to ring. This will be terrific pressure on you, will you be okay?'

I would have to be.

'I'll publish it with a headline, once the issue gets going.'

And there it is on 26 April 1973 in the bound copies of *The Age* in the State Library of Victoria, the personal statement enclosed in the legal, practical, political, even the constitutional realities, with Graham's headline.

Present Conditions Terrify

Sir,

The arguments of the Anti-abortion lobby would be so much more convincing if they went further than treating a woman as an incubator and dealt with life after birth of the child they demand she have.

You point out appropriately that these arguments do not sound well from those who oppose the only efficient readily available contraceptive (*The Age*, 18th:4th).

In their literature these people say that 100,000 abortions are currently being performed illegally in Australia. I have had to have two abortions, and I suppose that most of the other abortions are performed under the same sleazy and terrifying conditions. Do these people imagine that they will prevent people having abortions by their guilt-provoking inaccurate literature? Of course not. All they want is to prevent women having abortions under sterile and safe conditions.

In the ACT in the last election the voters, men and women,

had the opportunity to vote for a Labor candidate who ran
against Kep Enderby on this issue alone. Mr Enderby believes
abortion is a question for the woman and her doctor – his
opponent was against this view, while endorsing every other
Labor policy. The anti-abortion candidate lost his deposit.
The McKenzie-Lamb Clarification Bill will not affect Victorians.
Both the lobbyists and the politicians should remember this,
and look to the views of the voters in the ACT.

Judith Pugh (Cottlesbridge)

How to achieve fame overnight without ever wanting to.

I'd thought that mine would be one among a number of letters
published from women who'd had abortions; but no, for three very
full weeks it appeared I was the only woman in the country who was
admitting in print to this experience. In the main body of *The Age*,
Melbourne's paper of record, there were a few opinion pieces. A
number of the state parliament election campaign stories mention the
issue, but within the context of women's rights, which were becoming
more mainstream; the candidates attended a public forum organised by
WEL at which one older woman became very angry and said that she
had to have a number of abortions, but no one seems to have followed
this up.

I rang Rosemary again, she congratulated me on the letter. Any
problems at the school? I'd hated every minute of the place, but because
she was disabled, the nuns were patronisingly good to her. Nevertheless
I thought they might make life difficult.

'No,' cheerily, 'they haven't mentioned you. We came into class and
there was a letter on the blackboard for us to copy out and send to
our MP or to the paper. I put up my hand and said that I wouldn't be
writing any letter, I wished I hadn't been born, and that it was unfair for
Mum to have had to have me, I hated my physical condition. Then the

rest of the class said they wouldn't write either.'

'You know I'm glad you're alive, don't you?'

'Oh yes, I know you are, it's just that I'm not, a lot of the time.'

The decision to be sterilised had been easier because Rosemary was fifteen years younger than me and I expected to care for her when she was older.

The letters columns and MP's letterboxes were flooded with letters. Most of the debate in the print media was conducted in the letters columns. The vivid public argument was on television and radio, and I was lucky to have observed Clif handling those media. I was interviewed constantly on both. Fortunately, it was a story the journalists wanted to tell effectively, and if the interviewer is sympathetic then it is easier to put the message across.

1960s Police Rounds. A young journalist, committed to exposing corruption, saving the world, you spend quite a bit of time watching the police ordering the town at night; two drunks fighting ineffectually, their injuries almost accidental, men and women your own age sprawled unconscious in smashed cars. You see wounds from vicious assaults and sad murder victims, accidental drowning. You learn that when a suicide hangs himself his neck stretches, and that when a drunk camping in the park rolls unconscious into his fire the neighbours will smell him cooking. You understand that vomit, blood, piss and shit are the constant sights and smells for the police. You see prostitutes on the street, how they are at risk, that a brothel offers some shelter, and you come to understand why they are tolerated; the impulse to turn a blind eye to what is in fact illegal conduct.

You go with the police to see the corpse of a woman who has died from a backyard abortion, and it is a woman who was desperate, and her distraught husband is comforting the other children, and you see why it is better to allow a doctor to do it with sterile equipment designed for it. And you see how easy it is for these tolerances to be exploited, for the doctor or the madam is vulnerable to threats. They need police protection on the side; that is, they ask for help as they are providing a service. A police officer risks career openly to tolerate criminal activity; the police are underpaid, money changes hands, a system of protection develops almost inadvertently, blackmail is possible, the areas of tolerance are extended, and in the end evil gently becomes systematic.

Journalists wanted abortion to be legal because they understood, from observation, how its illegality corrupted the legal system. They also understood that the argument could not be made in these terms to people who lived in the suburbs and mowed the nature strip and who worried about pre-school education and the mortgage. Television, film and the internet have integrated images and understandings across the culture now; it takes an effort to deny them and denial is ineffective, but we were only then beginning to live through and with television, so polite formal language was the key.

I know this consciously now, it was instinctive then.

There was very little time to organise any form of public support, but Beatrice and her Abortion Law Reform Society were flat out; she had always been very well organised. Sydney journalist Teresa Brennan and I wrote a statement and asked a series of public figures to sign a letter stating their opposition to abortion laws, and this became a full page advertisement in *The Australian*, and a news story. I decided that we needed a sporting hero to emphasise that this was an issue that affected everyone, that it was not confined to any particular class, it was not aspirational, not about popularity or style.

Footballers in those days were famous: muddy, but never celebrities. The footballer Ron Barassi had a silent number, but I rang the operator on the enquiries line. She telephoned his number and explained who I was and why I was calling. His wife took my call.

'Ron believes in that, yes, he'll sign that.'

Clif took the petition to a meeting and the Australia Council members signed and, remarkably, the Governor of South Australia, Sir Mark Oliphant. Well, perhaps not so remarkable. His Premier asked him to.

To this time all the focus of our publicity had been on Clif. I'd been in the occasional photograph, celebrating the Archibald, offering to help Whooper fight conscription, nude on the telly, but that was for Clif, or for the ALP. The personal spotlight was intense, with some difficult and some positively weird results. The postmaster at Hurstbridge rang, telling Clif there was a parcel for me as well as the daily bundle of letters we were getting, and he'd called the policeman, could Clif come down? They didn't think it would be good for me. It was the smell that alerted them; someone had gone to the trouble of parcelling up a rabbit foetus and mailing it to me.

After one of my first television appearances I was walking to a seat in a lecture theatre and a woman approached me.

'Did you see Judith Pugh on television last night?'

A moment of reflection on my own reality, and not wanting to be impolite, 'I think I am Judith Pugh.'

Indignantly, turning her back as if I'd offended her, 'Oh, so you are.'

Both Clif and Don encouraged me to see the funny side of this sort of incident, and the positive side, as I had to debate people who kept asking if I understood that tiny foetuses were cut up. Not that either of them knew about that conversation, that was hidden, taken out and considered when I was alone at night. I was waking up in the early dawn now, and when no guests were about, wrapping myself in a blanket on a window seat, waiting for Wombalong to come out of her burrow for an early morning cuddle. To make abortion polite, so it could be talked about openly and not hidden away, to take the shame out of it for the families who were hiding it, would allow something to come out of nothing.

The vote was lost. That was predictable. Race Mathews tried to deflect the entire issue into a 'Royal Commission into Human Relationships', which bizarre concept, instead of deflecting it, became a sort of floating focus of frustration as it toured the nation taking submissions. Clyde Cameron wanted a Catholic judge he said he could trust as president of this commission, but I didn't trust any judge or any Catholic, and after having some fun with telegrams from Whitlam, 'My Bishop trumps your Judge', had the Anglican Bishop Felix Arnott appointed to the job. Clyde was focussed on changing the law; I wanted to change the tone of the debate, as I couldn't see what possible outcome the ramshackle idea would have. What was unpredictable was that I'd somehow gone too far.

On the Thursday evening before the Friday vote the ABC current affairs radio program *PM* had played an interview with me. It was recorded at Dunmoochin, and there had been a television crew there too, and I'd said to wait and I'd make some tea before they headed back to town. I'd been talking about the law, not morals, about the way unworkable laws corrupt, the mantra that it was about choice, no one wanted to force women to have abortions, the same arguments that are always made.

Then the journalist asked, 'How did you decide to have an abortion?'

It was the way she put it. *How*, not *why*; so the question was not limited to 'What were your reasons?' I stopped to think. I wanted to answer so that I brought the issue back to the human. I didn't want to be personal in the sense of detail, because I had not been desperate at the time or raped, but I didn't want to seem callous . . . '*Always remember, you may not like what the interviewer asks or says, but you are not talking to the interviewer. You are talking to the audience. Use the question to say what you want.*'

I saw the sound man wait, and then as his hand moved to switch off so that we could start again, I just said, 'In tears, I think, the first time . . .' and we all sat for a moment contemplating that, and he turned off, and one of the television journalists clapped, and another one said,

'That will do it.'

We all knew he didn't mean get the Bill through; he meant that little phrase would change the atmosphere. The *PM* program that evening was devoted to the issue and then just before the end the announcer said, 'We're going to play the credits now, and then we are going to play the last interview after that, before we go off air.'

And they played the credits, left the silence, and then a longer silence afterwards, and then, softly, the music with which the show always ended. Graham Perkin heard it and rang to congratulate me. So it all seemed worthwhile.

For four days. The three weeks had been exhausting, and such a relief when it ended. Or when I thought it had ended. My understanding of the function of fame had been quite sophisticated enough to know that it would help Clif get the public to focus on the anti-war message, and on what we were doing to our environment. Fame and celebrity render one a mirror of expectations and desire, and for Clif it was manageable because the life he was living was about the issues on which he spoke out. He was a painter, it was about art; he painted the narrative of life in nature and nature's rhythms, it was about the environment; he was an ex-soldier, it was about war. My issue had been educational funding, that was in hand, and otherwise I worried about the things in society that concerned him. He could do all the publicity, he was credible and he'd achieved his position through skill and commitment and years of hard work. If I had a career at all, he was my career. I didn't have any urge to continue to campaign about feminism; there were women with careers, there were women who were philosophers and really good historians to do that. I wasn't even a lawyer, and abortion was about the law.

But inadvertently I'd become a symbol, and what I'd done was be too effective. We went to an opening in Melbourne on the Tuesday after the Friday vote. In a not even very radical analysis, women were at the time the underclass, are the underclass culturally even now, and it is a truism to say that if you represent the desires of an underclass you had better be careful what that underclass will think. The happy gossipy noise of the opening was loud through the closed glass doors as we arrived at Réalités Gallery that evening, and it was surprising that they fell silent as we walked in. I looked around to see who was behind us but no, it wasn't that. Then from the centre of the crowd a woman's voice.

'I suppose she thinks she's the only one ever to have had an abortion.'

As the implications of this hit me, Clif was there, walking me on, towards someone sensible, and saying quietly, 'It's good, it's good, you've made it popular.'

And that was true. But for me, it wasn't good.

We both now had public personae that were at odds with our selves. He had not wanted to be in arts politics, I had not been ready to theorise in public. But through force of circumstance, we were famous, alone and together.

22

GOING ON

*Iceberg lettuce, well-hung beef,
an extra glass of brandy*

The abortion law campaign had brought us back almost to where we started. Clif had been encouraging and protective, never letting me down; through those weeks there had been no difficult angry nights, so I had hopes that the worst time was over. A show of his pictures was touring the Victorian regional galleries in 1973, and we decided to travel to the openings. Eric McIlree had told us that trainee commercial pilots who wanted to get up their hours would fly without charge; we only had to pay for fuel, accommodation and meals, and we could travel from the local airstrip. This gave a pleasant rhythm to the year, visiting the paintings every few weeks, seeing the history of the towns through their buildings. We could see the state from a different point of view. We stayed with charming energetic families across Victoria, and my new public persona took the burden of speaking from Clif, who was constantly asked, but who did not enjoy articulating things except in paint. There was one slight problem: the baby's death had left me with physical damage, so that every month my disabling pain had to be controlled by morphine. When these events coincided with the show, my degree of suffering depended on the local doctor.

But the year was also to be broken up by Australia Council meetings, and these were not a force for good in our personal life. Once it became apparent that Nugget Coombs' agenda was to continue as before, in spite of the careful policy development by Clif's committee, Clif began drinking and becoming angry again. Australia was out of Vietnam, so the focus at first was blurred. It would start with denunciations of people like Coombs who wanted power, but who did not exercise it properly. This would lead to the worst irresponsibility, to take a country into war. Then the horror stories were repeated, his own war stories, and then one in which Japanese prisoners were shot and killed.

This story had begun as a symbolic tale, an example of how bad things could get, how war made beasts of everyone; it was reported, a sort of army myth. It had happened in another battalion, another company, another unit. He knew men who'd talked to the soldier murderers; then he'd talked to them himself.

And as it got nearer it became more detailed. I could see the gully where the Australians camped; I knew that the light was pale even at midday, because of the green of the jungle. I knew the stream at the bottom could be heard at night. That the orders to hold your position were tiresome, because the enforced stillness meant that your body wanted to relax; yet the need for caution was almost more urgent when you were camped on the edge of enemy territory than when you were on the move. I knew what it was to creep down to the stream for water, never at the same time of day, because the enemy might be watching.

I heard the astounding sound of the Japanese soldiers banging their tin cups together as they approached the stream, and then I heard them talking loudly. With my companions I waited, some time after they left. Then tentatively, watchfully, the others on guard, two of us went to the stream with our cups rattling. I knew that this developed into a routine, and the Japanese soldiers waved to the Australians, and that each group casually went down for water each day for several days.

Then they came down in file, all of them, and up the side of the gully where the Australians were camped. And there they surrendered, and were made welcome. It is astonishing how much you can communicate with goodwill even with very little language in common. You can discover that the enemy is not the enemy, but a young man just like you. That he believes, as you have believed, that he is fighting to defend his women from you and his country from invasion by you. That he and his fellow soldiers are not depraved subhuman monsters, but ordinary people who are sick of fighting. They have read the leaflets dropped by the RAAF that say they'll be taken care of when they surrender; indeed, he and his companions have brought one of these leaflets with them. He is so relieved that the leaflet has proved true, that he needs no longer go hungry, march in fear. Kill.

You all camp together for a couple of days. You know you should have started off through the jungle, there are standing orders about prisoners. They are to be treated well and delivered to base camp. Which is some miles back, through territory in which Japanese soldiers, still committed to their emperor, will shoot at you and at your new companions. But this is a holiday, you are all relaxing. There is no rush.

And then the radio crackles, and you have orders to go forward.

And somehow – it is inconceivable when you think about it now – somehow a decision is made that the trip back is not worth it. You break camp. You explain to the Japanese – no longer prisoners, just soldiers, friends – that you are taking them back to base, because you've had orders to move on.

They say goodbye to the rest of the unit. You pick up your pack and your gun.

And you take them out, and shoot them.

And come back to your unit, and say that they tried to escape.

And you all go forward, and you never speak of it to each other.

I don't remember when I was certain that Clif had been the murderer. Because the anger happened to me, and the fear, I wasn't objective, in the sense that a counsellor or even a friend might be. There was such obvious despair. The tough, strong man crumbled, staggered, before the cold angry man appeared. Early on, the bouts of anger had happened when we were alone for a couple of days in a row, and because this was quite rare, they'd been intense but infrequent. In late 1971, they had been more frequent; chaotic and rambling, but at that time the murder story was still in the third person.

I think the story crystallised in 1973. When the Amors left for the Mornington Peninsula, we were alone; and before the Australia Council we were very happy. Clif always loved the late summer, as the grass became silver-gold, the days long. He had money, from the book and the Archibald; we re-hung the house together, because so many of the paintings had left on tour. I had decided to return to Melbourne University, to see if I wanted to resuscitate the law degree I'd turned into a Bachelor of Arts; classes gave structure to the week. This gave us a reason to end the regular all-comers Sunday lunches, so we had more control over the house and its quiet spaces. He had what he'd wanted: unassailable reputation, money, a comfortable house.

But when we get what we want, particularly when we have struggled for it, particularly when what we have is so much more than we asked for, we have to deal with it. Despite comfort, and love, and money, he was still the young soldier; the struggling artist; his mind telling him not to rest, even though he was still. Even though the enemy had surrendered.

After the election and Australia's withdrawal from the Vietnam War, the bad nights happened often when dinner guests left, or when we came home after an opening or party. I learned to keep neutral: containing my thoughts in the hope that he would be engaged with a conversation or an idea and stay content, or really enjoy himself and be full of delight and affection on the way home.

I never managed to develop effective techniques for deflecting the mood, or preventing its development, but every now and again I could make him laugh so that he forgot the anger. We'd arrive home after a party and I'd drive round and around the roundabout, or as we went into the house from the drive I'd strip. If I could get him to talk about the Contemporary Art Society and the Reeds, or to tell me what the people we'd met that night were like – the elements of their character that he could see in their faces and hands – that would sometimes work. Oddly enough, if I could get him to tell the stories of the war that were about having fun that worked, too; although it had its obvious risks. If he began to drink when we were alone I'd try to sleep in the guest bed; if he calmed down before coming upstairs to bed he didn't wake me, but if he hadn't calmed down then it was frightening and unpleasant.

His conflict was made worse because he first painted Tom Uren at this time. He loved the company of this big, exuberant man, but all the while, at the back of his mind, was the image of Tom as a young soldier, captive, taken by Japanese soldiers to a prisoner-of-war camp, but not killed; that the enemy he'd abused in his letters to his mother had behaved correctly, when he had not.

He didn't admit his involvement at this time. The story became personalised slowly, amid a chaos of anguish and fear. The anger itself toughened me and made me still, giving me the power to listen. I suppose he was afraid that if he actually admitted it to me I would tell people, or even go to the army, or the police. He knew I thought about the relationship of such acts to society. He knew that somewhere in the jungle were the bodies of his victims, and that they had families, who did not know where they were lost, who were owed an apology. He knew I thought about the human element. He must have feared I would leave.

But in 1973 the realisation kept me there. Once I understood what he had done, I knew I should stay; to help him through it and to face it. I thought it was why I was there, to let him tell the tale and, by exposing it, deal with it.

How to proceed would take some thought.

Meanwhile, there was our daily life; full of interest, friends, food; the beauty of the autumn in the bush, the animals, and opportunities to use a growing number of public occasions to talk about the environment. Best of all, to get to know the country.

Barney Davis rang, to say it was raining. The Coopers had flooded; when it receded we could use his truck to go up and have a look, it had four-wheel drive. I was relieved to hear Clif tell Barney that we'd be up the week he was supposed to go to an Australia Council meeting. Was Clif going to miss the meeting?

'No, he said he'd get them to kill a beast so we could have a barbecue. In that case we'll go up a week later than he expects us. I'll ring Barney the day before we were to leave and say we're delayed a week. This will give the beast a week to hang; we'll be able to chew and swallow it.' We would leave our car with Barney, and head north.

One of our guests said how lucky I was to have such a holiday. Such was the conception of our life at home and, as it were, abroad. But I wouldn't actually be on holiday. My kitchen at Dunmoochin was efficient, but I was still catering for many guests with minimal water, cooking on two Bunsen burners backed up by an electric wall oven. Our nearest village, Hurstbridge, is almost a suburb of Melbourne now, but then it was a sleepy rural place, with few shops apart from the post office and the police station. The general store stocked iceberg lettuce and tomatoes, but for supplies for our constant visitors and houseguests I drove to Melbourne twice a week. Housekeeping was about monitoring water in the tanks and gas in the bottles, keeping the wicks of the kerosene lamps trimmed and the glass clean in case of electricity failure, maintaining stores, disposing of one's own rubbish, travelling to the Melbourne markets and particular shops to buy healthy interesting food.

Holiday, if I ever had one, certainly wouldn't be camping. Although this trip would not be holiday, this was Clif's longed-for country, and he had been tranquil there. To avoid a drunken night on the train, I drove to Mildura. I also wanted to see the changes in the landscape as we travelled. I was learning to observe the European overlays, to understand Clif's indignation at the ecological impact of exotic farming, of superphosphate and massive irrigation, how this affected the look and the state of the land: the colours, the harsh marks of the roads and angles of the fences, the glare of aluminium agricultural sheds. He disapproved even of the older marks of settlers, the way nineteenth-century cottages snuggled into the folds of hills, the softened red roofs, the gentler oaks and quinces around them. He knew I responded to these, but what he wanted was the bush or the empty desert. For me it had been harsh, that first Tibooburra experience, and as the softening grey gums and the autumn wattle gave way to scrub and orange dust out of Mildura I imagined the next few weeks as endurance.

People in Tibooburra kept talking about the drought breaking. To make conversation I asked how long since it had rained.

'Forty-five years.'

'That's not a drought,' I remarked to Clif, 'that's a condition.'

'Yes, they aren't farmers, they're miners. They don't plan, they pick up the soil. It's not harmony with nature. In their minds they haven't left Europe. They'll overstock the country now. This trip will be important because we'll see the growth that comes after rain before they get the chance to spoil it.'

After a couple of nights of barbecue and roast mutton, we left the car with Barney, loading our supplies into the back of the ute along with petrol and water for the journey north. This was long before four-wheel driving became a lifestyle choice; we would be alone for most of the time. The Tibooburra policeman had radioed to the stations along the route to Cooper's Creek to say we were coming; people would expect us to call in, or they'd come to look for us. Everyone was eager to know about the journey: the rain had been such a phenomenon and the flood hundreds of miles wide.

I was to drive, as usual, so that Clif was free to look at the landscape. While Clif secured the load, Barney explained that the truck had a few idiosyncrasies. The steering was a bit slack, so you had to spin the wheel fast to get a grip, five to seven times would do. He showed me how to engage four-wheel drive, and as an afterthought, mentioned the brakes. They needed a bit of pumping. I pressed my foot straight on the floor.

'Barney, there's no resistance.'

'No worries, just keep pumping, once you get going she'll be right.'

Oh. I hadn't driven a four-wheel drive before; perhaps that was the difference. If it had even been a normal country road ahead of us I might have demurred, but there were instead only empty miles, no other traffic but kangaroos and dingoes. The only people on the road would be those looking out for us. Steering was not as relevant as usual, nor perhaps were brakes. When in the outback . . . Clif got in beside me, and I drove down the main street, onto the gibber plain towards the Queensland border, where Ernest Cooke had paced, all that time ago. I felt his grandson relax beside me as I pointed the truck towards the rabbit-proof fence.

Although I'd known it was a fence, I realised as we approached it that I'd thought it was a metaphor. Or at least I was surprised it was so fence-like, so apparently flimsy; and that it had a gate. Which we nearly hit. Clif was surprised, but he supposed that, after all, I was unfamiliar with the truck. He was irritated by and rude about the wild swerves as we met the first of the seventy miles of sand dunes that differentiate New South Wales from Queensland, but insisted that I didn't need to engage four-wheel drive, as it would use too much petrol. By the end of the first day's driving I had the hang of the truck but I was rather exhausted, as the wheel-spinning to get a grip made each jolt an event; each slight deviation from straight ahead a great deal of effort.

Because I was concentrating on the hundred or so metres in front of the truck, watching for the smallest variation in the track in order to deal with it, I didn't see the country. In mid-afternoon Clif saw somewhere to camp and directed me off the road, which required intense concentration on the spot exactly in front of the bonnet. I pulled up as directed, got out of the truck, and there in front of us was a lake. Our arrival had startled a flock of parakeets that swung above us like a green cloud. The grey-green scrub was full of birdlife, the orange soil covered in small flowering plants.

I had thought I would endure dust and heat, eking out water. But this was Arcadia.

There is rarely silence in the evening in the desert: the birds are nesting, animals call to each other, the fire crackles. The sweetness of the air and the scent of the smoke made the food seem perfect, and we slept in the open; the rain had stopped. I woke when it was cold, just before dawn, and built up the fire. We hadn't brought any wine with us, and over the billy coffee the night before we'd talked about space and time, about what the land meant to Indigenous people and to us, whose culture opposed it but who loved it and wanted to live in it.

There were bad times with Clif, but he was one of the most interesting, intelligent men I had met, and my life with him extraordinary. The sorrow about the baby would always be there, but I might as well use the freedom that being childless brings: my life would not be structured by parental responsibilities. I could travel the country and learn about it. I had freedom to speak out about things that concerned me. I could wake in the illimitable space and stretch as one could never stretch in the city. I could watch the sun come up across a temporary lake, see a mob of kangaroos come to drink. I could feel perfectly happy.

I don't know how long the journey took. Clif spoke of time as local in that country, but for us it was more than local, it became personal. In the desert, when we were alone, he was never angry, never bitter. As city and market and politics dropped away we talked at night, about history, about ideas and the place of painting in relation to them, about the purpose of an artist. He had listened in the desert to zoologists and palaeontologists, to stockmen in pubs, and over many years he'd made his own observations. And he had read and thought. These times brought us close and their gentle depth held us against the pressures of the rest of our lives.

Clif adopted an extremely blunt and apparently uneducated, in fact apparently unread persona on social occasions, and was focussed and blunt in public. People often patronised him, and I would look across and wonder that they couldn't see it as a technique to see into their souls, or their shallowness. During the days of that journey we didn't talk much at all: I drove, he looked, we thought, and the track took us up the country. We called in at a couple of stations; silent families offering cups of tea. We camped early each day so Clif could 'look and put', always beside water. I could watch the pelicans circling overhead, and a heron on a branch over the water drying its wings, one and then the other, slowly, as if it was examining its own abstract shapes.

The driving got easier except where the Coopers had crossed the road. The surface consisted of soil impacted over many years, so several centimetres of apparent road remained in place. But the water had undermined it, and as we drove, the upper layer would give way and the truck drop; on one occasion we got out to see what damage had been done, the hole was seventy centimetres deep. Still no four-wheel drive, though.

I knew he made ridiculous demands. For me it was something about face, about meeting and overcoming each challenge without appearing even to notice it was a challenge. Performing impossible tasks without flinching was a transaction in power, and to make the task seem effortless amused me. Besides, life is a continuum; it offers its own rewards. Sometimes when we labour patiently something delightful happens.

We came to Innaminka, where the publican had been expecting us. The pub was the only building, rough, of corrugated iron. The men in the bar knew that we were the first up from Tibooburra since the rain. They asked Clif about the state of the road, and agreed it was rough going. He talked about the difficulties, the way the track was undermined; anyone who heard him would have thought he'd driven at least some of the way. It was pleasant to be quiet and reflect on the way men get the message across to each other about how tough they are by talking about tough conditions.

Then the publican asked if we could move the truck, he needed to unload some casks. I'd left the keys on the bar and went to pick them up, but Clif had them and was out the door. I wondered if he'd remember what I'd told him about the brakes and steering. Obviously one couldn't rush after him to remind him, he might lose face in front of all these blokes. Corrugated iron is fairly flimsy, so I didn't think there would be too much damage. I moved beside one of the sturdy trunks holding up the roof. Sure enough, moments later, he drove the truck into the bar. I had an extra brandy, in quiet celebration.

23

DOUBLE DISSOLUTION

Fresh caught fish, red wine

I think of it as a life in sections, each lived separately but at once. There was Dunmoochin, the wombats and the emus, the kangaroos. There were our friends: old friends, and some we met as portrait subjects or elsewhere in the art world, some through political activities. I made the mistake of agreeing to attend an abortion law conference to talk about political strategy, and was rescued from a group of radical feminists by Carole Baker, the first woman mayor of North Sydney, and Judith Malcolm, an immensely witty and practical member of Women's Electoral Lobby. They gave me a base in Sydney less committedly masculine than Rudy's gallery. There was the business of the art world; there were Clyde, Tom, Lionel and Don coming to stay, telephoning, sharing politics and ideas; Tom Lewis, the Premier of New South Wales, asked Clif to make him a book plate; David Williamson and Kristen moved near us. The stream of visitors continued, journalists and television crews were about; there was the fun of marketing with Barbara Tucker and of feeding the artists after their days with models or en plein-air.

Clif's raging nights were a small part of life that I isolated from the rest along with the sorrow. I thought that the anger would go away once he spoke about the murders in the first person, and I told myself that this would mean joy again. I hoped I could get him to talk about it with some professional, providing he could be persuaded that the painting would not be affected.

The problem with anger in a relationship is that the object of it retreats: actions are automatic, affection becomes conscious and purposeful instead of spontaneous. And one longs for comfort and to be able to be oneself.

I'd found a compromise to cope with the evenings of anger and misery, which was to find a gentle married man unlikely to leave his wife, and spend time with him. The intuition was split, which was not good, but it meant on the one hand I could keep Clif from noticing; with my lover, the intuition was so focussed that we never needed even to telephone to arrange to meet, we knew where we'd be and at what time.

And at least the intuition was back. At this time I dreamed everyday life in advance, so accurately that I sometimes forgot what was dream, what was not yet reality. Clif had always liked this. He would remind me, in a perfectly matter-of-fact way, sometimes across the dinner table as I commented on an event, 'I think that hasn't happened yet.' Oh, that's right. They were usually convenient, comfortable dreams: about who was coming to dinner unexpectedly, or where to go for some food, what material object would be in my life.

Then one night in a motel, early in the summer of 1974, as we travelled via Gippsland to Merimbula, I had a dream of utter terror. During the day, as I drove through those tracts of giant trees, Clif had become very quiet. Perhaps he wasn't well? 'I'm okay,' gruffly, and I thought perhaps it was the dark, the overhanging trees, the lush wet forests that reminded him always of the war.

The dream that night was quite abstract, but quite specific. I was alone, completely alone, disconnected from everything familiar. Without Clif, or family, or friends, or anything or anyone I knew.

I woke up, sweating in fear, heart frantically pumping.

On to Merimbula, where we were sharing a house with the journalists Maximilian and Geraldine Walsh. The next night, the same dream. But as I woke the second time I understood. I had to go through this; it was some kind of process, to imagine what it would be like to be absolutely alone, without resource, where I had to cope. I had to stay asleep throughout the dream and to manage, to deal with, to master the fear.

It should have been a tranquil holiday: card games and fishing off the pier, reading and swimming, particularly because the local pubs were still in the early 1960s. There had been a travelling salesman through from a winery years earlier, and each pub had bought a case or two of a very good red; and no one, it seemed, had ever asked for a bottle, nor had the publicans noticed its current retail price. We casually pub-crawled our way along the coast, Max and Clif taking turns to 'take the lot off your hands, mate . . .'

But every night I had the dream; there was urgency to this, as if I had a deadline to meet; it was like training for a competition. In the dream, I grasped for points of reference: cutlery, a sewing box, a scarf; the staircase and rooms in the house; the beach of my childhood, the town hall; the dream stripped each away as soon as my mind delivered it. I was without people, familiar systems, language, money, food, or the means to get them, and I had some huge responsibility on which more than my own life depended. So I took to going for walks every day, alone, consciously recreating the fear and making myself face it.

Back to Dunmoochin, and to the Australia Council.

My lover had seen me walking, thinking, on my own. 'You had a look on your face, I hadn't realised you were ruthless.'

So his gentleness would be gone, too; how could I explain the dream and its message?

The public campaign to oppose Coombs had taken on its own

momentum, but Clif, bearing its brunt, was taking the fight too seriously. His moods swung from the present anger and frustration to bitter drunkenness, a chaos of war images and of old political fights: how the Dunmoochin Co-operative broke up; how, when the Contemporary Art Society at last had a space, Clif and Arthur Boyd on behalf of other artists argued at the committee meeting that it should be somewhere for artists to meet, work and exhibit. But the Reeds wanted the space for a museum, and Clif and Arthur lost. In the short time he'd been involved with the CAS he'd decided that politics interfered with his work, and yet here he was, on the Australia Council, dealing again with people he knew to be out for power. Politics is a game of compromise and he was not a compromiser, yet he'd allowed himself to become involved again.

If I didn't manage his drinking, if he drank just a bit much at dinner in Melbourne, if I couldn't focus the mood on the trip home so that we went straight to bed, if he began to drink again, or had just a few too many before I got us away, the focus would be the murder, and I would suffer.

Barbara Tucker dropped in one morning to say she was going on a packaged trip to Bali, to the Tjampuhan, a simple hotel built on terraces in the mountains. Bali at that time conjured images of the musical *South Pacific*, rather than surf and bars. The hotel had been built in the 1930s, she believed it would be very simple but restful and quiet, the meals were local style. It wasn't expensive. Bert was staying home, and perhaps Clif didn't want to come, but would he please send me with her? Clif said he would come. I should have realised he was reluctant and have thought about the reasons, but I wanted to get away. I visualised rice paddies, meals cooked, no washing up. I thought about cool mountain air, and picturesque villages, and an elaborate culture. I imagined ancient tiered valleys, misted in the morning. But I didn't think about *jungle*.

While I practised being alone and unaided, anticipating and extending the dream every night, the Opposition Leader, Billy Snedden, was

Barbara and me

fulminating against legislation that had been part of the ALP platform, using the Coalition majority in the Senate to block it. Whitlam called his bluff, and another election. All our systems were in place in the Victorian marginal seats, where campaigners such as Brian McKinley in Greensborough were running a continuing campaign. I'd been less involved on the local level since the abortion debate and the Australia Council had taken over our lives. But Kevin Childs from *The Age* rang in the first week of the campaign.

'I've got seven Snedden stories and no Whitlam stories; it will look as if we're deliberately supporting the Coalition.'

So I gave him a couple of locally based ALP stories and rang Ken Bennett, the assistant secretary of the Victorian Branch of the party.

'Who is doing your media liaison, Ken?'

'Oh, that sounds like a good idea.'

They gave me the use of the Melbourne office of one of the Victorian ministers. I rang the Cabinet ministers and asked those who weren't from Victoria to let me know if they were coming to Victoria, or when they could come, and I began to campaign. I was lucky to have the on-the-ground knowledge and the confidence of the Cabinet. Joan Child had preselection for the marginal seat of Henty, but she had no public profile. She was a charming middle-aged woman, obviously sensible and intelligent. The opposition had focussed on the economy, so I wanted to make sure a reliable and down-to-earth image was presented. I rang Joan to ask if she shopped regularly at a local supermarket. Yes, she did. Could the Treasurer Frank Crean go shopping with her? A creature of my own culture, it had not occurred to me to ask Frank if he did the family shopping. I'd expected he might explain something to her about international market forces, while looking like the kindly rational man he was. But there they were, each with a shopping trolley, in the middle of the aisle and on the front page of the papers and across the television news; the Treasurer liked to shop because it kept him in touch with prices, and he knew that the price of frozen peas had gone up this week.

The Minister for Transport, Charlie Jones, rang. 'Judith, you don't need me, do you?'

Race Mathews had been campaigning for an interchange at Box Hill, and he had a campaign bus; the local newspapers and the dailies loved the minister in his cap, driving the bus. Tom Uren and Clif talked about the environment policy, wombat in attendance. Television and print media celebrated the work of the federal ALP government. It was a relief for Clif to get back to his real issue, the environment.

He resigned from the Australia Council; my media campaign was finished, interstate ministers making their way to their own electorates for the election. We were booked to Bali a couple of days before the election. We could leave and return refreshed after the ten days break, to take up normal lives again. I knew I would be refreshed, because I had at last managed to stay asleep throughout the terrifying abstract dream, calmly, without my mind resorting to any people or objects or even ideas, and calmly to contemplate the emptiness and take up the burden.

Brian McKinley rang to say have a great trip: they hoped to retain Diamond Valley, as the previous Liberal incumbent had refused on principle to stand against David McKenzie until he'd had one term. It had been an exhausting campaign but now it was virtually over. Brian was relaxed and amused. He told me that Bill Hartley, the ex-secretary of the Victorian Branch, had just been in to ask if there was anything he could do to help, but he couldn't stay for long as he had a plane to catch. It was a running joke; Bill always offered at the last minute and with this proviso.

In the last week of the election campaign Ranald McDonald, at the time a director of *The Age*, rang. Could he bring a couple of people up for lunch, just with Clif and me? Of course. Two cars arrived, one with Graham Perkin and Ranald, the other bringing Sir Warwick Fairfax, the chairman of the company, and a driver. At the table Sir Warwick turned to me and asked who *The Age* should support in the coming election. I turned to Clif, but, 'No, young lady, I am asking your opinion.' So I said that, for me, the issue was the set of conventions at the heart of the Westminster system translated to our constitution. I thought that the ALP government had often appeared chaotic, had done too much too soon. But I thought, I hoped, that the chaos was peripheral rather than central, and I hoped that winning a second election might settle them down; whereas, if they lost, it would simply make them and their supporters cynical. That a bitter parliamentary party would not be a healthy opposition, and that a disillusioned electorate would be bad in the long term.

Nor did Snedden strike me as necessarily better equipped in personality to take the country through what looked like harder economic times ahead. And this was not only because he was greedy for power, apparently unable to accept that the Labor Party had actually won the right to govern, but for another reason. He was prepared to stretch the convention that was central to the system, that the government should be formed by the person with the majority in the Lower House, that the Upper House was only a house of review. I thought that these delicate conventions were crucial to the way in which British democracy developed; they were the scaffolding on which we negotiated changes to the structure.

Sir Warwick reached into his pocket, took out a document, signed and dated it, and handed it to Ranald.

'That is my proxy, Judith. Ranald and Graeme are going back to Melbourne, where the board is meeting to decide who we will support. I understand your husband knows a great deal about birds. I am a birdwatcher. Do you think he would be kind enough to take me out locally?' Off they all went in their different ways, and I packed for Bali: just a couple of long cotton dresses to keep off the sun, sandals, swimsuit, a hat.

Bert drove us to the airport the next day. Clif had all the traveller's cheques and both our passports and the tickets, so when at the airport he disappeared for a very long time 'to use the toilet', there was no use Barbara and me trying to board the plane. He turned up finally and wasn't looking well.

'Are you okay?'

'Yes,' bluntly. And off we went.

It took about an hour from the airport at Denpasar to get to the Tjampuhan, but it was just as promised. The dining room was at the top of the little valley, our bungalow on the lowest level, the price of privacy only a couple of hundred steps. The hotel was exactly the unpretentious place in which really to relax. There was a rock pool in which we could swim. In our room were two beds, bedside tables, two little kerosene lamps, and a small table on which our charming waiter set our breakfast the next morning. Our room had tiled floors, and in the bathroom one poured water from a ewer. Beautiful necessities, nothing more.

Our tour packages entitled us to two days with a car and driver, so we went with Barbara the next day to see temples and monkeys and tropical jungle. Clif cashed a traveller's cheque so we could buy a couple of china dishes. He was interested in carvings, and ordered a set of doors. But he was moving slowly, and looked pale. I was worried about the effect of the jungle surrounding us, but perhaps after a few days a return to it would dilute the old horrors. Before the evening meal I suggested he have a massage, hoping it would relax him . . . He called out that the masseur wasn't gentle enough, and when I went in with the English-speaking manager the old masseur working over Clif's chest was obviously very worried, but the manager could not translate the concern. Clif complained he was in pain, so the massage stopped. I climbed up to dinner alone, with my one-person kerosene lamp; Clif just wanted to go to bed.

I was pissed off. No matter what my physical condition I'd always been with him, leaving hospital to appear on television, cooking for dinner parties after days in bed. It seemed somehow mean that now I had time to relax without having to worry about him, I had to worry about him. I stopped on the way down to our bungalow, watching the lights go out across the hillside. Such a wonderful feeling, to be ourselves, alone; where the culture was indifferent to us, without worrying about the election or the Australia Council. Clif had his paints in his suitcase and all our needs would be met for the next ten days.

He was in bed in the dark when I found our hut. I put my lamp on the table, looked into the velvet night, and opened a notebook. Clif said something, but I hadn't been listening.

'Sorry?'

No reply.

'What did you say?'

Still no reply.

He doesn't sulk. I left the table, tapped him, shook him, called his name loudly. He was quite still. He didn't move.

I tried to find a pulse. No pulse, still no response. I pulled him flat on the bed because I had seen it on television and I made fists and I raised my hands above my head and I hit him very hard in the middle of his chest and it made no difference and I did it again, and a third time, and then he mumbled something, so I stopped.

He wasn't conscious, but he was alive.

I took my lamp and went outside, but there were no lights on at all, I couldn't remember where Barbara's bungalow was. I didn't want to leave him. His temperature was going up very high and then down, after he'd sweated profusely. I thought he might be having a repeat of one of the three kinds of malaria he'd had during the war, or the dengue fever. I wrung out a wet towel and put it on his forehead, and I sat beside him all night, changing it and checking his pulse when he became very still.

In the morning he woke, but was still very drowsy, so when our breakfast arrived I ordered the car and driver again, found Barbara and told her Clif was ill, and that I would take him into Denpasar to a doctor. The Tjampuhan manager told me that the Bali Beach Hotel had an English-speaking doctor, so after Clif had slowly climbed the more than two hundred steps to the road, that is where we went.

For four years I had relied on Clif's judgement of people. By virtue of his age, his status, his personality, the culture, he had power in the relationship; I could only on occasion assert myself, often only to my own amusement. It had never mattered.

We walked into the doctor's rooms at the hotel and I looked at him and thought, 'Unreliable alcoholic.'

When he said that Clif, who was losing consciousness again, might be very very ill and should go straight to the hospital, I was concerned, but not worried. He gave me a bundle of syringes.

'Hepatitis is rife here. Don't allow them to use any other syringe on him and get him to Australia as soon as possible.'

Back in the car, Clif looking very pale again. The hospital was like an old Australian country hospital, one-storied, deep verandahs, and like any public hospital there was a long queue waiting to see the doctor. The driver came in with us. We sat on a bench and waited, and Clif suddenly fell sideways. The driver grabbed him, and I ran to the front of the queue and demanded to see the doctor immediately. He was very upset but I could see he thought I might make a scene, so he came with me and then called out, and four orderlies arrived with a stretcher, lifted the quite unconscious Clif onto it and brought him into the surgery. Two nurses connected him to a machine and began taking his blood pressure, while I gave his details to the doctor. Then one of the nurses called out and ran across with a printout from the machine. The doctor looked at it and said, 'I am very sorry, he is dying.'

I asked what of. And he said, 'Myocardial infarction.'

I said I didn't know what that meant, and he said it meant heart attack.

Heart surgery was then in its early stages, but I had a vision of bright lights and operating theatres and lots of equipment.

'Well, I don't want him to die, how do we stop him dying?'

He said, 'He must give up smoking.'

I went across and took the packet of Camels out of his pocket and threw them in the bin. 'He's given up smoking, what now?'

He asked if I wanted the hospital to look after him.

'Yes, please.'

'Would you like a first-class room?'

Still assuming this would be after the imminent surgery I said I would. He wrote out a prescription and gave it to me with the printout, and called the orderlies and Clif was loaded back onto the trolley, and off we went, our driver following.

To a room off a wide verandah. A single hospital bed, and a hole in the floor to an open drain with some shit in it, bloodstains on the sheets, and one thin pillow. I had visualised more pillows. The orderlies slid Clif onto the bed, and then they left. I looked for the white starched nurses and the surgeon and then it sank in, this was it. I asked the driver if he could find out where the hospital pharmacy was, and he came back and told me there wasn't one, I would have to go into town. I gave the driver a note telling Barbara what had happened and asking her to send down our suitcases, and to tell a doctor friend of ours who was arriving that day. There were Bemos, little three-wheeled taxis I could hire.

Christopher and his partner visited Bali every year, and they knew the system. I went back to Clif, who seemed to be sleeping quietly. 'I am a doctor, but sleep is the great healer,' my father used to say. I took the money Clif had cashed from his pocket so I could pay for the prescription and the Bemo ride, and I took his passport and the traveller's cheques and put them in my bag.

Then I realised: this was the dream.

24

GROUNDED

Valium

I was holding the equivalent of about thirty dollars. I had to pay for a taxi, for medicine, Clif's hospital room. I had to find an airline office and book us back to Australia. I had no money. I had no contacts. I had no language in common with the people around me, I did not understand the system I was in, and here was Clif, entirely dependent on me. Those were the difficulties. But the dream had entirely prepared me and I was calm and resolved. The hotel doctor had said to get him to Australia, and I could see that not only was there no treatment available but that we would be a strain on such resources as were in this place. I would wait until Clif regained consciousness and explain I'd be away for a bit, and then I would get a Bemo, and get the medicine.

After about an hour I heard people speaking English and coming towards me along the verandah was a group of young people, obviously Australians. They were deciding to kidnap a friend who had come to the hospital for treatment for a leg ulcer and the doctors had admitted him and wanted to do surgery on it, and they thought they meant to amputate it, why would that be? The staff had been adamant it was urgent but they couldn't understand why. I told them I'd be getting Clif on a plane, and if they wanted I'd get their friend on, too. They said that with the oil crisis all the planes were overbooked, and if you missed your flight you might not be able to get on one for a week, it was as bad as that. I said I could do better than that. Fame has its uses, they knew who we were, obviously believed I could do what I said, and decided not to kidnap their friend unless it appeared he was about to be anaesthetised. A couple of them would sit with Clif, a couple would stay with the friend.

I went into the courtyard where the drivers were waiting for customers; how cute these little Bemos would be if only I could stop to enjoy myself. I said I needed to go to a chemist. The drivers looked blank. I said simply, 'Chemist,' but to no avail. My mother taught English as a second language, and our house had always been full of migrants and refugees and foreign students. I knew verbal was not the only technique, but mime or drawing are difficult when cultural concepts are involved. Then I remembered all the apparently-only-of-academic-interest lessons in English Language I at Melbourne University. I tried pharmacy, no response, and then I thought, 'This was a Dutch Colony,' so I hardened chemist put the emphasis on different consonants – *kemist*, *kemeesT* – no joy, and then I hardened *pharmacy*, again with no effect. Then I thought, okay, older words for *pharmacy* and I tried *apothecary*, but that brought no reaction, so I began to harden it, *a-pot* and 'Apotik!' with great delight, so off I went with the first driver who got it.

The chemist spoke English and gave me the valium that had been prescribed, and then he looked at the printout, called it an electrocardiogram, and said that he didn't know much about them but that it looked very serious. I asked if I was being either silly or arrogant to try to get Clif to treatment at home and he said no, there was in fact more sophisticated treatment, surgical intervention, other drugs, but that the Dutch had left with most of the infrastructure and there was no treatment available here, and yes, I should try to get him out. He thought carefully and said it did look very serious and I should perhaps take the valium myself when I needed sleep. I asked where there was a public telephone. This was 1974 and there were no mobiles, and he said that if he had a phone I could use it but he didn't, there was a phone at the Bali Beach Hotel but no public phones in the street, a telephone was of itself a luxury. I saw a bank and went in to ask how I could change Clif's traveller's cheques. They agreed that if he signed them they would cash them.

'You have an honest face.'

This was a Saturday and so I was worried that the airline offices would be closed. I knew from the young Australians that there was a Qantas flight that night, and I planned to be on it. The driver knew the Bali Beach Hotel, it was at the time the only modern hotel on the island, and the Qantas office was there. There was a very pleasant man in the office. Yes, there was a flight that night, but he thought that with heart patients there was a problem; he thought the reduced oxygen in the plane was bad for a heart patient and it might be better to have Clif stabilised. I asked where the public phone was in the hotel; I had very little money, as Clif had all the traveller's cheques in his name.

'There is no public phone. There are phones that can be used by people who aren't guests but there's a ten per cent surcharge payable in advance for reverse charges calls.'

He let me use the Qantas phone, so I rang my father. There was a delay in the signal, and I could hear the Indonesian operator talking to the Australian one as they tried to connect me.

'Denpasar, you're through, go ahead.'

'Thank you, Melbourne, go ahead please, Ma'am.' Dad thought I was ringing for the election results. I explained that Clif had had a heart attack.

'How do you know?'

'They did an electrocardiogram'

'Have you got it there? Okay. What is the number there?'

The very nice man, I think his name was Stewart, spoke to my father for a moment, and said, 'No, don't ring back, that's fine,' and gave me back the phone. Dad and I worked out a grid so that I could convey the electrocardiograph information over the phone. He checked it with Stewart, and then Stewart looked worried and handed the phone back to me.

'Jude, this is very serious, very very serious. You will do everything you can to bring him back here, but you must think all the time *he may die*. Now, he can't get on a plane tonight, this is damage to a muscle, but unlike other muscles it can't rest. It needs oxygen, and if it doesn't have it the damage will get worse. Because planes fly at reduced air pressure there is less oxygen, so initially it would put too much stress on his heart. If he is still alive after today I think you should try to get him home. I'll ring my partner, he's the medical officer for the Air Line Pilots Association, the Qantas Pilots Union, and I'll ring you back if he disagrees with any of this. Now can you get him any morphine?'

I explained that the doctor had prescribed valium.

'No, don't give him valium, adrenaline from the pain just might keep him alive. Morphine would be good, because it delivers oxygen to the heart, but it will mask the symptoms of a new attack.'

'Um, Dad, mask them from what? Clif will presumably notice, but there is no one but me observing him, and a kid who should be on the beach. And I won't be there much.'

'You're right. See if you can get some morphine.'

No point explaining that that was unlikely, that in fact the only place for morphine would be a casual beach encounter, and not only did I not have money, but if the gaols were worse than the hospital I didn't think that was an option. My mother came on the line. She had developed a system of taking professionals into their workplaces and teaching them the technical words they needed to access skills and information.

'Jude, I just trained a cardiologist who is based in Bali, I'll do what I can to get him to you.'

Dad took the phone again. 'Now remember to think *he may die*. Good luck.'

Stewart was quiet when I put down the phone. I asked him if Dad had told him Clif should not fly tonight. He was looking at me in the same way as the doctor in the hospital, and the pharmacist. What was the expression? Compassion. But I didn't need compassion, because I knew with the same casual certainty that I'd known I would live on the top of the hill that Clif was not going to die. I thought however that there was no reason to explain this, as the compassion of itself would make people encourage me rather than try to stop me; they'd think it would help me to survive Clif's death.

Stewart spoke. He'd made a decision, one could see. 'Yes, your father said it looked as if Clifton is very ill. We have guidelines about who should travel and when, I thought it would be bad for him. Okay. Now, I'm leaving this job today so I won't be able to help you much longer. I wouldn't be telling you this if he wasn't Clifton Pugh and if you weren't so calm.

'This is the situation. All planes are overbooked because of the oil shortage. You won't be able to get on a plane. You'll need to bump off passengers. That means that the airline has to pay for those passengers in a hotel until they get on another flight. At the moment because there are no spare seats this could create an endless expensive cycle.

'There's not another Qantas flight until next week. There's a Pan Am flight on Monday night; it goes to Sydney. You should aim for that. You'll need to put pressure on Pan Am, they won't want to take him, the guy here is fairly rigid at the best of times, they'll have the same guidelines as us, and Clifton is not a US national. And they had the crash here only last month. The local Pan Am manager had nothing to do with it, but in all big companies a trouble spot becomes a trouble spot, so he's going to be particularly uninterested in getting you on. So you have to get Qantas to put pressure on Pan Am at a very senior level. The way to do that is to get a Hercules from the RAAF promised to collect him. You don't want that, I know for sure that the noise in those things is very very stressful and would probably kill him, but you need the RAAF to tell Qantas they are coming for him; it's a matter of fuel allocation. The RAAF has a priority on fuel allocation and so if they did come they would get Qantas's fuel, and Qantas would have a whole plane full of passengers to offload and huge expense. If you get the government to say they will send a plane then Qantas will put pressure on Pan Am, and it will be easier for you to get him on. The name of the guy in the Pan Am office is van Dommelen, Mr van Dommelen. Come back if I can be any more help, but remember this is my last day.'

Mr van Dommelen was in the office and I said I'd like to book two first-class seats to Melbourne on Monday. He said the plane was overbooked and he could put me on a waiting list. I said actually I needed priority because my husband was ill. He said that they could not take people with infectious diseases, and I said no, he'd had a heart attack. He said in that case the guidelines were quite clear and he could not book him until two weeks after a heart attack and that he would even then need a medical certificate.

'You should understand that the plane trip might worsen his condition and if he dies then other passengers might complain, and sue the company.'

He looked harassed, poor man, as I stood there in a cotton dress and sandals, a woman in the age of men, in the culture of the coloniser, and half his age.

'What do I need to do to get him on the plane?'

'You will not get him on the plane.'

'But what would I have to do, as a matter of theory, to get him on the plane?'

'You would have to move two governments, and an airline. The Indonesian Government, the Australian Government and the American Government would have to order Pan Am to take him and Pan Am would have to agree.'

'Is there anything else I would have to do?'

'No, that's all you would have to do.'

'Thank you, Mr van Dommelen. I'll be in later.'

I went back to the Qantas office, and asked Stewart if he would help me arrange with the hotel for me to reverse charges without the surcharge. He found a manager who agreed to let Qantas be my backer. I then rang Teresa Brennan, who thought I was ringing to get the election results. I could hear her telling the Australian operator to tell me that the election results were not in, so I said loudly to the Indonesian operator to tell the Australian operator that Clifton Pugh had had a heart attack, and I heard the Australian operator tell Teresa, who took the call.

'I take it hospital conditions are not good?'

And I told her the story and why I needed the government to promise, without delivering, a Hercules. I said I'd ring Don Chipp, who'd been Minister for Customs in Gorton's government, she said she'd ring Tom Uren, could I ring back? I was very worried about Clif, and balancing the time to and from the hospital and the money I had. I said I'd wait for an hour and then I'd ring in the morning.

I rang Don Chipp, who thought I was ringing to get the election results. I could hear him telling the Australian operator to tell me that the election results were not in, so I said loudly to the Indonesian operator to tell the Australian operator that Clifton Pugh had had a heart attack, and I heard the Australian operator tell Don, who took the call. I explained about the RAAF Hercules and he said that he would speak to Snedden, who would contact Whitlam. I was not to worry, the Coalition would make no trouble about it, and to take care, ring if he could help at all in any other way, and good luck. I went to the coffee shop in the hotel to think and to have something to eat, but realised that I had to do this without food, until I could cash traveller's cheques. If I imagined this as a campaign, as politics, it would give me a structure through which to think and plan. Make a list. I had the overall strategy in place, involving the Australian Government, and once they agreed to help I'd have pressure on Qantas. I'd need them to ask the American ambassador to put pressure on the Americans to ask Pan Am to overrule their rules, and perhaps to chat up the Indonesian ambassador too.

There was something that had been niggling at me since van Dommelen's speech. Grass roots. This was a campaign, who in these circumstances would be my grass roots? The passengers. Where would they be? Well, many in the Bali Beach Hotel. Think about how to mobilise them. Meanwhile, give Stewart an update then back to the hospital. He was with someone in the Qantas office as I arrived and the telephone rang. Stewart gestured to me to answer it.

'Qantas, Denpasar . . .'

Before I could finish Tom Uren said, 'Judith, give me Stewart.'

The surprise at hearing a familiar voice brought some emotion. 'Oh, Tom . . .'

'Give me Stewart, Judith,' and I realised that I was somehow to blame either for the heart attack or relative inaccessibility of treatment. Stewart carefully explained, as I am sure Teresa had explained, why we didn't want the Hercules, but when Tom got off the line Stewart was worried about whether Tom had followed; he was keen to get one up here. I could cover that with Teresa next day, it was back to the hospital now.

At the hospital I reassured my little group of Australians that their friend would be on Monday's Pan Am flight. Just as they were going off to see their patient, an orderly appeared and indicated I should follow him. So they said they would wait with the semi-conscious Clif. I was led to a room where a telephone sat on the desk, the receiver beside it.

'Hello?' It was my mother. Throughout the time in Bali only my parents managed to get through on the hospital phone. My mother had spoken to Professor Moerdowo, who would call in to see Clif. My father came on the line. He had spoken to the Pilots Association. They had an idea, and were contacting the American Air Line Pilots Association. They would be in touch when they knew more. How was Clif?

'Judith, he's suffered a great deal of strain on an essential muscle, it pumps oxygen to the brain, if there is no change that may be good, he may be stabilising. Remember to think *he may die*.'

Back in the room, and alone with Clif. Barbara arrived, most concerned. We decided that she would take her hire car, find the Australian painter Donald Friend, who lived in Bali, and ask him for help in getting Clif on the plane. She'd then go back up to meet our doctor friend Christopher when he arrived at the hotel, to ask him to come down and see Clif.

During that long night I didn't even have water to cool Clif, or food or drink for either of us. Several times he seemed to be unconscious, rather than asleep. It was not that I couldn't sleep or struggled to stay awake; this was the dream, I was alone, without resource, and I was simply alert all the time.

Christopher in the morning. He examined Clif and looked at the printout, and wept. I told him what I was trying to arrange, and he agreed that if I could get Clif back to Australia it might help, but emphasised I must not expect too much. Clif became lucid enough desperately to ask Chris to arrange payment for his doors and to have them brought to Melbourne. Chris agreed, and as Clif settled down from his obvious distress he went to see if he could find Clif's admitting doctor. He came back with an orderly carrying a remarkably industrial oxygen cylinder, which did seem to provide some pain relief for Clif, although two people needed to hold it and it soon ran out; and two phials of morphine, one of which he injected.

He arranged for Clif to be moved to a VIP room, where to my delight an English-speaking Dutch social worker was in the other of two beds, and where there was a cardiac monitor, just as featured on television. The social worker was very kind; fortunately he was having rest for a back injury so without suffering he could communicate with the nurses who had appeared at this level of the hospital hierarchy. Chris connected the machine to Clif and, taking another note to Barbara, went back up the mountain. I sat on the tiled floor in the bright room and had begun to rest for a moment when the alarm on the machine went off. A nurse rushed in and looked at it, turned it off and on, and the alarm started up again. She called out to another nurse and they repeated the turn off/turn on, with the same result. Then they turned off and unplugged the machine.

'What if he has another attack?'

'Then we will attach the machine. We must not waste electricity.'

Oh well.

Encouraged that with oxygen and morphine Clif looked better, I decided to tell him he'd had a heart attack and needed to get home, and what I'd done so far, and produced the traveller's cheques and asked him to sign them.

He became very agitated. 'What? And have you buy clothes and other useless things?'

'No, it's that I can't use the phone or pay for the seats unless I have some money.'

'But you said you had been making calls.'

'Yes, but I am supposed to pay a ten per cent surcharge and I have to get the government to talk to the US and Indonesian ambassadors and . . .'

'Look, Judith, you are doing perfectly well without money, and frankly I think all you'll do is go out and spend. I need to keep you on a tight rein, this place is too tempting.'

He was becoming even more anxious; breathing fast. Not wanting to upset him any more, I stopped discussing it. He became semi-conscious again.

That night I sat on the floor until he seemed to sleep more deeply, although in the evening his temperature was again up and down. On the verandah occasionally a gecko dropped from the ceiling, the cool air of the tropical night was soothing. I had to struggle to remember that *he may die*.

25

ALIVE

Chicken porridge

The next morning he was still alive, but still half-asleep, half-conscious. Just enough money for two more Bemo rides. Back to the hotel the next morning. The social worker would keep an eye on him. The Qantas office was closed but I was able to telephone Teresa from the hotel. Good, that system worked. She'd found a cardiologist on the golf course, there would be an ambulance meeting the Pan Am flight, the message had got across to the ALP and the RAAF was prioritising the fuel. So now to the grass roots. Start on the top floor and door knock my way down. No South Australian Premier this time.

'Excuse me please, I am sorry to bother you but I am wondering if you are booked to Sydney on the Pan Am flight tomorrow night?' If the answer was yes, 'Well, this may seem a strange question, but would you mind if my husband died on the flight? You see, he's had a heart attack and when I told the local Pan Am manager, he said we couldn't fly, because passengers would object if he died, and they would sue the airline. I thought if people did object I could explain the difficulties in getting treatment here in Bali, and that people might change their minds.'

It is always best to turn an opponent's weapons against him. Mr van Dommelen had not considered the effect of his remarks on his own market, which was, in the main, composed of middle-aged Americans. All of whom identified with the idea of being ill and stranded far from home. My grass roots were sympathetic, then wished me luck and closed the door. I would get as far as one or two more doors along the corridor and they would emerge, usually with a companion or spouse, asking me to repeat what I'd told them. They would go back into the room and emerge again, confirming Mr van D's name and whereabouts, and head for the lift.

In the middle of the afternoon when I took a break from door knocking to use the phone again, there was the poor man with quite a crowd in his glass-walled office. Barbara, who had arrived at the hotel to tell me that Donald Friend had no solution, came with me to visit van Dommelen; her constant tact might be useful. Would he allow Clif to board? Could Clif walk onto the plane? That, Mr van Dommelen had decided, would show he was fit to travel. Barbara sounded so reassuring as to Clif's condition I found myself wondering what the fuss was about. She left for the Tjampuhan, and I rang Sydney.

Teresa was organising the lobbying of the United States and Indonesian ambassadors. It looked as if the ALP was back in and the DLP might have lost its Senate majority. Yes, I was coping. There was a call from another journalist. There was a call from Bill Hartley, who was in Djakarta and had heard the news. The moment of near connection with the outside world was so encouraging. Bill asked if there was anything he could do to help. But he couldn't talk for long, as he had a plane to catch.

My parents were again on the hospital telephone when I got back. The American Air Line Pilots Association had decided to assist us by asking for an extra crew on the Monday Hong Kong–Sydney flight. There would be four first-class seats waiting for me if I could get Clif to the plane, which meant past van Dommelen. I asked Dad to mention the boy with the ulcer. He would. He didn't know what would cause

Clif's temperature to fluctuate. I was doing the right thing, but I must keep thinking *he may die*. Another quiet evening; I was used to the geckos now and the floor. No sleep or food yet, but only a day to go.

The next morning a lovely surprise. The Tjampuhan had sent us a 'chicken porridge': rice and chicken mixed in a billy. They had realised we had no food and that I would have no way of procuring it.

'In Bali, the family brings food to the hospital, and we are your family here.'

Not useful to cry. Chris had told me to keep Clif sitting up, there were lots of pillows, so he could eat comfortably, but that morning he was still very dozy, so I still dared not ask for the traveller's cheques to be signed. I sent another note to Barbara, asking if she would come that afternoon to the hospital and bring Clif to the airport that night. Then I left again to keep door knocking.

That afternoon in the Bali Beach Hotel café an Australian woman approached me to ask if I was okay, would I join her family at the next table? The O'Keefes were on holiday from Queensland, had seen me sitting alone without eating since Friday, and were concerned about me.

I explained why, and the husband said, 'I'm a GP. I run a small intensive care unit in the Nerang Hospital. Why don't I come and see your husband?'

'When she's had something for lunch,' said his wife.

We got from poor beseiged Mr van Dommelen the form of medical certificate he would need.

'If your husband had recently recovered from a heart attack.'

'Yes, Mr van Dommelen, but you will be hearing from your head office and this requirement will be waived.' He obviously thought I was delusional. Better than thinking I was mischievous.

Victor O'Keefe managed to imply that having the certificate might somehow distract me. He hailed a taxi and we arrived at the hospital at the same time as Dr Moerdowo. Dr Moerdowo gave me his card, which read 'Professor of Fine Arts'; I had a moment of thinking that perhaps because Clif was a painter . . . then he turned it over to the side that gave his medical qualifications. Clif was irritable at being examined by Dr O'Keefe, complaining that every time he woke up I produced another doctor. He announced he would be getting up to go painting that afternoon but Dr Moerdowo tactfully managed the situation by telling him my mother had shown him some of Clif's work.

While the two artists spoke Victor quietly pointed out that while he could sign and it would not affect his reputation if Clif did die, the situation might be difficult for Dr Moerdowo. We needed to give him a reason to agree. Outside the room they conferred. They agreed that the damage to his heart was very serious. Dr Moerdowo said that it was usual for people to rest for ten days after a heart attack. He didn't want to offend me by referring to the fact that the treatment was rest, and I didn't want to point out that if Clif had another attack then surgical intervention would, in Australia for people of our resources, be immediate. Besides, it wasn't that I thought that somehow being near some stainless steel equipment and an endless supply of sharp needles would be better than the casual calm of this tropical care, or better than Dr Moerdowo's expertise.

This was cultural difference, but not only between first and third world, colonising people and colonised. I knew that the muscle was repairing and would be threatened by flying, but I had recognised something else. That I had to get Clif out of the jungle, that what would diminish his pain was not just morphine and rest. What he needed was to return to an endless supply of eucalypts. So I spoke about place, about the need for Clif to be in the bush. Turning over Dr Moerdowo's card, I said that in this case the side to consider was the artist.

'This is so.'

Dr O'Keefe added 'psychological necessity' and they both signed the certificate.

I took our suitcases to the Pan Am office in the hotel lobby, where the passengers were assembling for transport to the airport. Our bags were seized by enthusiastic passengers. An American, a Mr Donovan – white seersucker suit, white hat, white shoes – explained: 'I've more or less been elected spokesman for the passengers on tonight's flight. We will take your luggage with us and check it in. Do you plan to collect your husband from the hospital?'

I explained that Barbara would bring him once I knew he would be allowed on the plane.

'Please come out to the airport, even if you don't hear that van Dommelen is able to put your husband on the plane. At the very least we can deal with your luggage.' He left to board the bus.

Wondering what I was going to say, I took my certificate to van Dommelen. Whose telephone rang just as I was called to the hotel phone. It was Tom Uren. As he spoke to me, van Dommelen was being told that the company wanted Clif on the plane, if he thought Clif was fit to fly. I went back to the office. *Make sure not to humiliate him.*

'Mrs Pugh, I have arranged with my company that I can overlook the regulation that would prevent your husband flying if in my opinion he is fit to fly.'

'Mr van Dommelen, that is wonderful. I have the certificate here, do you need it now, or shall I bring it to the plane?'

'You must understand, it is my decision, it is in my hands.'

'Oh quite, of course, it will be your judgement, thank you very much for making this possible.'

'He must come to the airport, I will see him there.'

'Of course.'

I rang Barbara. We were off.

The passengers had about a half hour's start, and I was surprised to see a huge queue at the Pan Am counter. Mr Donovan explained as he took me to the head of the queue that they had agreed not to allow the plane to take off unless I said so, that they had sent a group through to the transit lounge to explain the delay to the other passengers, who were really into the act. Dr O'Keefe had the boy with the ulcer in a wheelchair, he was concerned he might have cancer, and we had another person to get on, a miscarrying woman brought to the airport by my young Australians.

As we reached the counter a woman snatched her ticket back from the attendant.

'Seat allocation?' to her companion.

'Mabel, what is seat allocation? I don't like the sound of that.'

Mr van Dommelen was there, and I said I would like two first-class tickets on the flight to Sydney.

'And how will you be paying?'

I said my husband would pay by traveller's cheque when he arrived.

'Then I cannot issue tickets.'

Mr Donovan put down his American Express card. 'I'll be paying.'

'Mr Donovan, I won't say no, but we will reimburse you.'

'Oh, it's worth it, I want to see how far you can go.'

Every now and again I would see myself through someone else's eyes: penniless, bare-legged, in sandals and long cotton dress, and then I would want to cry. And I would think *he may die*, and then I would pull myself together. I took the boy in the wheelchair to the plane, and the woman. Mr van Dommelen asked if he could now board his passengers, and I said that I trusted him to wait for Clif, and Dr O'Keefe and Mr Donovan said they would wait on the tarmac with me, and everyone else boarded.

The Pan Am hostess said Captain wanted to have a word, so I went to the cockpit.

'I can make the decision to fly your husband once he's aboard, so all you need is to get him up the steps. The crew will do what they can to help.' The first officer and the engineer took up positions on the steps, with two of the stewards.

A delivery van of a very old sort was coming across the tarmac to the plane, and none of us was really paying attention, even as it backed toward the forward gangway. I was thinking how like a film: the night, the men in uniform, the way the coloured lights reflected on the metal steps, when someone said, 'God, it's the ambulance,' and went to open the door, which fell sideways as it opened, and a stretcher slid out, with a body on it.

Barbara threw herself across the stretcher to stop it, and Clif's head lolled sideways and she said, 'We nearly went into a ditch.'

And someone put their hand on my shoulder and said, 'You did all you could.'

And Clif, who was greyish-white, moved his head, *he may die*, but he is now alive, and Mr van Dommelen said, 'He's unfit to travel.'

And I said, 'No, look, he can sit up.'

And went to lift him.

And Dr O'Keefe said, 'He seems fine to me.'

And van Dommelen said, 'No.'

But Barbara had her arms around van Dommelen, pinning his hands to his sides, saying, 'Thank you,'

I gestured to the orderlies to take the trolley to the steps, and the crew grabbed him and carried him up and Mr Donovan and Dr O'Keefe followed, and I said goodbye and thank you to Barbara and went up the steps and the door closed and we took off.

26

HOME

Baskets of fruit, an apple,
an orange, the Copenhagen railway
station buffet.

The hospital in Sydney met all my expectations: lots of machines and nurses. However, the contrast between systems was not all in favour of the Australian, which relied on institutionalised processes rather than observation and common sense. But artists knew what an artist needs to normalise his life, and they delivered paints and paper, and soon Clif's room resembled a studio. Trolley for paints and water, trolley on which to lean a board holding paper, trolley with the bunch of flowers being painted, the walls covered with paintings: of the view through the window, of his baskets of fruit. There was no telephone in the hospital room, but *The Australian* newspaper ran a front page picture of Clif with the cartoonist Bruce Petty, so everyone knew we were back and that he was alive; I only needed to telephone Marlene, the art world network would take care of all the rest.

Clif was monitored, comfortable, fed. Oxygen restored his colour and reduced the pain, he slept at night and was conscious and coherent during the day. When we arrived I slept on the floor at Teresa Brennan's, but she needed her space and her time back, she'd been more than generous and had to write. My immediate concern was to get some shelter and warmth for myself.

There in the hospital, while I made him comfortable and he began to recover, we both must have understood that a fundamental shift in dependence, therefore in power between us, had taken place. But we didn't talk about it. It would have been rare for a couple to discuss such things, even for men my own age, then; and a man brought up by Clif's mother and then by the army would not have contemplated it.

Such a shift had not taken place in financial matters. The surname Pugh meant that people assumed we were married, but we weren't. De facto spouses had no status, and I had no idea whether he'd made a will. My residual fears from Bali, *he may die*, focussed on paying the hospital bill if he did die, and the phone bills I'd run up, and the fare. I knew when I got to Melbourne I'd be able to give a list to his sensible accountant: but I still felt as if I wasn't home. Optimism and comfort to Clif was prescribed by each hearty doctor and he was attached to a machine that manifested his anxiety in a noisy and spectacular manner, and therefore attracted the attention of the nursing staff to any upset.

Sydney was cold, it was late May, I had only thin cotton dresses and no money for a hotel. Clif's attitude to his traveller's cheques had changed from 'You'll spend it all' to 'I want to keep them because the American dollar may go up, they're an investment'.

This was frustrating, as I actually did need warm clothes. This was the first time I saw how distasteful it was for him to behave badly to me. I'd only characterised it in this way previously when it was directed at someone else. But no coming-to-consciousness took place. My defence against this meanness was to ignore it, to think it was part of post-heart-attack depression. I rang Alan Greenaway at Travelodge. Alan was away, but his secretary immediately offered me a room, and I put up with the inadequate clothes; it wouldn't be for long.

Clif cheered up when he found his dear friend Laurie Thomas was in the hospital. Laurie had been an academic, deputy director of the National Gallery of Victoria, director of the Art Gallery of Western Australia and of the Queensland Gallery. He wrote clearly and sympathetically about art and could be a very tough critic. He was not only an early and constant supporter of Clif's work, his larrikin independence made him a soul mate; and the fact that he'd served in Army Intelligence and New Guinea gave them a common understanding. Laurie had had a lung removed, he had cancer, but he was cheerful and positive about them both living much longer.

When we came back to Melbourne the disadvantages of celebrity were at once apparent. Clif was told to take it slowly, so we cancelled appointments for a time, looking forward to some tranquillity. But complete strangers drove the hour from Melbourne to knock on the door with flowers and cards. We hid our cars and shut the main gates. They came over fences and through windows. This was not about the press, no paparazzi, just well-wishing strangers. The phone rang constantly, he could not settle. We went to Melbourne to hide at the Williams's.

There Clif began to relax, painting and etching with Fred. I modelled for them, watching their contrasting techniques, intrigued by the mechanics of Fred's colour wheel. It was cold, so I fetched a kimono that I had been given years earlier when I stayed in Japan with a Japanese family. How astonishing it is, when accidental objects and moments reach into history and consolidate with imagination to produce material things.

Dunmoochin was embraced by the bush, by nature. The birds called, the trees rustled at every window, creatures snuffled about. Its subtlety, or the more absolute colours and narratives of the desert had filled Clif's painting since he'd left the Gallery School; the techniques he'd learned were somehow embedded in the imagery, so until this moment it had been hard for him consciously to think about the ideas raised by the pictures he'd seen in France. There he had particularly responded to Vuillard and Bonnard. And here in the city, even the architecture a reminder of Paris, was a coincidental series of images to bring both artists to mind, together with a technique that resolved the issue he'd worried about: how he would incorporate into his own work the ideas produced by theirs.

The white walls and dark fittings of Fred's austere studio were lit by pale winter light. In the centre, I was a pearly pink occidental woman, grey-blue eyes, pale reddish-gold hair, wearing the heavy silk garment from the nineteenth century. I bring it out now, hang it across a chair, and remember the challenge it posed against my body, and how they talked about the problems, and techniques for resolving them. The silk itself is patterned, geometrically, in a number of shapes, so that its sheen catches the light erratically. On an apparently bland salmon background appear patches of deep dark pink and reds, and oranges, in contravention of all the western rules of taste and design. The sleeves are lined with tangerine. The fabric seems to be randomly splashed with colours that should clash, or should subdue each other: they are paintings of flowers and fans, themselves outlined in different colours. Cadmiums, yellow and orange, and green; here lemon, and creams, and rose, and scarlet; pillar-box red and carmine, cobalt, a dash of ultramarine, here olive, there the most delicate sea green. The effect should be chaotic, but the design restrains each into a harmonious pattern.

The challenge of painting the folds of silk, the form of the body, the texture of skin and the veins beneath: both he and Fred were used to that. The kimono added the element of oriental imagery and pattern that had so engaged Clif in Paris, together with the technical issues faced by the artists he admired. How to celebrate and *exploit* the work of an artist from another culture, to learn his techniques; how to make the exuberance of the Japanese fabric work in a painting against the very pale pearl of my skin?

In that heady nineteenth-century period, colour theory had developed, and the use of the colour wheel in art began; Fred always had a colour wheel beside his easel. Painting in the studio with Fred, talking colour theory with him in the evening, gave Clif a way to manage the design, to add to his tonal technique. It also gave him a way of seeing and painting beyond the marginal colour blindness, to 'see' red and yellow earlier than he had been able to before.

The heart attack became old news, to the public and to us. Fred gave Clif a colour wheel when we returned to Dunmoochin, and although he used it only for a few weeks, the work he did consolidated, through two surprising series of pictures, the ideas that derived from his time in 1970 in Paris. In the two series he brought his human figures indoors, or, rather, created an ambiguous space in which they moved. This was a departure, as was the incorporation into the paintings of recognisable individuals. Although in the main he used animals or birds for narrative, Clif's non-portrait paintings had included human figures in the past, and would on occasion include them again. Ordinarily, when figures did appear, in the *St Francis* or the *Penitents* series for instance, they are unidentified: archetypes, shapes almost.

These paintings were different. Clif had begun a portrait of Clyde Cameron before we went to Bali; Clyde and Doris stayed with us often, but none of us expected Clyde to appear in any other paintings.

The *Assassination* series derived from a newspaper photograph Clif had stuck on his studio wall, of the shooting of Alabama Governor George Wallace. In the first picture Clyde, the master politician, watches as a female figure gestures ambiguously to the suffering male figure, a cracked mirror or pane of glass emphasising the immediacy of the event. In the second the injured man's arm is outstretched: the woman may be striking him. In the third, she watches as he falls. The play of dark and light in the blurry image on the studio wall echoed Fred's studio in the winter; the *Assassination* paintings play with colour but also with abstract forms in dark and light. The figures merge into the background, as if Clif were thinking of Vuillard's concentration on the elements of light and shadow. In these paintings Clif's tonal technique meets the colour wheel.

And then there are the *Copulation* paintings. In them the colour wheel is most apparent. My lover and I float in space; in this series Bonnard's interest in flesh, and his flouting of the rules about spatial relationships, was uppermost in Clif's mind. The colour balance is maintained by broad panels of colour and by the use of food: a green apple, a bright orange, three cherry cakes.

I didn't recognise the woman in the *Assassination* paintings: her fringe and black shoulder-length hair must have represented someone, she is drawn, not invented. I did wonder when she'd come into the picture, if his indignation about Don was hypocritical, but it seemed pretty clear she was out of it now. Clif cheerily showed visitors the copulation paintings, explaining that he was thinking about me one week while I was away. Most of them struggled for a comment, it is unusual to have to think about sexually explicit paintings while being offered a drink by their subject, and if anyone noticed that the skin tone of the man in the paintings was exactly mine, and not the golden tan of Clif's, they didn't mention it. Except for my matching pale pink-skinned lover, who was quite unnerved.

In a group of people looking at both sets of paintings, Clif stood in front of the *Copulation* paintings and pointed to the *Assassination* painting of Clyde, asking my lover, who was exposed in the paintings, 'Do you think I'm predicting something?'

I don't want to suggest that Clif intended the work as a weapon; his process of painting was nothing like that. On his feet at the easel, he blocked out studio paintings in broad strokes, thinking, feeling, drawing, all at once. But the images that arrived from his imagination were from observation, invention, and intuition, and often had a meaning that he, and I, only understood later.

Winter came, so we went north again, again to the desert after rain.

Clif understood about the truck now, and was far less demanding about driving; what is more – great luxury – the road had had a grader over it.

All our Tibooburra journeys sing in my mind, with detail but not sequence, and I have no way of sorting them. Writing this book, I made another journey, to the Australian National Library, where, in the manuscripts room, I think to my younger self that she should have kept a thorough diary. The research in Canberra is inconclusive: our diaries are of appointments, destinations, without detail except for the occasional comment, a message from one of us to the other, a reminder note.

On 8 March 1974:
'Missing Judith like buggery. Stuck all on my own in Newcastle.'

Tears in my eyes surprise me: he did love me.

On one Tibooburra occasion, maybe it was in 1974, we flew up for a few days with Clyde Holding and Clif's friend Ann. In the pub we were told that some Aboriginal peckings were to be found near Mount Stuart, so off we all drove the next day, with some archaeologists who were working nearby. The place was in a gully, about a hundred metres wide in places, the walls about twenty metres high. This was a stony place, layers of red and orange, the sun had dried out all the night's moisture, the air seemed to crackle. I knew I'd burn if I wasn't protected, and went to the one softer place, a slight cutting in the side of the gully, where a single tree struggled to make some shade. Clif set up nearby to paint, and the others headed across the gorge to climb the rocks and look for marks. Peckings are the most primitive of marks, tiny scratched drawings of emu feet, the most minimal of patterns made with rock on rock.

I looked up from my book and watched the climbers struggling for a foothold in the heat on the unforgiving stones. And wondered why, in what seemed a place unchanged for thousands of years, any human, no matter how familiar with the country, would want to draw when really uncomfortable, or to make marks that could be seen only by other intrepid climbers.

If it was about art, or ritual, it would be about communication, audience; I couldn't see why what had been described would need to be secret. If it was about information, then even more would you expect it to be accessible. If making marks was an after-hunting activity, then the shelter from wind, even some from the sun, would always have been the place where I was sitting. So I went over to the nearest rocks. Which were covered in tiny drawings. I called to Clif.

'I think we should find a way to let them discover them,' he said, 'You have to give the scientists their dignity.'

Even in company a desert trip gave us a sense of being together.

When we came back to Dunmoochin the drunken nights gradually began again, and the moody anger, although it was more subdued, within his fear of another heart attack. It was still too soon to confront the reasons. I wanted to wait until he was physically well, and for the Australia Council to be less immediate an issue. The advantage of the heart attack was that people stopped lobbying, our life was calmer and more our own. And as it seemed we were now both without lovers, or perhaps unthreatened by the idea of them, we were confident together in daily life and in bed, so I could put aside the anger and enjoy cooking, introducing friends to clients, working with the marginal electorates, speaking to groups and to the media about abortion laws, the environment, feminism, about the political issues of the moment.

The Tibooburra gouaches and the *Assassination* and *Copulation* paintings were to be shown at Rudy's in Sydney in September. We took the train up, and another really ghastly night eventuated. This time the couple in the next compartment tried to intervene, their rest was disturbed, and the expression on the wife's face helped me to see that this anger should not be directed at me. When we arrived in Sydney the real explosion happened. It was the day before the show. Rudy's building had a gallery upstairs and one downstairs: one expected the impact of an exhibition immediately on entering the narrow lower space, and there, instead of the two series of large oils, were the gouaches, and Rudy had put *Assassinations* and *Copulations* upstairs.

'He is my father, he is my father, he denies my work.' Clif was almost in tears, and I knew the mood could swing from misery to anger in a moment. I was exhausted. It was a sort of reflex to try to calm him down, a reflex, and a strategy to defend myself. He went off to lunch and I walked to Bonython's, where the first of two things happened that kept me with Clif. Brett Whiteley was at Kim's, having a coffee. I asked him to come and see the work and tell me what he thought of it. If Brett, much younger, with none of Clif's training or background, and already well known locally and internationally, liked the new paintings, I would feel confident.

We weren't close friends, but I had reason to know he'd be straight with me. He, like Clif, like all of our artist friends, assumed that a partner was there for support and encouragement, part of the whole of a creative person, and that if there was some crisis of capacity or vision then the partner should know. I knew, too, that he could not avoid being honest about the pictures. There is an integrity; to do, I think, with the resonance between the visual part of the brain and, somehow, a need to acknowledge its truth. This means artists don't lie about visual things, especially about works of art. A bitchy untrustworthy artist will try to upset a rival, or to steal a client, to cheat a dealer; I've heard remarks designed to cast doubt about another artist's work, to undermine another artist's confidence. But whatever they say about a picture or a sculpture or a drawing or a print is accurate. The difference between encouragement and derision will be to emphasise strength or weakness.

A lovely moment followed. Brett went upstairs alone, and then came down and looked at the gouaches, then asked Gwen where Clif was. He was coming back to the gallery with Rudy. Brett would wait. I assumed he was going to be polite, or he'd have left. In walked Rudy and Clif, and Brett went up to them.

'Mate, I went upstairs. I wish I could paint like that.' And they went up to talk about the paintings. So I rang Clyde Cameron and told him the problem, and very soon the gallery was full of a television crew interviewing Clyde in front of his assassination picture, and Clif talking about it and the Tibooburra gouaches.

Perhaps because I'd rung Clyde, who showed concern for me, perhaps because I was back in Sydney, but that afternoon while everyone had a drink before the gallery closed I went for a walk and wondered what I would do if I did leave. I was beginning to resent the moods and the fear of him striking out. I loved the man who saw things clearly, to whom I could listen in the desert as he talked about delineating space, about time; who was so brilliant a judge of character, who let me have the intuition and left me to manage the house; who encouraged me to work in politics and supported me when I expressed myself. Most men were institutionalised in Australia then; well, that hasn't changed. They seem to learn to 'be' a person, as if it were a style: barrister. Most of them had expectations not just of the role of women in work and the home, but did not want a companion who spoke up or for that matter made jokes. Clif enjoyed both of these things.

I walked back up the hill thinking about these qualities, his capacity to see and bear the truth in daily life, and I told myself that if he could face and bear his own dark truth we could get through it. Bronwyn Thomas had dropped in to the gallery when I got back; she and Laurie lived just down the hill, and she wondered if Clif and I could call in to see Laurie, who was in bed, sick.

Their terrace was narrow and the stairs steep; I climbed up first to realise that Laurie was dying. He was all bones, propped up and barely breathing. My instinct was to protect Clif, to say he was asleep, but Clif came in, so I took Laurie's hand and said, 'Oh Laurie, I am sorry to see you're not well.'

And he said, 'I am looking forward to seeing the show,' and I said how much I hoped he would, and then from behind me, calm, absolutely sober, utterly clear, Clif spoke.

'No.' He gently moved me aside and sat on the bed and took Laurie's hands in both of his, and said again, 'No. Laurie, you can go.'

And Laurie said, 'Oh, Clif. Am I dying?'

And Clif said, 'Yes, old mate, you are dying. Goodbye, old mate, goodbye, old mate.'

And I was weeping and Clif took Laurie in his arms and said goodbye again, and that we would go, so he could go.

And Laurie died that evening. Although I bore the brunt of the grief, I knew that I wanted to be with a man who could deal with someone's life face on, despite his own hatred of death, and the scene with Laurie decided me to stay with Clif, to help him face his own fears.

Some of which were about mortality, and this was obvious to a man of his own generation. Steve Dattner suggested he should 'get back on his horse', that is, go overseas again. In October Steve and his wife Kay had to be in Paris for the 1974 leather fair, then in London, and suggested we go with them. Steve and Kay had met during World War II, she a general's driver, he an intelligence officer in the British Army. Steve's family had been furriers in London since the sixteenth century, and Kay was born in India and then sent home to the United Kingdom to be educated. Young, single, capable, intelligent: the perfect couple, the wartime romance. But there was a problem. Rather than tell his mother he was marrying a woman who was not a Jew, Steve and Kay migrated to Australia. They brought confidence and urbanity with them. Cherry Trees, their comfortable Eltham property, was a place of constant welcome, the two working together to introduce people and encourage talent, to smooth the unsophisticated ways of the artists with whom they mixed. It is still unusual to find a well-educated businessman not intent on being involved institutionally, not wanting accolades for supporting the arts. Kay was a painter, Steve and Kay enjoyed the company of creative people, and, as they were amusing and enthusiastic hosts and guests, the pleasure was mutual.

We agreed to join them. It seemed a good idea to get away from the residual arts politics issues. The DLP had indeed been wiped out in the half-Senate election, we'd picked up an extra seat in Victoria, and it seemed clear that the electorate had endorsed Labor policies. The conservatives would have to allow the passage of the Medicare and other fundamental legislation, and there seemed to be no campaign urgency for the party. I'd begun interviewing people for the Labor Hour, which Brian McKinley was now running on the Melbourne ALP-owned radio station, so I could see about doing some interviews in London, and we could talk to André Kalman about Clif doing a further show with him.

The Dattners always travelled first class overnight to Singapore and stayed for a few days, and then took a flight across the Himalayas to Copenhagen. On our first day in Singapore they invited us to dinner in the glamorous restaurant in the Shangri-la Hotel.

Kay, like the great-aunts of my childhood, said, 'And, darling, you should wear your pearls.'

'Kay, I don't have any pearls, I had my grandmother's, but they were stolen.'

'No pearls?' It was inconceivable.

Clif confirmed it, adding firmly, 'She doesn't need pearls.'

That evening before dinner the Dattners gave me a thirtieth birthday present in advance. A lovely string of pearls.

'You really will need pearls in London,' explained Kay.

When we arrived in Singapore Kay and I had some clothes made; tailoring was traditionally good and cheap. Steve suggested that Clif might have a safari suit tailored; they were fashionable and cool and would give him something to wear on slightly formal occasions. It simply didn't occur to Steve, Kay, or me that he would choose bright blue.

He emerged resplendent from the fitting room, and I had one of those moments when it is essential immediately to ditch a host of preconceptions and attitudes. I realised I was used to the subfusc of his jeans and army shirts, therefore had assumed he'd choose khaki or navy for the suit; that was what men did, it was what men wore, it was what men *were*. But he looked so pleased my views revised immediately. This was what he wore, what he was – a brightly coloured happy artist – so I told him it was good. Steve glanced at me and, understanding as ever, agreed.

Often Clif presented me with a problem to deal with, and then made the problem more complex. I had dimly begun to recognise this process as evidence of a need to control me, which was instinctive rather than deliberate. But the blue safari suit was innocent, unconscious. It would be a very interesting obstacle to navigate, to move in British social circles with a man not so much eccentrically as mistakenly dressed.

Copenhagen and Paris before London, though. Clif took advantage of the free alcohol to get very, very drunk and be generally unpleasant on the long haul across Asia, and we were not a happy group when we arrived in Denmark; it took the joy of the Copenhagen railway-station buffet to restore cheer. Steve took me aside to ask if these binges were regular; he was concerned on my behalf. He thought the problem was not the heart attack, but success; he would try to talk to Clif about appropriate behaviour. As when Clif had been unpleasant to Clyde Holding, I could see the tastelessness of the behaviour when it was played out in front of me. I stayed in Paris when the others went for the day to Versailles.

I knew the issue was deeper than success, but I was defining more clearly to myself why success was indeed part of getting drunk in general, as opposed to getting drunk because of war crimes, which was personal. Clif was a very practical man, a physical man; a builder, planting trees, making sculpture. He loved beautiful things, he would happily pay for them, even though he could be mean about me wanting clothes. He enjoyed luxuries like good wine and delicious food. He took a practical approach to daily life and money. He had planned for money and for success, they weren't accidental. The drunkenness was a fairly new phenomenon; he wasn't known for it, in the way other artists such as John Molvig or John Perceval were.

The image of the prisoners' murder had been overlaid for so many years by immediate concerns: about survival, the difficulties of the marriage to Marlene, the sheer daily business of making his reputation as a painter, and also the activity of painting itself. Success, time, the distance that life allows us from our younger selves, had softened those layers, and the Vietnam War and his letters penetrated them. However, success raised problems: it was not just a matter of getting used to money and comfort and managing fame. The personal problem was how to deal with the persistent images of the friends he'd killed, the implications of that for his own moral personality, his public moral stance. The business question was whether the edifice of reputation and money would be affected if he admitted publicly what had happened. So the fear was related to, but not of, success.

He came back apologetic from Versailles, bringing me two heavy copper pans for my kitchen. Steve was reassuring; he'd had a word about bad behaviour, after which Clif had bought them. It was hard to stay cross in the Hotel California, to be determined in Paris to be unhappy. So he showed me his galleries, his Paris. Kay and Steve showed me theirs. Steve's to do with food and wine and furs, Kay's about clothing. And we set off for London, full of images and delight.

27

UNITED KINGDOM

*Champagne by the side of the road,
garden vegetables and fruit,
venison, baps, kippers*

London this time was different for Clif. He had no purpose, no exhibitions, he wasn't meeting his past or his own familiar images. The Tube was no longer a place of individual welcome. The autumn at first was not mellow for him, but melancholy. We'd made the mistake of letting our travel agent put us into the Inter-Continental Hotel while we found somewhere to live. High off the ground in air-conditioning in a city was not what Clif wanted.

We found a flat to rent; surprisingly cheap. To overcome housing shortages, the Wilson Labour government had made it possible for anyone to take up or continue residence in an unoccupied dwelling, provided that it was not the only UK residence available to its owner. This made residential property a redundant investment. As the courts had ruled that services – gas, electricity, water – had to be connected by the authorities to any inhabited dwelling, London was full of squats. Foreign visitors were therefore preferred as tenants: if a UK citizen left home on holiday and returned to find his place occupied, it was necessary to go to court to prove your home was your only dwelling.

Rents were, however, high for the few available furnished places. The agent seemed hesitant to offer us the cheapest place on her list, but it looked fine to us, a basement flat in a late nineteenth-century corner block, the street quiet, near the Tube and buses. It had a little garden and a light room where Clif could set up to paint; his mounting anxiety was in part a withdrawal symptom from the studio routine.

As soon as we moved in we realised why the rent was so low. I wrote out a number of postcards with our new address, stamped them, and went out to look for a pillar box to post them. There, directly opposite our front door, perfectly positioned to explode into the hallway, was the box. The IRA terror campaign was intensifying at the time we arrived in the United Kingdon in early October: there would be thirty-four bombs in England, twenty-eight of them in London, and a number of kidnappings and shootings by the IRA, before we left at the end of January. Australia by then had its own terrorist attacks, but this was the first time we'd lived in a city where bags were searched at the entrances of large stores, and where one consciously lived with terror.

In November that year the British parliament passed the Prevention of Terrorism Act, which proscribed the IRA, and allowed the police to detain people without charge for up to seven days. Clif and Steve were mystified as they listened to the debates. They'd both worked in intelligence and knew, from experience, from their training, and in Steve's case because he'd taken an interest in the history of intelligence gathering, that the effect of making organisations illegal and allowing detention like this is to drive fanatics underground. When an organisation is illegal its members have reason to be paranoid, and the reliability of your sources is questionable, not only because members become secretive, but because the market comes into play, and informants will be likely to invent or enhance information.

Steve and Clif thought the police would be under pressure to produce results, and innocent people would be at risk. Innocent people were promptly arrested the day after the legislation passed, for bombings in Guildford. They were tried and convicted and their convictions overturned fifteen years later. Another group of men were arrested for bombings in Birmingham, found guilty the next year, and freed in 1991 with huge compensation payments. Good detective work and alert citizens in the end caught the terrorist–murderers, as only it and they can. Nowadays, in Australia, as our politicians react with the same style of terror laws, one can see, as Clif and Steve knew, that such laws are about political expediency, and have nothing to do with good policing or control of violence.

London is a city of deep history and sophistication, and although cynical politics allowed the laws to pass, the atmosphere for me was wonderful. We were welcomed by people who had looked after Clif years earlier, the same liberal intellectual circles of artists, writers and clients in which we moved in Australia, and which intersected with each other in so many ways. Don had said that as soon as I arrived I was to telephone his friend the actress Miriam Karlin; he'd told her about me.

She said, 'Come round now. Write down this address, but not in your address book.' Puzzled, we took a taxi to the address she gave, to find her sitting on the pavement with three champagne glasses and a bottle of champagne. She'd unpacked the glasses from the removals truck and sent her moving men to the pub for a couple of hours. Now she gave us her new address for our book. We would come with her to the new house and have dinner at a restaurant that night.

When I protested she said, 'Judith, I have spent Christmas alone in New York, because I was the star of a show and everyone thought I'd be busy. The absolute rule when overseas visitors ring is "Come round now".'

Miriam had been to Australia and worked with Noel Ferrier, and we'd seen her in the television series *The Rag Trade*, but we had no idea she was a serious actress. Clif started a painting of her, and I began by asking what roles she preferred, to be surprised to find she did Mistress Quickly with the Royal Shakespeare Company, and had recently been 'doing some Brecht'.

'Oh, how interesting, what?'

Whereupon in a dark operatic voice, she sang Mother Courage. I remarked on her deep notes and she explained, 'I was in *Fiddler on the Roof* with Topol, we have the same range.'

Miriam was great friends with Peter Jones, the other *Rag Trade* star, and we got to know him and their friends Spike Milligan and the Australian actor John Bluthal. Going to the theatre became a constant London habit, often with Miriam when she was not performing, so we would go was backstage to meet Nureyev and other friends. Through her, I saw the glorious city of Brighton: when she was doing Albee's *Who's Afraid of Virginia Woolf?* she invited us to stay there and come to the opening night.

I was very lucky to be introduced easily into the London scene, and the pearls did indeed give confidence with clients. Kay had insisted on the clothes for me in Singapore, but I still had the same weekly allowance from Clif as I'd had in 1970 at Dunmoochin, and by 1974 everything was more expensive. The pearls helped, as all costume does, with connection across culture.

I was not at all apprehensive about communicating in Britain, but every now and again I'd see a moment of irritation on the face of the person I was talking to. Oddly, this happened more frequently as I got to know people, and they seemed . . . snappy. One day I snapped back a reply and had in return a beam of delight; I realised that they speak very fast. It wasn't that they were rude, but that they were puzzled, because they automatically slowed down at first to welcome a laconic visitor, and having welcomed me, expected me to speed up. One of those cultural details that is not seen by those wearing it, but which provides a comfortable uniform. A common language can be a greater barrier to communication than attempting to understand across languages, when one is of necessity on alert.

I made friends with Robert Jeffcock, who had a gallery on the Isle of Man, and who offered us his beautiful flat in Mayfair. His principal place of residence was on the Isle, and he therefore faced losing the flat to squatters if it was empty. He kept a room in the flat for his London stays. We made friends, and went to stay with his family on the Isle, where Clif painted his quintessentially Celtic wife Fenella in an almost mediaeval picture.

André Kalman wanted Clif to have a show in 1976, and gradually as he began to settle in and paint in the lovely South Audley Street flat, he seemed to be enjoying London life. Steve gave me a thirtieth birthday party before he and Kay left for home, and I realised that Clif had not been drunk since we arrived in Britain; we were close and happy. We developed a routine: each morning I'd go to exercise classes or to ride in Hyde Park, then come back to get breakfast for us both; we'd drop in to a public gallery for an hour or two, or to commercial galleries, or drop in on Kalman, then have lunch; in the afternoon he would paint and I would wander about the city, and we would have dinner with friends or go to the theatre. We met the ornithologist Sir Peter Scott, and arranged to see Leo de Rothschild again.

I picked up the phone one day to hear, 'Lady Mitchison speaking,' asking for Clif. It is naff to use one's own title, and I thought how pretentious. But she was inviting us to Scotland, where I longed to go, and it would be country, if not bush. So we drove north, finding our way eventually to Carradale in Argyll, to a large grey nineteenth-century Scottish house at the edge of a fishing village. Clif knocked, as she'd told us to, at the back door, which faced the entrance drive. Repeatedly. No answer. We drove into the village, the pub the only place open.

'Och, go in, Noo's expecting you . . .'

I was reluctant to go into the house, but Clif did so, coming out a little while later with a broad smile. I followed him through the commodious kitchen, the wide hall, and into the drawing room, where on the couch sat a very small woman with a very large plaster cast on her arm.

I was indignant. After all we were strangers, we might have been mad. She'd had microsurgery on her wrist after damaging every nerve in a fall, she was seventy-seven. 'How could you?'

'Och, I looked at my bull, and I knew it would be alright.'

This was Clif's painting of the bull that her husband had bought from the Whitechapel show.

Of all the people I met with Clif, Naomi (Noo) was the one with whom I had most in common. We were both born in big comfortable houses, in circumstances usual then for upper-middle-class professional families. In Richmond we'd had four live-in servants, a man who came to do the brass and an odd-job man, who, like the gardener, came a couple of times a week. Because domestic staff lived in the house, we both had an expectation of sharing our private lives. Naomi had seen, as an adult, the changes I saw when a child: how education, domestic technology such as refrigeration, reduction in class barriers, availability of housing, secure work for decent wages, all meant that this model of life was over. Embarrassing to have been a child of privilege, but that is how it was, and I was a beneficiary as a child, because I had the affection of a number of women instead of only one, and the run of a big mysterious and beautiful place where I was perfectly safe.

Naomi's parents, like my parents, entertained a great deal; family and friends came to stay all the time. Like them we rarely sat down to a meal as a family alone; this prepared Naomi for the life of a politician's wife and me to be the wife of an artist. As a consequence, we both filled our houses with guests. There were no servants in Carradale when we arrived, although there were employees: a woman came in from the village and people worked in the garden, and Naomi's ghillie was her dearest friend.

Naomi and Clif

Naomi pointed out that we'd come through the kitchen, which she hoped I'd enjoy. We took our bags upstairs to a room looking down to the bay, and which would be my room on all my stays thereafter. As Clif built up the fire I made tea and looked for cake.

Scotland's bare hills and the wild country suited Clif, and the autumn colours gave him plenty to paint. We walked each morning, but mostly after I helped her dress I sat with Noo in the magic drawing room where she wrote at her desk in the bay window, and I wrote and read on the couch, and then wandered into the walled garden with its seven glasshouses for herbs and vegetables and berries and fruit, and cooked fish and venison and made cakes and puddings. We had baps, a sort of light roll, and kippers every morning. Clif didn't get drunk, and at night Naomi and he talked about politics and painting and books and people, and I could not have been happier.

She'd grown up in Oxford with Aldous Huxley and his brothers, her uncle had been Asquith's Chancellor of the Exchequer, her father was the physiologist J. S. Haldane. When she talked about her childhood she talked of the changes in science from a domestic, personal point of view.

'In my father's day every laboratory had string and sealing wax.' The discipline had grown exponentially and shattered into different areas during her lifetime; her brother, J.B.S. Haldane, could truly be called the last 'all-round' scientist. Her sense of history in science, and its connection to politics, was a delight for us both. She married the son of family friends during World War I, and through that marriage, with its initial sexual difficulties from mutual innocence, and a lot of babies in quick succession, Naomi became interested in feminism, sex education, birth control. Because Dick Mitchison became a politician (he was a minister in Harold Wilson's first government), she was able to become politically active. By the time we met she'd published more than thirty novels, several works of non-fiction, and collections of short stories and poetry. As I wrote on the couch in her drawing room I leaned on a lion skin given to her by the Bakgatla tribe of Botswana; she was Mabakgatla, mother of the Bakgatla. And I used as a knee desk a copy of the private edition of *Seven Pillars of Wisdom* given to her by T. E. Lawrence. Carradale became my constant place in Scotland and Naomi one of my dearest friends.

Back in London in the new year, Clif began to have chest pains. His cardiologist could find no cause for these, but I was very worried, even though this foreign country had a perfectly good health system. In order to cheer him up I followed up a suggestion of Michael Parker's, that Clif should paint Prince Philip. His secretary did not seem to know about the suggestion when I telephoned, and Clif was upset, but I arranged a meeting and set off for Buckingham Palace, leaving Clif with a babysitter in the person of the Australian High Commissioner, John Armstrong.

'Buckingham Palace, please, driver.'

'I've always wanted to hear that.'

'Well, we need the Privy Purse Door.'

'I'll ask the guard.'

It didn't occur to me that it was a bit of a call, ringing the High Commissioner to ask him to keep an eye on a husband while one went to the Palace. Clif and John Armstrong were great mates; he'd been sacked as Lord Mayor of Sydney before Clif painted him, and had temporarily to 'knock off' the robes and chain for the portrait.

As I left, John, a wily ALP politician, said, 'Remember the rule when you're seeing a subordinate. Take what you can get and then negotiate with the principal.'

There are times when to be young and uninformed serves one best. It simply did not occur to me that there would be any question except when Clif would paint Prince Philip; whether he would do a portrait was not an issue. Well, not for me, although Lord Rupert Nevill was very unsure about whether or when. He seemed confused as to my expectations and to think that this was an official commission; when I airily replied that Clif didn't take commissions he appeared to be taken aback.

I learned later that the Queen and the Prince are painted twice a year; that the usual arrangement is that you get an hour with the Queen, and the rest of the time a model in her clothes. No wonder the portraits lack life. I had no concept of this sort of constraint; I knew that royalty was formal, but I had simply no idea how the system worked.

'Is the portrait for a charity?' asked Lord Rupert, and he seemed amused when I explained it was, if you like, for Clif. Clif had met, liked and admired the Prince, who was an early and committed conservationist, and when Michael suggested the portrait, Clif thought it would be interesting.

'Well, will he give the Prince the portrait, so the Prince can present it to a charity?'

Now I was bemused, why would a charity want a portrait? 'Do you mean the National Portrait Gallery? I don't know anyone there.'

The Prince could arrange that if necessary, but would we give him the portrait? I thought . . . what am I doing here? I'd really not considered such a request, but just began to see that, although in Australia almost everyone regarded it as an honour to be painted by Clif, this wasn't quite the reality in the United Kingdom. Or at least not in Buckingham

Palace. And I thought well, if we do this portrait, I can tell Kalman, and Kalman can arrange other portraits, and that will pay for us to come back, and we don't have to settle in the UK for ages. Clif wanted a regular market in London, but he needed the nourishment of Australia, not to be away from the desert and the bush for too long.

So I told Nevill this, and he said, 'Now we're speaking frankly.'

Then arose the question of timing. The Prince has a diary session twice a year, and the sittings – it was not possible to say there would be more than two – might be able to be arranged, *might* be able to be arranged, for the Northern Hemisphere autumn of 1975. *Take what you can get and then negotiate with the principal.* I felt I'd got as far as I could, so I walked back across Green Park. How to consolidate the arrangement? There would be competing portraitists, and I wanted Clif at the top of Nevill's list. Back at the flat I asked Clif to dedicate a copy of *Death of a Wombat* to Lord Rupert Nevill with a little drawing, and I borrowed John Armstrong's copy of *Involvement*, and sent both to Nevill with a note asking him to return the book of portraits to the High Commission. And had a note in return, saying that the sittings would be arranged in the autumn.

28

TRAVEL

Mouton Rothschild, caviar, spinach soup, Repulse Bay breakfast, beer, rubber beef, bacon and eggs, toast, coffee, coddled eggs with fresh herbs

My directness had worked; one is lucky sometimes that cultural expectations are relaxed for foreigners. I was very, very careful to do in London as the Londoners do, but, every now and again, it worked to do as Australians might be expected. It worked for Clif, too. We had dinner with Leo de Rothschild before we left London. Just as the guest on my left remarked, 'Delicious wine, pity we can't ask what it is,' Clif said, 'Good wine, Leo, where did you get it?'

Leo reminded Clif that he'd telephoned earlier that week to ask who were Clif's favourite painters. Clif had said Picasso and Kandinsky. That was why the wine bottles were masked. Unwrapping them Leo explained that his cousin had all the Picasso, but these were bottles of 1928 and 1929 Mouton Rothschild, the labels by Braque and Kandinsky.

We left for a drifting trip home. Rome first, where Frank Hodgkinson had arranged for us to meet his friend the writer Richard Mason. Mason was indignant when Clif said we wouldn't be visiting any churches, as he, Clif, didn't believe in religion. Mason took me about Rome as only an erudite resident could.

In Athens the manager of our hotel was a returned migrant to Australia, who didn't even bother to enquire what we wanted to do. We arrived at 1 am and went straight to bed, only to be woken a few hours later in the dark by pounding at the door, and 'Get up, get up.'

We threw on our clothes, thinking there must be an emergency.

He led us to the street, gave me a torch, and said, 'Quick! Follow that path!'

Quite disoriented we started out, and the path climbed and climbed, and Clif said, 'Bugger this, what could be so exciting at the top of Athens?' And I had realised what was, but I said the view. The manager had timed it so we could be at the Acropolis at dawn, and we were, alone, watching the sun touch the city and the bay. We came back to a beaming host.

'Good scene for an artist, eh?'

We'd spent a week in Rome and two in Crete, and because Clif had visited the Middle East in 1972, he wanted to see Esfahan. All our warm clothes went home ahead as unaccompanied baggage, because Tehran was desert, and never cold. Clif was in charge of geography, so it had not occurred to me to question the temperature, and I was miffed to step off the plane wearing sandals, jeans and a cotton top and find snow swirling about me. Tehran is about twelve hundred metres above sea level.

Before we left home Rudy had told me to buy a tin of caviar in Tehran. We were met by embassy officials who advised us to leave as soon as possible, not to go to Esfahan, because the situation was unstable. When we sat down for our first meal I saw that Beluga caviar blinis were on the menu, at the price of a piece of steak in Australia, so

I ordered them. And Clif countermanded my order. It was an automatic response, somehow from his past; he hadn't looked at the menu. The moment was crucial in our relationship.

I heard myself, suddenly crisp and cold, asking him to remember that I was the person who managed food, I was the cook, and that I was never extravagant in restaurants. And then I left the table, returned to our room, and ordered spinach soup from room service.

I was so cross that I ate nothing but spinach soup (quite delicious), all the time in the hotel. Suddenly I felt my own anger. I'd cooked since I was seven years old. Food was communication, and welcome, cooking focussed my creativity and nurture. It had made his life a delight, centred dinner parties, softened arguments across our table, given political rivals common ground. Insulting my judgement about a menu was to hurt the seven-year-old making scones on her wood fire in the garden, and the girl who'd made breakfast for his son, and the woman who had entertained his clients and his friends and his lovers. Clif became comically apologetic. Perhaps he was beginning to listen; he bought a tin of caviar duty free as we left.

The new crisp voice was in my own head when we boarded the plane for Hong Kong. British Airways was the carrier and we were, as always, in non-smoking. The only other passenger in the whole of the first-class cabin was sitting directly in front of us, so when he lit up as soon as we'd levelled out I leaned forward to tap him on the shoulder.

Suddenly Clif was bossing me about again, saying, 'Judith, sit down slowly, very slowly.'

I didn't obey orders. As I turned to remind him of this I saw he was looking past me at the gun in the hand of a man in the aisle, and the man was pointing the gun at my head.

Perhaps I'd reached a point of no return when Clif had intruded on food, and become again the boy trained by my father and uncles when they were fresh from the armed services and full of ideas about equality. This was the first time anyone had ever pointed a gun at me; I doubt

I'd seen a hand gun except in films or on television. I did not find it amusing. My paternal grandmother had lived in gloves and chiffon, but she'd left me an operatic voice. I didn't think, I didn't respond to Clif, I just yelled, 'That's a gun,' and when the gunman stepped back I stepped forward still yelling, 'How dare you! Don't you realise those things are dangerous?' and he looked at the gun, and I thought *This must be a terrorist*, and simultaneously remembered, *If the other bloke has a gun and you haven't got a gun, you have the advantage. He is focussed on the gun, and you can think about everything else* and began walking purposefully towards him so that he had to back away.

No point in stopping when you have the advantage, terrorist or not, and he hadn't shot me yet, so I went on yelling at the top of my voice.

'This is an aeroplane, this is a cabin, it's pressurised. If that goes off and makes a hole and we lose pressure we could be killed. Do you understand?' while backing him up the cabin towards the cockpit, where I thought the crew would hear me, and could bop him on the head from behind or lock themselves in the cockpit and land the plane. Two stewards emerged from the galley and ran down the plane towards economy. Well, they're no help, what if he has brought some friends and this is an organised group and not some pathetic individual? And almost immediately two of his friends did arrive with their guns, and I realised that although the scene had drama – the costumes and personnel, young woman wearing jeans and embroidered cotton top, pearls, silver rings, hair by Mr Clifford of London; men wearing business suits and beards, accessories by Colt or Smith & Wesson – it also had an unexpected comic element which could be quite distracting.

I must not lose the advantage. By now my initial adversary was backed up where I wanted him, so I yelled at his friends to get in line, and to my astonishment they did, and I began to dress them all down about the dangers of guns on planes, and they were looking at their guns, and at me, and at each other, and I was wondering when it would occur to them that they were the ones with the weapons, I only had the voice, when beside me was the chief cabin steward.

'Is there anything the matter, Madam?'

Well, that is cool calm and collected for you, just what one expects on British Airways, so I thought, let him set the tone, we'll treat this as a problem about cabin luggage.

I said, 'These men are carrying guns on the aeroplane.'

'Yes, Madam, they're Prince Faisal's bodyguards.'

'Well, that is no reason to point guns at other passengers. You might ask them to explain, I nearly had to disarm them.'

It turned out that Prince Faisal was the chap smoking. I explained why I'd tapped him, and the steward explained he expected to smoke wherever he liked, and I suggested that in that case he could buy his own plane, and then, in perfect English, Prince Faisal offered to move and we were all happy and settled again.

The incident made Clif very happy and very amused, he wasn't critical at all. That night we spent in the wonderful old Hong Kong Repulse Bay Hotel, and in the morning on the terrace was Margot Fonteyn. She'd known Clif for years, and we'd had supper together in Melbourne, so we all had breakfast looking across the bay. To be there with this graceful charming woman seemed to seal the contentment of the journey.

After a visit to the Australian Embassy in Djakarta we went to lay a ghost, or rather celebrate the lack of one, at the Tjampuhan in Bali, and then we were on the plane to come home, and there was the familiar orange of the soil, and the apparently dull grey of the scrub and the eucalypts, and it was good to be back.

The ABC's *A Big Country* wanted to film Clif in the desert, and we decided to go to the Naryilco gymkhana. We meandered north, picking up the truck in Tibooburra. The diaries show us stopping at Orientos and Napamerri stations, and the Collumarra waterhole, meeting

Marlene and Ray at Innaminka. We camped by the Coopers, swimming each day among paddling pelicans, and then drove together down to Naryilco station.

I was dismayed when we arrived at Naryilco. The desert alone was wonderful, and Marlene and Ray were fond company. But here was a chiller, a huge truck, full of beer, another of just-killed beef, a sort of flavoured rubber, and nothing else to eat or drink, no shade. When in Naryilco . . . I went to look for a list of events, and the chap at the stand asked if I wanted to compete. Buck jumping . . . no. Roping a steer . . . no. Riding one . . . no. But the Lady's Broom Throwing Competition . . . I asked if there were many experts, and last year's champion was pointed out to me.

There was to be a dance that night, assuming anyone was left standing, given the quantity of beer and the likely accident rate of the events; the few women who were around were preparing for it. Outback, you order clothes by mail, and they'd ordered whole outfits. Last year's champion wobbled across the ground on her obviously unaccustomed white high-heeled shoes, wearing a white crimplene suit, already a bit dusty. Her hair was up in rollers. I was wearing an army shirt, jeans and boots. I paid the entry fee.

First the steers. One thought, naturally, of Hemingway, the masculine outdoors American sensibility meeting with such eloquence the passion and ancient drama of Spanish rituals: the beautiful women, the intense emotion, the delicious food and wine. The bulls especially bred and managed. The annual building of the stands to watch the running of the bulls. The picturesque bullring.

Here the ring was made up of vehicles, plenty of space between. The animals at Naryilco had been rounded up by helicopter and motorcycle the day before, the first occasion on which they'd actually seen a human, such was the size of the run. They were in a truck, each let out into a metal pen before its turn to be ridden or thrown.

The lack of fence was not exactly a problem, as we just zipped behind cars or on top of them when the steers approached, and the local horsemen rounded them up easily enough and sent them off into the bush. Unfortunately the competitor who'd been injured the year before couldn't move his wheelchair fast enough, and was tipped from it by an unusually determined beast. At this point, the crowd lost its enthusiasm for the steers. We were called over to throw our brooms, which were ordinary household brooms, a bit longer than a metre. I adopted a javelin approach, and managed about twenty feet, best of three, two hitting the ground in front of me on the first two tries: I was quite pleased with myself. Out staggered the champion in her crimplene, twirled the broom above her head and threw it three times as far. The crowd was delighted.

The afternoon was hot, beery, dusty, no shade, and as the day went on, after barbecued sausages in sliced bread for lunch, all I had to look forward to in the evening was more beer and too-fresh steak for dinner, and no conversation. Where was a Hemingway character when you needed to be rescued? The horses were saddled up for the race, the last event of the day. Bored and irritated but still trying to get into the swing of things, I had a bet, then climbed on top of the cabin of a truck. From which vantage point I watched the horses trot into the distance for the start. I was whingeing to myself about the discomfort – the heat, the dust, that everyone, especially Clif, would be drunk that night; that the scrubby country offered no delight; that the twentieth-century sheds and the trucks were so crass, that I wished I were back in Scotland – when into my peripheral vision came a cloud of dust.

It was as if some genre painting had left a billiard-room wall and come alive, turning the flat back-country into something utterly romantic. The sun was low across the plain, catching the tops of the trees, and made shadows just as the horses appeared. In the centre of the picture was a cloud of dust gilded by the sun, and from it, apparently racing against it, stretched the thoroughbreds, galloping as they'd been bred for centuries; the boys intent on winning balanced on them and urging them on, and everyone was yelling and then there was the pounding rhythm of the hooves, and we were all choking on the dust, and the crimplene was made pink forever.

Night is very cold in the desert, so we always slept beside a fire. I woke just before dawn and built it up. Clif was still asleep, but once the sun comes up you wake with the heat, so I put the billy on for coffee and watched the sunrise. How very curious: where on earth did we have the ring, where was the racetrack? How could I not have noticed all these rocks? Had we moved so far away from the house to camp? No, there are the house and the trucks. Clif was stirring, so I put on the bacon and broke in some eggs, and found the toasting fork. The sun was up now, and as I watched, and the scent of the food and coffee drifted, the rocks began to move, and I realised that people had just passed out wherever they were after the dance, for which event the champion had not remembered to remove her curlers.

After breakfast we drove back to Tibooburra. The *Big Country* people were delighted with their film; Clif had been able to talk about climate and the delicacy of the land. They wanted me to sing my Tibooburra ballad on camera, and when they came up to Dunmoochin to do more filming asked to interview me – 'You're part of the story' – but for me it was all about Clif. At this time, I could not see beyond wife, and wife was only a supporting role.

We went on to Adelaide with Marlene and Ray, where I was offered another view of our relationship. Clif only once hit me when anyone could see, and it was on this trip. It was evening, and they were in their car behind us. Clif had been drinking, I was driving, and suddenly he lashed out. Moments later with lights flashing they drove up beside us, and I pulled up, quite relieved that some issue, a failing tail-light perhaps, was intervening. The passenger door opened, Ray hauled Clif out, and Marlene got in beside me.

'Drive on.'

She asked if this had happened before, and when I told her, she said I had to leave, women should not be hit, Clif had never hit her. She dressed him down over dinner and from that time on Marlene did her best, whenever we were together, to keep him calm and sober.

But I couldn't leave, and I couldn't tell Marlene why not. She asked me to lunch when we got back to Cottlesbridge, and told me gently, over coddled eggs with fresh herbs, that no one had to put up with that sort of thing. And I thought that Marlene had never seen the blind desperation I was seeing, and if she hadn't then she didn't know why he was doing it, and it wasn't for me to tell her the reason. It was his secret, and he had to deal with its implications. I felt I had to stay until I could get him to speak about it, and I had to cope until that time.

29

1975

*Peking duck, Beluga caviar
and accompaniments*

The Adelaide visit had yielded an invitation for a retrospective at
the Festival in March 1976. I found that I was pleased to have some
structure, knowing where I'd be a year in advance: the Kalman show was
already organised for the London spring that year. I was working during
1975 with Brian McKinley on the Labor Hour, which was becoming
a soundscape of feminist and social discourse. This was assumed to
be subordinate to the demands of Clif's career. In all our Labor Party
activities there was this understanding, that Clif was the priority.

Spontaneity was a habit for Clif, who could go to the desert or to
a client for a portrait almost on impulse, and it was incidentally a
convenient controlling mechanism. But Carl Wood had asked me to
develop a teaching program for the Monash Medical School at the
Queen Victoria Hospital, and I began to have regular meetings there:
a way to make sure that what had happened to me did not happen to
other women. Clif might have objected, but he knew that the work

I did with consultants and students derived from the loss of the baby, and was a way, for me, of going forward, making something out of that acrid place in my heart. He couldn't complain, and could hardly feel threatened by it.

We'd been very focussed on the ALP; the death of Clif's mate Harold Holt had left him without a close connection to the conservatives, but in 1975 the Premier of New South Wales, Tom Lewis, asked Clif to design a bookplate for him. It was a happy connection. Tom kept the portfolio of Minister for Lands when he became Premier. The ninety-nine-year leases on the three stations at the Corner, the north-west border of New South Wales, had come up for renewal, and Tom was enjoying the opportunity to resume them to create a huge national park. He was the old-fashioned kind of conservative premier, the state run on advice of public servants, steady-as-she-goes, with Tom calm and sensible. Dick Hamer in Victoria was managing effectively in the same mould.

Most of Clif's friends had accepted me, and we'd returned to Australia from the United Kingdom very much a couple. 'Sexual freedom inside a committed marriage' is the way Naomi Mitchison's marriage had been described to me; it was what Clif had articulated early on. It was not what I wanted, but I didn't expect life to deliver what I wanted just because I wanted it. I hoped for intimacy, but intimacy comes with trust, and until he'd talked about the jungle crime, trust would have to wait. He was always going to be on guard, and while I was the target for his anger I was always going to be on guard. Patience is a very useful virtue, you learn a lot if you wait and watch. In the meantime there were affectionate and happy lovers.

Who never humiliated Clif. That was a rule that we all somehow learned: from novels, perhaps; it wasn't taught in ethics classes or handbooks of etiquette. The other fundamental rule, again never articulated, was never to make a pass at the partner of a close friend. In one of those moments that reveal understandings I had a phone call from Clif when I was in town. I'd been looking after a prominent feminist in the same way I'd looked after Di Yerbury, collecting this woman from Melbourne when she visited, letting her relax and recover at Dunmoochin, and she'd suddenly approached Clif for dinner. He wanted to know if she'd rung me. I rang to accept for both of us, and it was clear her assistant was embarrassed. She cancelled.

'Even I think that's bad behaviour,' said Clif, 'and I'm not a feminist.'

No more contact with her, then.

I don't want to use the word abuse, or to avoid the word love. Some affairs were intense and I thought of taking them further, particularly when Clif was drinking repeatedly, when it seemed as if we could never get close: but then we'd go to the desert or out of the country and, alone, be easy together again. Some affairs were fun, we had a lot of fun. It was a very relaxed time in our circles.

No longer involved in policy committee work, Clif was happily painting. My work on the campaign, weekly Labor Hour, and medical school commitments filled the days, and the evenings resumed with dinner parties and all the business of the art world. Dr Moerdowo had an exhibition in Melbourne, we were able to thank him at length for his help in Bali. Denis Wren began plans for a new book with Ivan Smith, the *Death of a Wombat* author: it was to be called *Dingo King*.

Our ordered and productive lives were in stark contrast with the federal government. Jim Cairns had fallen in love; we had a treasurer behaving like an adolescent, he'd appointed his lover as his secretary. Such manifestly silly behaviour would not have been tolerated by the conservative premiers, but Whitlam let it go on. It had become clear that he was no manager, and he seemed never to take seriously what could be turned into fun; a fatal flaw in the big personality. The government was productive, reforms that had been canvassed in two elections – education funding, fault-free divorce, the introduction of a national health scheme – were all introduced, but the focus, the media management, was not on substance.

Lionel Murphy and Clyde Cameron thought the government was not going to last. Lionel had himself appointed to the High Court in February. But he did not give up politics. Our telephone was beside the pantry, and he was as active on it when a judge – talking to political colleagues, giving advice and lobbying – as he'd been when he was in parliament. By mid-year Whitlam was trying to reorganise his Cabinet so they at least appeared adult, and replaced Jim Cairns with Bill Hayden as Treasurer in June. The reshuffle also removed Clyde Cameron from the Department of Labour, which Clyde deeply resented. Clyde had brought in the reforms he'd planned and, thinking that the party would not stay in power, he should have remained the urbane statesman and sought appointment outside the parliament, or even another portfolio. But he became partisan instead. Whitlam showed spectacular misjudgement, and when that June Clyde refused to resign, Whitlam had the new Governor-General, John Kerr, sack him.

I telephoned Clyde and pointed out that he'd spoken to me about the importance of compromise, that you had more clout in a group than excluded from it. I said he should stay in the ministry if he wanted influence, and Clif said the same thing: Clyde was sworn in as Minister of Science. I rang every scientist I knew, told them how intelligent he was and that Whitlam would have reason to fund him well, and Clyde was showered with telegrams and soon was surrounded by lively clever men and having a very interesting time.

That year Clif painted the Melbourne dealer Marianne Baillieu, and the beautiful ex-model Yvonne Rockman, wife of Melbourne's Lord Mayor; he was looking at women as people rather than symbols now, probably because Miriam and Naomi had taken me so seriously. And he began to paint Sir John Kerr. He went up on his own to Canberra to begin the picture, because I had to be at the Queen Vic. It seemed to go well, working alone again, but Clif was worried about the portrait. Kerr was relaxed and charming, but there was a sneer that kept getting into the picture, his painted lip kept curling. Clif would paint the mouth, work across the rest of the picture, and somehow have put the sneer back in. He asked Kerr to come down so I could talk to him.

The Governor-General naturally has a very formal program arranged months in advance, so he couldn't come to us for long, but he managed a day. Kerr was a big man, but the scale of board and individual wasn't an issue; this time Clif had started with a six-by-four board. Kerr arrived, ebullient, and we had a very good session. But I was concerned. He talked about politics, about legislation before the parliament, as if he and Whitlam were part of a team. Unusual enough to have a High Court Judge behaving like this, but Kerr's role was by definition above politics. I worried aloud about this when he'd left. Clif was puzzled for a different reason; the sneer, which went as Kerr charmed me in the morning, had returned in the afternoon exactly the same.

In the meantime we put aside the portrait and the education of doctors, and went to China and to Israel. Clyde Holding led a delegation from the Victorian ALP to what was then a country in the grip of the Cultural Revolution. My luck with caviar was not improving. I saw it on the menu in our hotel for 100 yuan, about one dollar; Clif this time ordered it. At the price we expected nothing, but the food had been very good, and the evening before we'd had wonderful traditional duck in the 'Peking Duck Shop'. A tin of Beluga caviar was produced and emptied onto a dinner plate. We all had a taste, very very salty, but it would obviously be delicious once the accompaniments came: the toast, the lemon, the sour cream, egg, black pepper. Except they didn't come, there were no lemons available, nor bread, nor sour cream; nor did we have a way of finding the accessories without looking like bloated capitalists. We had to abandon the caviar. Never was a lesson more deeply felt, about the uses of a demand economy.

Clif and I went on to Israel, where he painted a different desert. The trip was arranged by the Melbourne Friends of Tel Aviv University. Some instinct told me to ask if some of the proceeds could go to a Palestinian organisation, and this was arranged. With this gesture I unwittingly set in train the beginning of the end of our lives together, but our horizons were unclouded at the time in that pale desert.

We returned to a deteriorating political situation. Malcolm Fraser, now Leader of the Opposition, wanted to stop the supply bills, the acts of the parliament which spend money allocated in the budget, supplying the government with money. Fraser, hungry for power, saw that the team Whitlam had in place was now pulling together and beginning to look solid and tough; he didn't want to risk losing an election. But there were enough senators with independence and character not to refuse the bills; the tactic was delay.

Much of the drama on the issue was fought in public, and Whitlam misjudged his man. Clif was at Yarralumla painting Kerr when an official came in to say that Whitlam had said that Kerr would do as he was told. Clif came home really worried, saying, 'Kerr will act.'

I wasn't concerned, I believed he wouldn't. The Westminster system of government relies on convention, and the head of state acts on the advice of the prime minister, who is the person who commands the majority in the Lower House. Whitlam was considering a half-Senate election and needed the states to co-operate. Clif had asked me to drive up to Sydney with the painting; he'd flown up earlier.

The journalist Max Walsh was at dinner the evening I arrived, and he kept saying, 'Fraser knows something or he's on valium.'

Clif went on all evening, 'Kerr will act.'

The rest of the party was bored with them both.

We met the Lewises the next day for lunch. He seemed worried: perhaps the drama was affecting even sensible state leaders. I had always been very careful to keep my politicians separate, as it were; only initiating the most general discussions, and if they did make a remark like McEwen's about McMahon I kept it to myself.

Clif, bold on this occasion, asked, 'What will you do if Whitlam calls a half-Senate?'

Lewis replied, 'I'll instruct my governor not to issue the writs.'

I thought I should check. 'Do you mind if I tell Whitlam that?'

'No, do,' Lewis replied. And relaxed.

I enjoyed the Lewises' company, and put aside the question of the relaxation.

Clyde Cameron gave a party for us in Canberra on Monday 10 November. Whitlam sent his apologies, but his secretary was there, so I told him about Lewis' remark.

He rang Whitlam from the party, coming back from the telephone to tell me, 'Gough says thanks, and to tell you this decides it. He'll call a half-Senate tomorrow. He thinks it will be good to have a federal election without the people of New South Wales; it will show the country how far the conservatives will go.'

Meanwhile, very, very drunk, Clif was repeating that Kerr would act. Tom Uren said the New South Wales Government couldn't intervene, that wasn't how the system worked. No one was listening to him; lawyers and people with political science degrees, they all knew better. They explained constantly to Clif that the Governor-General did not have the power to act.

He replied, 'But Kerr will act.'

The next morning I rang from Richard Carleton's house, where we were staying, to confirm our appointment.

Kerr's secretary paused and said, 'I don't know if you know what's happening this morning?'

Well, I did. I didn't define it, I just confirmed that I knew.

The secretary said, 'Then you will understand that the Governor-General has a great deal of writing to do. He will be too busy to see you this morning, but perhaps we could postpone until this afternoon.' Then he said, 'He might need friends then.'

I thought a bit after I put down the phone. What would he be writing? What was this about friends? Surely the Prime Minister's department would prepare a document for Whitlam to present to the Governor-General for his signature? I rang the Attorney-General, Kep Enderby. His secretary said he was in Cabinet, but if it was important she could get him.

In 1973 Tom and Clyde Cameron had rung me after a Cabinet meeting, to say that an official had come into the Cabinet room and spoken to the secretary of the Prime Minister's department, who had told Whitlam there was a telephone call for him.

He'd said, 'Who is it? The President of the United States? Tell him I'm in a Cabinet meeting.'

And Sir John Bunting had said, 'It's Judith Pugh.'

And, they told me, 'We all said, Gough, you'd better take it.'

So it was not surprising to me that she offered to get Kep. I can see now that Clyde was trying to get me to take myself seriously when he rang in 1973, but two years later I still thought of myself as unqualified to comment without the imprimatur of a cause or, of course, Clif.

I thought, on 11 November 1975, that I might be getting the Attorney-General out of a Cabinet meeting to explain to me that the constitution states that all matters relating to elections must be handwritten to avoid controversy, or some such provision. I told her not to worry.

Clif was raving at lunch, on and on. 'He will act, Kerr will act.'

Our host, the lobbyist Eric Walsh, was telling me to take him away, when one of the party was called to the phone, and she came back to say, 'Kerr sacked Whitlam.'

I had never understood, when reading history, the instinct to rush to the parliament or the palace, the seat of power. But when our table disintegrated, I went to the parliament. There was a crowd, and some guards, who'd always before been unobtrusive. I smiled and said hello, and they let me through. I walked, as I'd so often walked, across the huge lobby. It was empty except for a couple more guards, and, coming towards me, three men. Malcolm Fraser, Ian Sinclair and the Leader of the Country Party, Doug Anthony.

Fraser, the man who had tried to refuse supply, had succeeded in turning over a convention and – without a majority in the House of Representatives, indeed despite a vote of no confidence by that House – had allowed himself to be appointed Prime Minister and had not resigned after the vote. I saw the look on his face that day. It was that of a sulky schoolboy. Anthony had the grace to look embarrassed.

I walked around the parliamentary offices. Whitlam was shocked, at the Lodge. Bill Hayden was in tears. Other offices were empty. Tom Uren was on the phone.

'Judith, get back to Melbourne. We've got an election to run.'

Which was already lost. Fraser's greed had its reward. In his later life his public concerns about the proper order of things, that the conservatives who followed him took the country into new territory, seem to be a kind of reparation. I remember his face that day, and that Malcolm Fraser gave them the map.

We were sleeping in the children's room that night at Richard and Susie Carleton's. Richard was interviewing politicians and commentators on live television, but rather than wait up I wanted to get Clif to bed, to calm him down. Our bedroom was the children's, Richard and Susie's was upstairs, and I heard Richard arrive home as Clif muttered on. Just as I was getting him into bed he began to let fly. Suddenly, in rushed Richard and Susie, he grabbed Clif and she took me upstairs. They had a baby loudspeaker and been about to turn it off when they heard Clif threatening me.

Richard tried to sit him down with a drink, but Clif would not be sat. He kept pointing to the curl in the lip of the picture, which was and always had been evidence that he was right. He announced that we should be violent, people should riot. He would set an example.

And he smashed the Carleton's plate glass windows.

At least politics was over.

For me, formally, as well. Clyde Holding offered Clif a seat in the Upper House of the Victorian Parliament.

'Mate, you don't have to do anything: it hardly sits, it's a guaranteed income.'

Clif, who hated public speaking. Clif who, for all that he was happy to help with policy, expected everyone else to do the legwork. Clif, who had an income.

Whereas I . . .

I saw that the party was a bunch of immature boys playing together, and decided they could play without my help. Clif refused the offer.

Thus the first five years of our life together were political. We found each other's strengths, and our loyalty. Another lovely summer took us into the year of his retrospective in Adelaide, another festival, and to the United Kingdom, a second exhibition, to spend time with Miriam and Naomi, to paint Prince Philip and the naturalist Sir Peter Scott.

30

CONSOLIDATION

*Wedding cake, tea at the Ritz,
dinner at the Pomme d'Amour*

When an artist has a deadline for an exhibition there can be period of concentration that produces work; then, when in the mind's eye there is enough to fill the gallery space, time to relax but go on, the mind disciplined and the co-ordination in place. Exploring undeveloped ideas, refining technique: they are joyous times. Summer at Dunmoochin was always good, and to accompany Clif's retrospective at the 1976 Festival, a commercial show had been arranged. He sent the pictures to be framed, and then painted through the heat of February, pictures filled with the understandings he'd learned from Paris and the colour wheel. Light, pale, happy paintings, to come with us to London.

We visited my family in the border country in northern Victoria, and he painted a landscape based on the lovely country where I'd spent dreaming times in my childhood. It was his entry into a competition: Albury was planning to present a painting of itself to its Californian sister city, in celebration of the American bicentenary in July. Then to

Adelaide and the Festival, with the Dattners: Miriam was out from London. Don introduced us to the Governor, Sir Mark Oliphant, and we decided to ask him to sit for Clif. We took a flat and stayed for the whole Festival, and I gave a party, inviting one of the little troupe of telephone agitators Mick Young had organised years earlier. Clif had invited some old friends and so had his dealer, and there were curators I hadn't met: it was a sort of open house. My old telephone-tree colleague had become the State Attorney-General; I was looking forward to meeting him. Perhaps the transaction sums up the era.

'Judith. Hello. Would you like a joint?' said someone I didn't know.

'Ordinarily, thanks, but better not, I'm expecting the Attorney-General.'

'It's okay. I am the Attorney-General.'

At the end of the Festival and the very successful commercial show we left for London, where we'd arranged in advance to rent a house. My parents were dropping in en route to Europe, so we found somewhere we could have them to stay, with a light pretty garden room for a studio for Clif. Settling in was easy this time, and then we left for Windsor, finding a comfy little pub to stay in. The studio for the portrait was to be Windsor Castle's Grand Reception Room.

Major Nash showed us into the space, where a sturdy and beautifully made easel had been set up at one end near long windows. But Clif was clearly worried. The Major thought he was nervous and approached this very tactfully.

'Now, Mr Pugh, you must regard this as your studio for the entire time you're here in the Castle. You have access whenever you like, and you must make yourself at home.' But it wasn't nerves. It was the colour of the walls and the light they gave. The decorative scheme of the long room is eau-de-nil, cool cool colour, and the elaborate carved decorations on the ceilings and part of the walls, the vast mirrors, are all gilded, so that the northern spring light was returned a hundred times, but never warm.

'It's the light.' He sounded quite dismayed.

I explained that adjusting from the light was slightly more dramatic for Clif than for painters without the red recessive problem.

The Major cheerfully suggested, 'Well, you should do a painting of your wife to get used to it.'

Clif was pleased: this was a good practical idea and it consolidated the concept of territory. But he was also worried about mess, and he'd need a table for his paints.

'An old one, please, it might get messy. And would you have a rug?'

'I'll arrange a drugget,' said Major Nash. 'And a table,' adding, 'everything we have is old.'

The next morning a substantial piece of canvas was stretched under the easel and to the trolley on which Clif was arranging his paints. The Prince's page came to make sure all was prepared, and soon after I saw Prince Philip come through a door at the far end of the room. When he arrived Clif was organising his paints, and already in the mood of painting.

'This is my wife, Judith.' And began to concentrate on his subject and the board.

There was a chair nearby and the Prince asked Clif where he should sit. I replied, unaware how very rude I was, that he should make himself comfortable, sitting or standing; Clif painted the person, not their appearance. That I would be keeping him occupied so that he could be himself. The Prince asked Clif again, and I replied a bit louder, thinking, *hard of hearing*. I explained that he should feel free to move around, stand or sit, that if Clif needed a moment to draw a detail, we would ask. The Prince asked Clif again, and I realised we had a problem.

I explained again that he'd be talking to me, I was sorry that we hadn't had this explained, but that he would find the painting would work best if he was relaxed. Clif paints the real person, not the look of them. And he said he'd heard all that before, and asked if he could bring work on Friday, and I pointed out that he could, but he was stuck with

me now, and I saw he was really furious, but he decided to put up with me and asked what I'd like to talk about.

'This is your home, and I am a guest in it. It seems to be a place of history, why don't you tell me about it?'

Half an hour or so later he laughed aloud at something I'd said and his whole demeanour changed. Kindly, urbane and very amused, he'd realised that I was in fact doing a job, that I hadn't turned up so I could tell my friends I'd met him, and that by extension the portrait might indeed be of the real person and not the idea. He thought it very funny that I should be surprised that he might think I was there just to meet him.

Then he explained how often he and the Queen are painted, and about the process, and in that explanation gave me an insight into what it means, and the strength of character it takes, to be part of the system of royalty. He did not articulate, but I understood why, from his point of view, it was so intrusive that I had just expected, unpresented, to chat. Everyone recognises you, every action is scrutinised. There is no privacy. Every opinion carries weight, and in particular there must never be any preferring of one place or group of people above another, nothing ever remotely political. The space of neutrality in the centre is essential for the British system to work; it was fascinating to see how it surrounds its members.

Clif had been concreting just before we left Dunmoochin, so I had the image in my mind of the recipe of sand to cement, the proportion of water, the problem of flat. The Prince was showing me the points of interest from the window and remarked that Elizabeth had built the flagged area directly below us. They were big pieces of stones, beautifully fitted, and for a moment I was surprised, but I supposed he meant designed – surely she wouldn't have actually bucketed the concrete?

'Oh it's very nice.' in the tone you use when someone has just built a barbeque. He realised what I thought.

'No, no, not *the Queen*, Elizabeth the First.'

To live as a constitutional person is to do so absolutely. I am not enthusiastic for a republic, when the Queen is the constitutional person who maintains neutrality, and has done so for so long. After all, it was she who said, after the dismissal of the Whitlam government, 'It would not have happened here.'

To be the monarch is, for the individual, to have sociality entirely separate from personality or character; to understand the constitutional situation at all times, to *live* in the constitution. I am enthusiastic to have as Governor-General a person with the intelligence and personality to deal with this, otherwise whoever is the head of state can become a problem.

After the awkward start, the portrait went very well, and Prince Philip seemed to enjoy himself, arranging for more sitting time, showing us around the Castle and organising for us to come to the dog-cart trials in Windsor Great Park so we could see him in a different environment.

Dog carts are open horse-drawn vehicles designed to carry a driver and at least one passenger and, in a cage suspended below, dogs. Prince Philip designed and showed the carts.

I'd thought our tiny bit of celebrity was difficult. We arrived in the park, Clif with sketchbook, and found Prince Philip standing beside a Range Rover. Encircled, at a distance of about ten metres, by people silently gazing at him. Instead of at the trials. He kept making remarks about the events, to which no one responded. It was like watching someone being gently tortured.

I thought: what are manners? There is protocol: you don't go up to a member of the Royal Family and initiate conversation. On the other hand, it is good manners to greet your host, it is good manners to set people at ease, and it is certainly not good manners to stare. Clif has to stare, but I don't. So I took a deep breath and walked across. To learn a great deal about horses in harness, dog carts and Windsor Great Park.

Clif was enjoying his studio, painting me and working on two versions of the Philip portrait. The Prince had asked if he liked the easel.

'Yes, it's terrific.'

The Prince explained that it was van Dyck's. Clif nearly dropped his brush. *Everything we have is old.* When twenty-first-century art historians write about the now contested area of portrait painting, in particular historic portrait painting, they always draw attention to the manner in which the subject's social status and wealth are celebrated by the artist; the implication that from the point of view of the subject this is crucial, the artist always constrained. I think of it as a negotiation, and one in which an artist is not only an active but an equal participant; that sitters can be cajoled into sitting, that their motives can be quite independent of self-aggrandisement.

'Van Dyck.'

'War,' said Prince Philip, and added, 'Breakfast.'

I waited.

'Poor chap. Charming chap. There were appalling wars, obviously didn't want to go back. *"He's finished my portrait; you'd better get him to do yours." "He did me with the horse." "Well, what about your wife, then?"'*

And the scene was there before me, in this same castle, van Dyck considerately protected, his dignity maintained. Certain families don't have to make something of their status, and have plenty of room for pictures.

Clif noticed a small symbol at the bottom of the painting. He painted it out, but, like the Kerr sneer, it kept returning. When Prince Philip, who is among many other things a painter, showed us his own studio, there was the symbol: it was his signature.

There was another question. The Prince asked who his portrait was for, and it was clear to me that the issue of ownership hadn't come up when he'd agreed to sit. I must have looked taken aback, as I explained that we thought he had wanted it. Sometimes our representatives can be a little too enthusiastic on our behalf. I changed the subject as soon as I made it clear that he could make a choice. He looked very thoughtful.

The next day I deliberately arrived late. Clif and Prince Philip had met before I came on the scene and they had a great deal in common; Prince Philip was a committed conservationist and I didn't want to be all the time in the front of the friendship. But I found Clif in a bit of a sulk. The Prince had decided which picture he wanted. I was concerned that either or both of his portraits might alter and urged him to choose when they were finished; but he was quite certain.

I suggested, 'Well, we should agree that if it doesn't end up as you expect, you can have the other one.'

Clif said crossly, 'That won't be necessary.' Prince Philip wanted the portrait of me. 'I've got to know the sitter.'

Later that day he suddenly remarked, as we talked about feminism, that he hoped that the movement would stop men hitting women. That it was never, never acceptable, no one should ever have to put up with it.

The Prince asked if Clif minded uniforms; there was a portrait to be painted for a regiment.

'Not on other people.' So Clif was invited to the Trooping of the Colours: an invitation thought through with great tact. His equerry explained that Prince Philip realised that Clif would not have his morning suit with him, so if he didn't mind being among men in morning suits, could he simply dress formally. There on the day, in the middle of a group of matching morning-suited ambassadors, was Clif, resplendent in the azure safari suit. When the ceremony flagged, the television cameras kept returning to the little blaze of colour, and the viewer could see that the group began by staring straight ahead, and ended up animated and enjoying their colourful companion.

The show opened at Kalman's and almost immediately sold out, and Kalman had a portrait client. The Jeffcocks again loaned us a flat in central London so Clif could have a separate studio, Ray and Betty Marginson moved in from a hot poky room at the Oxford and Cambridge club, and Judy Laycock from Dunmoochin was coming to stay. It seemed clear that we'd be coming regularly to London, so I began to look round for somewhere to buy. The Prince came to the flat for a last sitting, and also came to Kalman's to see the show, bringing one of his paintings for us.

Clif went to Ireland for a week with Ian Turner who, with his new partner Leonie Sandercock, was on leave in London; while they were away I found a three-bedroom two-storey flat in Palace Gardens Terrace in Kensington, and Clif made an offer on a nineteen-year-lease with Bert Tucker.

On the night the show opened Clif got very drunk; openings were always a tinderbox time. I was very distressed the next day and, emboldened by Prince Philip's remarks, made the distress clear. Clif suggested that we should get married, that this might make us both secure. On 29 June 1976 we were married at the Kensington Registry Office. The Whitlams were in town and Gough was Clif's best man, my childhood friend Susan Hoppe, then working in London, was my bridesmaid. My father insisted on giving a reception at the Oxford and Cambridge Club. When my mother and I went to make arrangements with the delighted function manager, he was clearly going to be very upset if we didn't have a cake.

Susan. The happy couple and Gough

'Two tiers, of course, Madam.'

'Two tiers?'

'The top one is for the christening.'

My mother had had the bright idea of explaining that I'd changed my name so we'd have the same name on our passports, but she told Clif there was no way to explain about being sterilised. Back in Dunmoochin we shared the top layer with the wombats.

Margaret Whitlam took the wedding party to tea at the Ritz between the ceremony and the reception, and the next morning we left for the United States.

Clif had won the Albury sister-city prize, and it paid for a honeymoon in California to present the painting on the day of the American Bicentennial. So there we were, on 4 July 1976, presenting a painting to Albury's sister city, Merced, in California, celebrating in the heat among the citizens of a small town: the local ladies' barbershop quartet of eight or so women in red, white and blue, the Mayor arriving on a bicycle in shorts, the town clerk and his wife in costume as George and Martha Washington.

'They always like to dress as historic figures on days like this.'

The Australian Consul in San Francisco asked us to present an Australian flag to the local B52 base, and we laugh out of a photograph across all those years, the anti-war activist in his ex-army shirt with the commander of the base and the huge-sunglassed young woman, holding up the Australian flag. If the China trip was fascinating this was extraordinary. In London we'd met Victor Carter, then the sixth richest man in the world, and he'd offered to look after us. When he'd suggested Disneyland Clif was appalled, but a society is a society and you have to meet it on its own terms. I knew Harry Roskolenko and André Kalman would organise the art and literary moments for us, and we knew where the galleries were. Besides, it is polite to accept gifts of this kind.

Carter had shares in Disneyland and Universal Studios. A limousine collected us at the hotel in which he'd arranged our accommodation, and we spent a whole day at Disneyland, and the next at Universal, where lunch was arranged in the Commissariat. Hollywood is all about contacts. It is a measure of my innocence that as really well-known figures, one after another, came up to introduce themselves I just thought *how friendly*. Clif had got the picture but he wasn't sharing it; from the point of view of the people in the restaurant we were an agent and an actress, and I was for sale.

I grew up in a culture of men when charm was a sign of effeminacy. My mother, herself a sensational brunette, had beautiful fair daughters.

She wanted us to use our brains and not our bodies to make our way in the world. So from the time we were very small she said, 'Men will tell you you're beautiful, but you are not, they are just trying to manipulate you. You are average but you'll never win a beauty competition. Never, never believe them.' For years I'd been painted by every artist who laid eyes on me, and complimented by the photographer Norman Parkinson on my complexion, and Prince Philip had wanted a portrait of me, and the penny had never dropped.

One of the directors, an Italian, came up and said, 'Has anyone ever told you you are the most beautiful woman in the world?'

I replied crisply, 'Yes', and went on with my salad.

Clif said, 'Sorry mate, we're not interested' to the poor bemused man, and although a couple of them followed us, he ignored their approaches and we went off to drive through an artificial lake and be attacked by a mechanical shark.

At the particular time we were in America the bicentenary distilled images of American history across the country. It was a wonderful journey: Carter arranged a box in the Hollywood Bowl and we saw that, just as in Merced where it was very local, all the film stars present – Paul Newman and Joanne Woodward, serious actors, producers – sang 'The Star-Spangled Banner' out loud, every verse. The happy honeymoon ended in New York, and we travelled back to London.

I have journeyed to the National Library manuscripts, to read my letters to Clif, to look at photographs; I have my own letters and many of our photographs here. The laughing couple at the B52 base. The photograph I took of Clif painting Prince Philip, using the camera the Prince loaned me. Boris, the grey wombat from Gippsland, gently blowing into my nostrils.

Here is Gough Whitlam kissing me on the steps of the Kensington Registry Office, the British press shouting questions about what he'd discussed with the Queen. Whitlam refusing to answer, them continuing to shout. Realising he'd come without staff, I stepped forward, thinking to myself, *they are British*.

'Please, gentlemen. This is my wedding day. This is no time for politics.' And having them apologise and walk away. Well, that was unexpected.

'Not Australian press, then,' said Clif.

The diaries record a wonderful summer in the UK. Naomi's daughter Val was radio critic for the *Guardian* newspaper and her son-in law, Mark Arnold-Forster, its foreign editor. She stayed with them in town and we became great friends. Their houses backed onto a park enclosed by the entire block. A cellist practised in one of the houses opposite; they thought it was Rostropovich. Naomi and I went a lot to tea, at the Ritz or to Browns, Clif and I stayed with Susan Peacock and Robert Sangster on the Isle of Man, and Clif showed there.

We travelled to Slimbridge to paint Sir Peter Scott, as famous for being the son of Scott of the Antarctic as for his yachting, scientific and conservation achievements. British modern architecture had an absolutely municipal air at the time and it was with some dismay that we approached Scott's home; it looked nothing like a sanctuary from the drive. But Sir Peter's study was literally built onto a lake on which myriad birds swam and preened and drifted; when he opened the long window a swan tried to clamber in. While Clif painted I had to keep reminding myself to concentrate on keeping the subject concentrated, and not look out the window.

Naomi had us all, my parents and the Marginsons, to stay; Clif and I went down to the Dawnays at Longparish House, where they invited a neighbour to meet us as he had wonderful eyes, and they thought Clif might like to paint him. Wonderful eyes he did have, and a reforming mind; he was Lord Denning, Master of the Rolls. Sadly he'd had a bad time posing stiffly for an official portrait and couldn't bear the thought of going through it again.

With Ian Turner and Leonie we went to Holland; out to Arnhem, bicycling through pine forest to the Kröller-Müller Museum, and in Amsterdam to see the first ever van Gogh retrospective. Clif was beyond himself with excitement, and began that evening to talk about what it meant to be an artist, what he and other artists had in common with van Gogh.

'Of course he killed himself; of course, he'd gone as far as he could.'

And about art in general: 'You see there are no straight lines in Nature.'

Ian, ever the rigid ideologue, interrupted. 'That's where you're wrong, mate, crystal spectrography has shown us there are.'

I was about to punch him when Clif replied, 'The magnification isn't strong enough.'

In the hotel that night as I waxed indignant he said he hadn't realised how much I cared about what he thought.

The diaries remind me that we were trying to make it work, we both thought the marriage a way to consolidate things.

Before we left, our new portrait client, Stanley Picker, took us to *Chorus Line*; the diaries list theatre, concerts, dinner parties, galleries, sheer interesting fun. On 25 August is recorded *Dinner Pomme D'Amour just us*, and I remember the sober discussion when I explained that it would be romantic to go out occasionally and not have him comment on the price, and him saying, did I not realise that the food was always better when I cooked it, and me saying yes, but he liked looking at other people's work and I liked trying other people's food, and him saying, 'Oh, I see,' and making the booking.

The next day we flew home, optimistic and comfortable. The surveyor was inspecting the flat, our offer had been accepted. We knew that next time we returned to London, it, too, would be home.

Bert and Clif

PARTY

Apple charlotte, little potatoes, herbs,
piles of asparagus, mounds of
strawberries, gallons of cream

Early in the seventies Marlene showed me a Drysdale drawing.

'Maisie Drysdale gave me that as a wedding present. Clif and I got married when we were going to Mexico, after we'd gone through all the shit about living together. She said that sometimes people get married in order to get divorced. She said I could sell it to pay for the divorce.'

I wanted a different story, for the structure of marriage to make it work. I loved the freedom I seemed to have. I loved Dunmoochin, the desert, Scotland, London. I wanted to look after Clif and for him to love me and let me love him. It seemed when we came back to Australia that the last hurdle could be overcome.

The appointments diaries continue in Australia full of a confusion of family, friends, events, and the notes we make that conjure up those events. We are in Sydney. We are in Melbourne, at home giving a party for the English actress Susannah York, who has taken up with Clif's friend, film-maker Tim Burstall. My mother gives a party to celebrate our marriage, and across the table I see Tim reach down to grind out his cigarette on the glowing surface of my parents' dining room table. I can't make him hear me over the noise. My sister Rosemary, who has the family reflexes despite her disabilities, slides her hand under just in time, and he grinds it into her skin.

Then suddenly looks down and takes it away, abashed. As I put ice on the burn, 'What did you do to get his attention?'

'I kicked him with my caliper.'

There is a Law Reform dinner. I sit opposite Lionel Murphy and Michael Kirby: Michael is now a High Court judge, we meet these days and remember our friends. I open an exhibition for Margot Knox, and Clif another for someone else. The Hawthorn Football Club wins a premiership; Betty Marginson as Hawthorn's first female mayor proudly celebrates them; Denis Wren finalises the *Dingo King* layout; there will be another promotion by *The Age*. The Tuckers come to dinner, often; we go to them, often; here are the Hodgkinsons and Clif's chess-playing opponent, philosopher David Armstrong, and my friend Julie Shaw, whose son is nearly four. There is a book launch and the young painters David Aspden and Colin Lanceley call in; there are portrait clients and Julie Dallwitz from Adelaide takes us down to the Baxter Provender: that long slow golden afternoon comes back as I turn the pages, but the apple charlotte was disappointing. We have parties in the little cottages Clif has bought in Macarthur Place in Carlton, and Powell Street Gallery shows the primitive artist Eric Stewart whom Clif has found; photographers arrive to photograph pictures, to photograph Clif, the wombats, me: us.

At dinner at the Rockmans for Susan and Robert Sangster, one of the models says that she too is a feminist, and challenges Robert to explain why mares are not as valuable as stallions. I am encouraged to go to the Melbourne Cup, but my lovely dressmaker Zsuzsi Korchma and I can't contemplate the clothes. The night before the race I dream of a very big

Premiership party

dark chestnut horse splashing through a great deal of water; I tell Clif
as we wake up in the gorgeous early summer with the scent of wattle,
and he laughs.

He is collected in a Rolls Royce by models floating in chiffon; behind
them on the spiky trees I can see the wisps of web on which the spiders
floated that morning. He arrives at the track and gets very, very long
odds on the big red horse that's good in the wet, and everyone laughs.
As the horses come out into the ring the skies open, and for the first time
ever the start of the Cup is postponed; the starter can't see the field. Van
Der Hum wins, and when I meet them that night, the models are smart
again, he is damp and very happily drunk. He peels wads of notes for

me from the huge bundle; he never gives me money, and I think it will always be wonderful.

Vogue comes to do a story, Norman Parkinson photographs Clif and there is a note: Patrick White; Harry Bluck comes to stay from Perth and the Murphys from Sydney, and Tom Uren, and Carole Baker. We go to meetings with the Aboriginal activist Hyllus Maris and philanthropist Sandra Bardas. My sister Rosemary has a birthday party, the winemaker Tom Lazar gives me a birthday party in Kyneton, and my friends smile at me from the photographs, Tom's ex-wife Veronique, and the partner she met at my twenty-first birthday party.

'What a lot has happened since then, Jude,' and we stay in Holbrook with the collectors Margaret and Doug Carnegie en route to Sydney and

Clif and Rosemary and Betty's portrait

meet Neville Wran – *Parliament House, Dinner*, says the diary – and we have lunch with Clyde Holding back in Melbourne.

On my birthday we have dinner alone, that is the rule, has been for seven years, dinner at Two Faces, and I always get drunk, it is my annual turn, drunk on champagne, and I sing, off-key, 'I'm forever blowing bubbles'. I always sing it, it's our song, and he always drives home to Dunmoochin, and we have more champagne, and we dance to my singing and do fishtails across the slates we laid in the big room, and I think of the terrace at Windsor and Clif as a young ex-soldier at the Palais de Dance after the war, and I think how we live in history.

The history of that year, our history, is full of laughing faces, and light, summer light. He hated the cold, and we'd had a northern summer, a drought in England, and now we have an Australian summer, and life was optimism and could be endless summers now.

Somewhere – a party? an opening? with Harry Stein? – I bumped into Frank Traynor the jazz trumpeter: maybe his band was playing, maybe he was just there. And he said, 'Judith, why don't we give Clif a surprise party?' and I felt a worry cross my heart, but Frank was looking so confident, and it was such a generous gesture, and I made the fatal mistake, and said yes.

Signe Thorsen from Merced came out to stay, and Tom Uren came down. The intuition was between Clif and me alone, so he knew what I was thinking; and I had to have a series of strategies to deflect him. I bought several presents and, apparently unable to keep them until his birthday, gave them to him. He told people who knew the secret that I couldn't keep a secret, and we all kept the secret. Each time I felt the little worry, but after all, it wasn't adultery, this would be such a splendid party, who could possibly argue?

I made excuses to be in town, and went to my parents with the housekeeper and cooked for days, and brought patés and terrines and dips to refrigerators across Melbourne. I marinated chickens, fifty chickens in three baby's baths, and hid them in the guest rooms. On the morning of the party we drove into town with Signe and met my sister Diana and two of her friends. We collected breadsticks and washed lettuces and herbs and hulled two hundred punnets of strawberries and steamed six hundred little potatoes and three boxes of asparagus, and went back to Dunmoochin to appear to give him a lunch and a last present. Then Tom and Signe babysat him while we made vats of mayonnaise and vinaigrette dressing, and we stored everything in the laundry and the guest rooms and Maggie's quarters, and I set the fire Diana would have to light in the old wood stove, and people dropped in to say *Happy Birthday* and while they were with him we got the electric frypans they'd brought from their cars. We would have chickens cooking on every switch.

'What if the electricity fails?'

'There's fuse wire in the possum cupboard.'

Every guest had a job, and a list, a parking map, and a clear set of instructions. Marie Davidson had agreed to be late, to miss the actual surprise, and she was having us for dinner. As arranged, Diana and her friends suddenly became bored sulky teenagers and refused to come with us, and she and I seemed to fight, and Clif took me out of the house, which was very clean but full of precious things, and needed to be set up for two hundred people to arrive, be given drinks and lots of hand-around food. The chickens had to be cooked, a gallon of cream decanted, all the crockery and cutlery unpacked, the band set up, and then all needed to fall silent and dark while we arrived.

I was okay at the beginning of the meal at Marie's, but the twinge of worry had mingled with anxiety to sit in my throat. Marie began to show signs of flagging at the pre-arranged time of half-past eight. Clif was pissed off.

'Marie, it's my birthday, you never get tired, what's up? Are you ill?'

'Clif, I'm an old woman now, an old woman. You'll know what it is some day to be old. Let me just give you some coffee and I must go to bed.' Tom had swung into sympathy and Signe was accompanying him when the phone rang, and Marie came in.

'Clif, you're right. It's silly of me to fall apart like this. Let's have some more pudding.'

I thought I would faint. What had gone wrong? In the kitchen while Marie made coffee she tried to keep me calm, it was just delay. I couldn't carry the conversation, but it didn't matter, Tom was magnificent; one could see why the man was such a success in politics. We ate more pudding, had coffee, Marie was on speed. Then the phone rang, and she went into a decline.

We drove off the bitumen and along the dirt road to the house, past the blue wren, which seemed as energetic as ever. Could a hundred cars have passed in the last hours? I had prepared lots of excuses as to why cars would be parked along the track. But there was not a car, just Tom Bruce, the Taxing Master of the Supreme Court at the bottom of our drive.

'Judith, my phone line is out. Can I use yours to report it?'

The house was in complete darkness. Perhaps it was all in vain. Clif decided we should have a swim in the pool, but Signe wanted a whisky first. He opened the door, stepped in, the lights went on, the band struck up, and two hundred people sang 'Happy Birthday'.

And Clif turned to me. 'You shit.'

He did have fun that night, greeting the sunrise with Frank's trumpet: indeed, after several hours of practising he was rather good.

But I'd set myself up. He'd begun to hear me, rather than make assumptions based on culture, so that we were beginning to work things out in daily life. He'd always known I couldn't hide from him in the essentials, that I'd only done so to protect myself. Inadvertently I'd shown him I could hide if I wanted to. I didn't want to, but the potential was there. The niggling worry, that the intuitive connection shouldn't be messed about with for something as frivolous as a party, had been right.

His birthday was on 17 December, so Christmas that year was a quiet family matter; the party had summed up the marvellous year. A journalist who planned a second biography arrived to stay; it had been a while since Noel Macainsh's lovely monograph. She didn't seem to be on my wavelength; she kept covering the table where we had lunch and dinner with the letters and papers she was reading and with her notes, although she had a desk in the quiet upstairs.

But the happiness of 1976 carried through into the new year: January on the south coast of New South Wales with the journalist David McNicoll and his wife and their great friends Snow and Georgie Swift was full of pleasure, not the least element of which was that the men on this annual holiday brought their wives breakfast in bed. David and Snow had complete control over Clif's drinking, which was becoming a worry again now we were back in Australia. The Vietnam War was over, Fraser had removed Coombs from the arts, so both of Clif's specific political issues were in fact resolved. Financially more than secure, his painting going very, very well, clients queuing up, another book on the go, portraits whenever he wanted; when he did drink and become morose he had little to complain about.

But this meant that the war stories were the focus, and without the screen of Vietnam. Back home in the heat of late January, secure I thought against all comers, I decided now was the time. So one night, as he began the story, I said that I knew he was the person who'd done the murders. I said I didn't judge him. I understood that he thought at the time it was wrong, but that he was very young and it was a long time ago. I thought that everyone would accept what had happened and that I knew he had spent his life regretting it. I said I loved him. I would help him do whatever he wanted, to make reparation to the families of the men he'd killed, to speak out because it was a way of talking about how badly people behaved in war and how it affected their lives, and their families' lives. Most of all, it was his decision, but I thought it would be good if he did admit it publicly, because I thought it was a burden that stopped everything: his work being truly free, him being able to be intimate. I told him I thought that having to control the memory and its implications would only go away if he faced it. But I would be there with him, whatever he did, even if he did nothing; and if he wanted to say nothing I would say nothing.

He just sat. After a while I went up to bed. And woke up some hours later as my eardrum split. This was the only occasion he really laid into me, and fortunately he was so drunk and unco-ordinated that I was able to get out of the room, down the stairs and outside very fast. I grabbed the distributor cap from his car, and drove away in mine, to wait by the side of the road. When I drove back the next morning he was already up, working around the place. Well, I had said that if he wanted to say nothing I would say nothing. Besides, I had only just raised the suggestion, one must have patience. And I got breakfast and we went on.

Steve Dattner arranged a dinner for us to meet John and Esther Handfield, journalists who had begun one of the first public relations firms in the country. Steve thought I should work with them, they were looking for someone to join the firm. Clif was entirely back in the rhythm of painting now, and portraits were a cross-current rather than the main force of his work, and I thought it would be the sort of thing I could take on project by project. I still hadn't managed to bring under review the question of the weekly amount he gave me. One of the anomalies of the relationship was that he was prepared to buy me Fabergé jewellery but not clothes; having no income of my own was tiresome. It is very easy to look back and see that it was about control, he wanted me there all the time. But I wanted not just to sit, and I wasn't ready to write, I wanted to be in the world, and the constant political meetings were over, so was the Labor Hour. Public relations would define and refine my skills, and, I thought, fit in with our life together.

He must have known he was on the verge of another heart attack, but this time I didn't feel it. He may have tried to hide from me as

I had hidden my unspoken thoughts from him. Perhaps I should have tried to delay the biography while we settled the issue about the killing. Perhaps I should have insisted he get a professional to talk to. But one can always look back and say *perhaps*.

On the day of the dinner he had a second heart attack. It crossed my mind to wonder, as the ambulance took him to hospital, if this had anything to do with wanting me not to work; but surely not. In the hospital, wired up, he apologised: I'd have to put off meeting the Handfields. I thought this concerned him, so although I had intended to put it off, I assured him I could go on my own, he was not to worry.

Facing again the possibility of his death, I was worried about my absorption in his life and career. While he was in hospital I talked to my friend Veronique and to Marie Davidson, and to my father. My father said yes, he had a shortened life span, he was going to die before me, well before me; after all I was twenty years younger anyway. Marie and Veronique thought I should begin work, it would not intrude on our lives. So I agreed to start work with the Handfields, part time.

Clif had a notion: to try to make contact with his first wife, June. He thought she lived in Adelaide. What did I think? I thought it would be a lovely idea. He wrote. The next day he made his usual run to the mailbox for the papers and the mail, and returned, surprised. There was a letter from June. After more than twenty years of silence their letters had crossed in the mail.

On my first day at work, I asked if they'd mind if I left early. Clif's first wife was arriving that day from Adelaide and I was having Marlene, his second wife, to dinner to meet her, and I hadn't had a chance to get to the market. The silence that fell on the office at this remark underlined for me that my way of life was still different from the ordinary.

It was lovely to see him with June; she was all gentleness and he became protective and gallant when she was around, they made sentimental trips to see their little house and their other haunts. Her second husband had died and so we arranged for June and her children to join us for Christmas that year; she and Clif would keep in touch from that time on.

The year was again filled with activities. He had hit me for the last time, and the jungle ghosts were apparently stilled. The drunkenness, however, hadn't gone. It now meant he focussed on other people. In some ways this was a relief, but when my brother was married from Dunmoochin, an otherwise very happy occasion, he abused Roger's new father-in-law and I had to get one of my uncles to intervene.

The round of interesting guests and travel to Sydney and the desert and of interviews and openings goes on in the diaries. In June 1977, lunch at the Florentino with the printer Bob Cugley; a book launch; dinner at the Florentino with Anne Purves from Australian Galleries and her friend Jean Gibson; Clif's old friend Barry Humphries was back from the United Kingdom and at the next table. To Réalités Gallery to organise a show: Fred Williams and Clif had insisted that now Marianne Baillieu had a good space, Rudy must deal with her; the scene was now professional.

There is life drawing, always life drawing, Gary Bradley and Bert Tucker come, so does Kay Dattner. Tom Uren launches a film about Saccho and Vanzetti, we lunch and negotiate with *The Age*; Rudy is making difficulties and they ask me to run the *Dingo King* show in July. Nina Christensen, who teaches Russian at Melbourne University, brings a Russian friend to lunch; there is a football match, and interviews with television in Adelaide and local radio and Christina Stead's seventieth birthday party at the Murray-Smiths': Stephen is editor of *Overland*. A new biographer arrives, and we see Hyllus Maris again.

It was about this time, and again at the suggestion of someone else, that I made another fundamental mistake. The Victorian Premier, Dick Hamer, asked me to look after Jill Robb, the newly arrived head of the Victorian Film Corporation. She came up, as Di had come, and Harry, and anyone else I was asked to take on, and watched me cook. And she decided I could sell the food. Her husband Brenton was at a loose end, and he would do front of house, and I would have a restaurant. And I agreed. Clif was keen – I think he thought it would be a place where he could bring all his friends – and so he and Brenton went off and found a very cute pub in Port Melbourne with an unused dining room, and we planned to set up there.

The Handfields retired, and so I decided to begin my own consulting business with the commission I would make from the *Dingo King* show at *The Age*. At this point the diaries change; I am paying a secretary, and she and the housekeeper manage a lot of the day-to-day matters between them, although we add and note things; Michael Elizur the Israeli ambassador stays for the weekend and arranges for Clif to go to Israel the next year. We have heard rumours about Palestinian refugee camps and Clif wants to get in to see for himself.

The July *Dingo King* show was, of course, a roaring success, the book launched at the opening of the show. This lead to huge publicity for the Réalités exhibition, which opened on 1 September 1977. It was the first opportunity that Melbourne and Clif's artist friends had to see the close-toned paintings which brought together all the new insights into colour and technique. There was to be another show, at Kym Bonython's gallery in Adelaide, and Clif had expected the paintings from Réalités to go across, but they'd all sold. He was already on the post-filling-the-gallery high, and painting unusually fast: perfectly happy about it, but something was a strain.

Two exhibitions, one a departure in subject and an advance in approach, the biographer, then another show, and I was starting a business, and he realised he'd encouraged me to start another one. We opened the restaurant on a Tuesday, the Adelaide show was to open on the following Friday. On the Monday night we were at dinner at Monsalvat when I realised he was having a heart attack and interrupted his conversation. My father had been unhappy with Clif's specialist, and had told me to get in touch if he had another attack. I rang from our startled hostess's phone, and Dad spoke to Clif and then to me; Clif agreed to see a new cardiologist. 'Don't fuss, just get him to his rooms tomorrow.'

Ted Kay examined Clif in the morning.

'I'd like you to come into hospital.'

'Alright, alright, if it will make Judith happy. I can probably come in next week.'

'Actually, I was thinking of intensive care, right now.'

'I can't, I'm too busy.'

'Clif, please, Dad says you should.'

'See? It's her fault, her father's a doctor. She thinks hospitals are the answer to everything.'

'Please, darling.'

'Oh, okay. I have a business lunch on, I can go after that.'

Ted turned to me and asked if I thought that would be okay, and it did seem that he was determined to be at the lunch. I gave Ted's secretary a note with Denis Wren's name and that of the restaurant, and off we went. Never has a negotiation been so amicable or so swift. Clif found no opposition to altering the *Dingo King* royalty terms, Denis agreed to my suggestion that a proportion of proceeds should go to the Australian Conservation Foundation.

The next day, returning with gouaches and paper and clips and board and jars for water, I was surprised to have him describe how the heart worked, that it was a pump; that smoking narrowed your arteries. My father had drawn for him, instead of just talking. The man was visual, this was the way to communicate.

This hospital experience proved quite different, and very positive.

'Hullo Mrs Pugh. He's had an electrocardiogram today; the result is on the floor.' Which seemed odd, until you understood that from the point of view of this uninstitutionalised group of people the result of a procedure was its effect on the patient.

I arrived at the hospital after a couple of days to be asked for a list of family members who were to be able to visit; his biographer, not telling me, had wanted to see him.

The great advantage of having close relationships with the medical profession is that when they close ranks they really close ranks. My father decided that it was best for Clif to tell the public that the attack, which had been worrying, had in fact been aborted, but to isolate him for ten days. He was to go home and remain isolated.

Clif insisted I stay at Dunmoochin. I was getting up at 5 am, an hour north of the city, marketing just south in Prahran en route to visiting Clif in Caulfield, south-east, going to the restaurant in Port Melbourne just west of the city to prepare for the lunch – we only did lunch – crossing town to the office in the Carlton cottages, just north, to check the mail and see my assistant, returning to Port Melbourne to cook lunch with my team of feminists, going back to the office, visiting Clif, and going home to Dunmoochin. He insisted I be in Adelaide for the opening of the show, although I didn't want to. And that night in Adelaide I fell into bed, but not alone, and realised that I was again very lonely. This time it did seem pretty clear that the new independent activity and the attack were related.

I had an anxious call from Marie Davidson on the first day back to work after Clif left hospital. She and my lovely next-door neighbour Lee Werther had offered to give Clif lunch and help the housekeeper keep people away, but could I come home?

When I got home he was drunk, the biographer had arrived and 'asked the big question'.

Which presumably should have been: *what made you an artist?* but which had, from the look on Clif's face, been something else. No point in being angry, I went to have a swim, and Clif, pale, sweaty and having difficulty breathing, handed me a list she'd given him, of men with whom I was supposed to have slept, and about which she'd sought his comments. Such was the price of fame. After that incident my father spoke to Clif forcefully, and he agreed to rest and paint.

He must have felt physically better, relaxing at the artists-versus-writers cricket match, and on Christmas Day with all his family – June, her children, Marlene, Shane, Dai – and anyone at a loose end. A trip to Tibooburra early in the month had helped, but I lost the friend who went with him; he'd made a pass at her, one of my dearest friends. *You never have an affair with the husband of a friend, nor should he try to have an affair with your friends.* She didn't articulate it but I knew, and Clif and I were back again to distance.

32

LEDA

Ham on a stand, trifle

In January 1978 Naomi Mitchison arrived for a visit that included the
Adelaide Festival, and an outback journey by air with Clif, and again
I had hope. We all went to Tasmania, and when the hire car broke down
on the top of a mountain pass, Naomi's and my enjoyment of the slow
wheeling of a pair of wedge-tailed eagles was interrupted by every car,
every car that passed, stopping to offer help or a lift or some food.

'Just like the Highlands,' said Naomi.

She stayed for some time and brought order to our lives, negotiating
with Clif for me about the usefulness of what I did. The restaurant
morphed into a catering business and regular clients; I cooked fundraising
dinners at the Howard Florey Institute and city stockbroking firms, and
displayed glazed succulent hams on the stand my mother gave me, and
piled cream on trifles for weddings. Catering was fun and controllable.
I had interesting clients in public affairs, mostly not-for-profit groups:
defining foster care from adoption for the Uniting Church Child Care
Service, producing a folio of lithographs to raise money to renovate
the Victorian ALP headquarters. The Australian board of ICI (Imperial

Chemical Industries) invited me to be its art advisor. I agreed, on the basis that I'd be taking advice from artists, and I set in place a plan to make it the most extensive corporate collection in the country, with one major example of every important artist's work. The little art committee and I had such a good time that its chairman, managing director Alan Hamer, kept increasing the budget.

There was to be a show at Kalman's in London in September. Clif went ahead, staying in Israel for July. I was to join him early in August, and spent a quiet month alone, drifting between Dunmoochin and the city. At these times I would see my own friends, Veronique, Margot, Penny, and write for my clients and make jam and think. Rosemary dropped in to my office in the Macarthur Place cottages with a present, a funny little matching paper-covered notebook and a vertical box for pens. I drove her back to Ormond College, where she was in her first year in law at Melbourne University. I went to see her room, full of posters; there were notes on the door from friends who'd dropped past while she was out.

She was in the Law Revue. When she was born they couldn't say she would even sit up; born missing sets of muscles, her tiny baby feet were twisted and her hands distorted. As she developed she needed surgery on her eyes, which weren't co-ordinated, and she had a cleft palate. My mother had been frantic, distraught; for all she claimed to ignore beauty she was obsessed with physical prowess, and when I was fifteen I'd taken a great deal of care of Rosemary. At the age of eleven, too slow to run, she'd been hit by a car; one leg stopped growing and she'd had to have the other shortened, so she was not in proportion. And here she was: a triumph. She had been turned down when she auditioned for the Revue, but they'd asked if she could write, and offered her parts as an understudy.

'My physical condition will always go against me at first.' So she had written and understudied, and now she was in the front row in the opening chorus line, and in several other sketches, three of which she'd written herself.

'You must be happy.'

'Yes, Jude, I am happy.'

Early in the morning on 30 July the phone woke me. I thought it must be Clif from Israel, but it was my father.

'Jude, has anyone told you? Rosemary collapsed and died at the party after the last night of the Revue.'

She'd telephoned him at the beginning of the week, with a pain in her chest. He had asked her to describe it. Weeping, he told me, 'I thought, I have to give her the choice. I said, "Rosemary, you know I can cure pneumonia, you've had pneumonia, and you know that pain. There are other things I can try and cure, but the cure can make people invalids. I can try, come home if you think you need me to try."'

She had repeated what he said: 'I should come home if I want you to try.'

Then she had gone out and bought a present for each of us, and then she had done the last three shows with the pain of the aneurism – he'd known it was an aneurism – and she had gone to the party and danced, and died.

I really had expected she'd have to live with me; we'd expected in the end she'd lose her leg. When my baby died, my consolation was that Rosemary would always need me, and that I would be an aunt to her children if she had them. Now I had lost her, and that continuity.

I kept trying Clif; the operators at the manual exchange in Jerusalem were sympathetic, the embassy tried, so did the Israeli officials, but it was two days before he finally rang.

I was in Macarthur Place, to be near my parents and to see Davis McCaughey, the Master of Ormond, about the funeral, and because it was cold alone in Dunmoochin. My secretary Maureen and friends could come round easily in Melbourne. I had the notepad and box on the desk, and there were a lot of flowers, and the telephone rang, and Clif asked, 'Which sister?'

'Rosemary.'

'I thought it would be Rosemary. I hope this doesn't mean you're not getting on the plane on Thursday.'

Maureen was watching me, and she took the phone. 'What is it, Clif? . . . No, actually she won't be, she has a funeral.'

And made a cup of tea.

Earlier that year, while we printed the lithographs for the ALP, into the busy scene – John Brack, John Olsen, Frank Hodgkinson, George Baldessin, printers, stackers – a woman friend of Clif's had approached me to ask if I would mind if he went with her to Spain the next year; she understood I wanted to go to Italy. That little public humiliation had felt bleak enough, but this response was really difficult.

Then I thought, he is always afraid of openings, he is afraid of death. Maureen rebooked the flight, and I went to London and had to mourn alone. The show did really well, and Judith Malcolm, who had gone to live with a fellow of Magdalen College, Oxford, was a bright lively presence in that beautiful city. Scotland was wonderful that year, and I slept and felt better and was writing a good deal, and once you have one grief another is easier. Our place at 28 Palace Gardens Terrace was exactly the place we needed in London, near Kalman, leafy green. Barbara and Bert agreed to join us there in 1979.

We had a routine: to Singapore for a couple of nights, replenishing our clothes – Clif now had orange and pink shirts which he wore under his black diamond mink coat (I'd given up taste, for colour) – then the Concorde to London and the Tube to Kensington.

Back in Australia, we were in Perth, then in Melbourne with Dick Roughsey, the Chairman of the Aboriginal Arts Board. Clif went to Point Wilson painting with Fred, to the Castlemaine Festival with the *1812 Overture*; a local farmer firing his shotgun into a forty-four gallon drum right on the beat. Clif painted Dick Hamer, I sang on my birthday as I'd always sung. The wombat, proving aboreal, sat on the top of the wall, reached down with its teeth and dropped firetongs on the housekeeper; this had to be observed before we would believe her. In Sydney we painted the Chancellor of Sydney University, Gordon Samuels, and the lithographs were launched, and it was summer, and cricket, and with the Dattners and our regular dinner companions we took to playing charades.

As I feel my way through the clutter of images thrown up by my notes from the diaries I remember the odd sensation as my life felt more and more hollow, while at the same time it was gathering momentum and envy. I'd always tried to focus media attention on Clif or a cause, but inadvertently became public again when a friend needed recipes and stories for a new job on a women's magazine, so we mined my life to keep her afloat financially. I was asked to speak at the 1979 Women of the Year luncheon in Perth, and I accepted because I had a new message: I'd seen a personal computer in London. These machines would obviously change utterly the way we did things; it was very, very important women should think about them at once.

What was Clif saying to the women we mixed with? My own friends he knew to be loyal, but was he looking elsewhere for absolute devotion now I had a business and he often travelled alone? What I hoped for was that if he came to respect what I did, then perhaps we could meet, as it were, on the top of the world. Before we went to London that year we were asked to take the Dean of the Yale Medical School and his wife, who were birdwatchers, to the desert. We flew to Tibooburra and the place was good again, the Berliners sophisticated companions.

I grieve for Rosemary, and for the baby; grief like this is almost comfort over time. I can write about Tibooburra and think of the reds and pinks and all the happiness. But there was on this journey a place of such extraordinary beauty that even as we arrived I felt a sense of loss. It was a small stony valley. The light was so strong that anywhere would have been pale, and as we drove up the track we saw a house bleached by years of sun. It was an inside-out place, the kitchen in the through corridor to get every breeze: there was no breeze. The verandahs were netted for sleeping, to let any moving air across: no air breathed. The people were as still as the air, a woman silently made us tea, and the light shone from the pale pale rocks and silence was all. It seemed as if time held the place, and us: as if work, society itself, was insignificant, and peace was tangible.

It stayed with us both, and I brought the subject up: what if we moved, found a place outback, where he could paint? It was possible, possible. We'd have to see how we could do it.

We arrived in London and settled in. The woman with whom he was indeed going to Spain telephoned and asked if I would mind booking their train journey to Madrid and a couple of nights in a hotel?

I went to the Kensington High Street and found a travel agent with a woman at the desk.

'I wonder if you can help me, my husband's girlfriend has just rung from Australia, she's having difficulty booking their train travel and accommodation from home, and she has asked me to do it from here.'

I could see she was having difficulty taking it in.

'I asked' (and I had) 'if she wanted a double room, and she said yes. I think they should have a very comfortable hotel.' I sat there and watched her understand me.

'Are they sharing all expenses?'

'I believe they are.' She said that she might ask some friends for ideas; why didn't I have a coffee and come back? When I did, her three phones were ringing. Travel agents across London were finding limousines filled with flowers and chocolates and champagne, to transport them from their first-class compartment on the train to the lavish suite in the most expensive hotel in town, where a wonderful dinner would already be ordered. The cost would be booked to his American Express card.

I gave them the tickets and a bland letter confirming their arrangements, just before they left in early July. They could settle up back in Australia. Off they went, innocent of their destination, and I have the plaintive card from Barcelona: *Missing you, the hotel in Madrid was very expensive although lovely, missing you (true), Clif.*

While he was away I had an unenthusiastic time with a lover and then, alone in Scotland with Naomi, time to reflect. It was fun, keeping face and having revenge, but it was cheap on one level, I actually didn't want this life. When we got back after the show we should try to find some way to be faithful and close.

We met in Milan, with Barbara, which was great fun. He went off to Israel, and I to Australia. Clif had finally put a piece of property in my name, a house on the Yarra – well, half of it, shared with a friend – and Maureen had moved in.

I spoke at the Women of the Year luncheon; Alwyn Birch had asked me to send him my speech before I left, and he wrote to ask if I would do a book.

Perhaps we could be equal.

I rang the number I had in Israel, but I couldn't get through. I tried over several days; I was really quite excited, this was it, this made it all possible between us. Finally, a couple of days before I was due to leave for London, Clif rang and said, 'Judith, I know what it is to be truly loved by a woman.'

All I could think was that I had just put lavender in between all the sheets in the linen cupboard. I realised that was pathetic, *pathetic*, and I was very angry and asked, 'What does it mean, Clif?'

And he said, 'Do you have to do this?'

And I thought, you bloody coward, you didn't even think to come home to talk face to face.

And then he said, and I could hear her urging him to say it, 'She says you can stay on as my manager, she just wants to live with me.'

347

And I felt myself think, he doesn't understand, he's never understood, perhaps if he can accept her love then I should let him go, and then I thought if he wants to, he will, and I said, 'I'll see you in London for the show. You must tell me what it means.'

In London, I was strong enough to raise it, and told him what I'd been thinking, that I too had had an affair, that we really should decide together what to do. He agreed, and even agreed to see a counsellor with me when we got back.

The show opened to the usual success, and London as ever embraced us and we did really try, I am sure he was trying, he was considerate and we bought bits and pieces for the flat. I was hopeful, all that autumn in London, riding in Hyde Park, going to see the Turners at the Tate, Miriam with Romy Schneider in *Bus Stop*, tea at the Ritz with Naomi. Rostropovich was practising with a pianist, perhaps it was Gilels, there was early snow in Scotland, dinner at High Table at Magdalen, concerts in the Wigmore Hall. But I was saying goodbye. On the last day of the show I went to Kalman's. The show was of Leda and the Emu. The first image he made of me was as Leda, with a swan. This new series was touching, amusing. A quintessential Australian bloke, the emu kept watching Leda, who sunbaked for a while, and then got into the dam, and he watched her from behind a tree, and he followed her about through bush, from painting to painting, until, in the desert, they became one.

He'd used all the gawkiness of the emu to indicate the awkward, shy man, unsophisticated, but longing.

I remembered Margot Knox, saying. 'Don't worry about what he says, look at how he paints you.' And I saw it: Leda had a widow's peak in her long black hair, and broad hips, and dark eyes, and she was clearly trying to seduce the emu. And I had pale gold hair, and narrow hips, and I had never tried to seduce him. I'd challenged him, I'd met him head on.

And now I was no longer in the picture.

I felt sorry for her, for them. She was older than me, a Jew helping the Palestinians. Political, intelligent and radical. I thought I should let them be happy. I suggested he bring her out to Australia. But the hopelessness had affected him, too. We were paralysed for a while, we went on trying to live together, and we went to counselling.

He sat on the bean bag, 'Oh Judith, not bean bags,' and said to the counsellor, 'How much does she want? I understand it's about money, I don't mind paying, I just want her to stay.'

And I said directly to him, 'It's not about money, it's about love.'

And years later I realised that for him money had come to mean love, and for me money had come to mean control.

The other women circled. I had decided no more lovers; he was supposed to have decided that too, while we tried to talk.

I talked it over with Veronique. She said, 'You can stay and you'll have a comfortable life. But you will have to pay a price.'

Early in 1980 I found him lying down. He couldn't see out of his right eye. He was pale and clammy and I rang Dad and drove very fast to meet an ambulance, but by the time we got to the hospital the effect had passed and Clif dismissed it. They said that they'd be able to ream out his carotid artery if he agreed to an angiogram, but somehow they didn't.

I asked my father what to do and he said that if he were the kind of father who thought about money, he'd say I should stay, because he thought Clif was going to die soon, and I had put a lot of effort into his life and I should inherit from him.

I said I thought that the tension between us was making it worse and that to stay would be to hasten the process, and I thought it wasn't ethical.

I said this to Clif, and we decided I would base myself in town and he would be based in Dunmoochin and we'd keep seeing the counsellor.

'Even with the bean bags.'

And of course I'd go up at weekends.

Then it became clear that one of the circling women had landed; on one level he was happier, and after all, I wanted him to be happy.

Dunmoochin is delicious, and it is at its best on a quiet still spring day, when the air is clear, and you can see the detail. It was on such a day that I collected the last of my clothes and drove down the drive. We'd agreed that I'd leave books and various other things until I settled, we would remain close, but that as I had found someone else and he had, too, it would be best to say it was over. I had life ahead, and so, it seemed, did he.

I decided to have a last walk down the drive. The delicate local wattle was out, soft lemon, not the vivid Cootamundra, and the hakea we'd scattered ten years earlier was in spidery creamy bloom.

He was teaching me, then: 'You have to burn the hakea. This is how the Australian environment works. The hakea seed pods are covered in a tough wax, and until it melts, the pods don't open to release the seeds. The bush burns, and the wax melts, and the hakea seeds blow around, and then they put down their roots, they don't need much nourishment, and the bushes grow up covered in spikes. The spikes protect native birds, and the blossoms, too.

'If you can burn away the tough wax and, if the seeds take in the sparse environment, and you wait while the bush grows; in the end, you get a thing of great beauty. You can miss it. You have to look carefully, you have to look at the detail. You have to be patient. That is what the Australian bush is all about.'

But there is an end to patience. And when your vision is blurred with tears, you can no longer see the detail. And you may as well get back in the car, and drive away.

SOURCES

While writing this book I consulted copies of *The Age* and *The Australian* in the State Library of Victoria, the papers of Clifton Pugh in the Australian National Library, (which include some of my own material), together with those of Sir William Dargie and the Rudy Komon Gallery, and Clif's tape made for the library with Barbara Blackman. Friends shared memories and reminded me of events, and I used my own collection of letters, diaries and photographs from the period.

I looked again at Noel Macainsh's beautifully written monograph on Clif (*Clifton Pugh*, Georgian House, Melbourne, 1962); Andrew Grimwade's *Involvement*, (Sun Books, Melbourne, 1968) and Traudi Allen's *Patterns of a Lifetime* (Nelson Melbourne, 1981). I confirmed some facts and dates from the Australian Dictionary of Biography Online and the online resources of the Whitlam Institute, and from Susan McCulloch's revised edition of her father Alan's *Encyclopaedia of Australian Art* (Melbourne University Publishing, 2000).

Mainly, though, I was there, and we were together. For ten years we talked. In bed, and in the car, over breakfast, and morning coffee in the studio; walking through the bush and beside the fire in the house and in the desert. We relived his journeys, and they became ours. Friends arrived and re-told his history, their histories with him and with the house and with the work; it always comes back to the work. Essentially, paintings and drawings and sculpture and prints are the diaries of an artist.

PICTURE CREDITS

cross the swift flowing Ninahau river during their advance to BUT. Identified personnel are: VX44906 Lieutenant Colonel A.G. Cameron, DSO, (1) NX34868 Captain H.G. McCammon, Adjutant, (2); SX29388 Private C.E. Pugh (3); NX138174 Lieutenant I. Norrie (4). Ref 079797. Courtesy the Australian War Memorial photographic collection.

PAGE 88: In 1972, Clif asked Harry Stein, 'Which bit would you like?' 47 cm x 32 cm, charcoal on paper, 1973. Collection Peter Fradkin. Courtesy Shane and Dailan Pugh.

PAGE 100: Left to right: (back) Frank Hodgkinson, Judith, Clif, (middle) Phyllida Hodgkinson, Barbara Tucker holding Leon Hodgkinson and (front) Patricia Hoppe at Dunmoochin, 1971. Photographer Albert Tucker. Courtesy Barbara Tucker.

PAGE 115: Marie Davidson at Dunmoochin in the mid 1970s. Photographer Albert Tucker. Courtesy Barbara Tucker.

PAGE 136: Don Dunstan with a painted Judith at the Adelaide Festival, 1972, photographed for the *Adelaide Advertiser*. Image supplied by Flinders University Library, Don Dunstan archive. Copyright News 1972.

PAGE 138: Kevin Childs, Judith and Clif in the dam at Dunmoochin, 1972. This was part of a series shot on 10 February 1972 for *The Age*, but was not published. Photographer unknown; any information welcome. Courtesy *The Age*.

PAGE 148: Boris with Judith at Dunmoochin in the late 1970s. Photographer Ben Frankel. Author's private collection.

PAGE 167: Clif's drawing of Judith feeding Wombalong. From *Wombalong*, first published in 1985 by Methuen, Australia. Courtesy Shane and Dailan Pugh.

PAGE 168: Judith and Clif with Wombalong and Wimpy at Dunmoochin, 1973. Ref: NLA, MS 9096, Box 12, transparency marked Australian News and Information Bureau. Courtesy Parliamentary and Media Division, Department of Foreign Affairs & Trade.

PAGE 177: Sydney suburban art fancier, Debbie Harris, looking at the award-winning portrait of Gough Whitlam by Clifton Pugh at the Art Gallery of New South Wales, 1973. Photographer Bill Payne. 1 photograph: black and white; 15.5 x 20.5 cm. nla.pic-vn3513833. Courtesy Department of Foreign Affairs and Trade and the National Library.

PAGE 197: Judith serving tea to Don Dunstan, Premier of South Australia, in the garden at Dunmoochin, 1973. Photographer Clifton Pugh. Author's private collection. Courtesy Shane and Dailan Pugh.

PAGE 205: Clif in Jerusalem, 1975. Photographer Judith Pugh. Author's private collection.

PAGE 231: Judith at the Coopers in mid 1970s. Photographer Clifton Pugh. Author's private collection. Courtesy Shane and Dailan Pugh.

PAGE 240: Barbara Tucker and Judith at the Tucker's in mid 1970s. Photographer Albert Tucker. Courtesy Barbara Tucker.

PAGE 258: Clif at his Balinese door in December, 1978. Photographer Mark Strizic. Strizic Collection.

PAGE 277: Judith takes tea at Raffles, Singapore, 1974. Photographer Clifton Pugh. Author's private collection. Courtesy Shane and Dailan Pugh.

PAGE 280: Clif working on a double portrait of Judith and Naomi Mitchison in London in the late 1970s. Photographer unknown; any information welcome. Author's private collection.

PAGE 290: Judith and Clif on Scotland, 1975. Photographer unknown; any information welcome. Author's private collection.

PAGE 296: Clif at Naryilco, in the late 1970s, wearing the 'not-an-akubra' given to him by an Aboriginal stockman. The akubra is the manager's hat. Photographer Judith Pugh. Author's private collection.

PAGE 300: See credit for front cover. Close-up of Clif's portrait of Sir John Kerr.

PAGE 314: Clif painting Prince Philip in his 'studio' at Windsor Castle, 1976. Photographer Judith Pugh. Author's private collection.

PAGE 319: Susan Hoppe, Clif, Judith and Gough Whitlam at Kensington Registry Office, 29 June 1976. Photographer Ray Marginson. Marginson Collection.

PAGE 321: Commander of the U.S. Air Base, Judith and Clif with the Australian flag, July 1976. Courtesy U.S. Air Force. Author's private collection.

PAGE 328: Clif and Rosemary Ley with a portrait of Betty Marginson as Mayor of Hawthorn at Dunmoochin, 1977. Photographer Judith Pugh. Author's private collection.

PAGE 327: Judith and Betty Marginson at a celebration of Hawthorn's premiership. Photographer Ray Marginson. Marginson Collection.

PAGE 340: Judith at the window of the Grand Reception Room at Windsor Castle, 1976. Photographer Clifton Pugh. Author's private collection. Courtesy Shane and Dailan Pugh.

PAGE 324: Bert Tucker and Clif in Kensington Gardens, London, 1977. Photographer Judith Pugh. Author's private collection.

PAGE 351: Judith among paintings at Dunmoochin, 1980. Photographer Rob Lovett. Author's private collection.

ACKNOWLEDGEMENTS

Without the Peter Blazey Fellowship I would not have begun this book. The deadline focussed me and produced the first two chapters; the prize gave me financial breathing space and, through the Australian Centre at the University of Melbourne, space to continue.

Peter Blazey and I danced together as teenagers in the gentleman's residences of polite, comfortable Melbourne, where the constraints were subtle, where people spoke softly so as not to offend. Peter spectacularly decided to speak up, and we are all the richer. I hope this book does justice to his model of directness and truth.

Many people have urged me to tell the story of these hectic years, especially Ros Hollinrake, Nick Hudson, and Tony Palmer; but it was Robert Manne who encouraged me to stop and do so in the middle of a doctorate. He and John Poynter stretched their supervisory role to include the memoir, and I am very grateful.

The staff of the Australian National Library, especially those in the manuscripts room, were encouraging and resourceful as I researched our archive and those of our friends. I was assisted by the Australian Parliamentary Library, the National Archives of Australia, the State Library of Victoria, the NSW Bureau of Meteorology and the Queensland Railways. Vincent Alessi and his team at La Trobe University, where Clif's collection can now be found, could not have been more encouraging, helpful and generous. The Australian Archives and the Department of Trade and Foreign Affairs gave permission to publish images now held by the Australian National Library; I thank that institution, the department,

ACKNOWLEDGEMENTS

the library, the Australian War Memorial, Flinders University and the United States Airforce for use of images they own or in which they hold copyright.

Liesbet Blomberg gave me shelter while I wrote, read the manuscript over and again, made coffee, made home. Jeff Berger, Shannon Boyer, Brigid Cole-Adams, Paul Craft, Stephen Davies, Kon Kadaras, Judy Koves, Deirdre Langenheim, Race Mathews, Alister McCrae, Robert Mendham, Cheryl Slatyer and Noel Simpson read and commented on the manuscript, which improved for their remarks. Much of the book was written as that precise and brilliant editor Patricia Ridley lay bravely dying; I beside her, she beside me.

Andrea McNamara was at the Blazey announcement for Allen & Unwin and picked her moment carefully to approach me. She has been a most tactful and helpful publisher, Teresa Pitt a committed agent.

I particularly want to thank Barbara Tucker for giving me Bert's lovely photographs, which portray so happily our lives together with Bert and Clif. I am grateful that Ben Frankel, Rob Lovett, Ray Marginson and Mark Strizic let me use theirs to describe that lovely time.

Shane and Dailan Pugh gave me permission to reproduce their father's pictures which, in the way of pictures, say more than any of these words.

INDEX